Donald Barthel

THE
TEACHINGS
OF
DON B.

The late Donald Barthelme was a longtime contributor to *The New Yorker*, winner of a National Book Award, a director of PEN and the Authors Guild, and a member of the American Academy and Institute of Arts and Letters. His sixteen books—including *Snow White*, *The Dead Father*, and *City Life*—substantially redefined American short fiction for our time.

VINTAGE

INTERNATIONAL

About the Editor

Kim Herzinger teaches at the University of Southern Mississippi. He is the author of books and articles on D. H. Lawrence, modern and contemporary literature, Sherlock Holmes, and baseball, and is now at work on a cultural biography of Donald Barthelme.

Also by Donald Barthelme

Come Back, Dr. Caligari
Snow White
Unspeakable Practices, Unnatural Acts
City Life
Sadness
Guilty Pleasures
The Dead Father
Amateurs
Great Days
Sixty Stories
Overnight to Many Distant Cities
Paradise
Forty Stories
The King
The Teachings of Don B.
Not-Knowing

FOR CHILDREN

The Slightly Irregular Fire Engine

THE TEACHINGS OF DON B.

THE
TEACHINGS
OF
DON B.

Satires, Parodies, Fables,
Illustrated Stories,
and Plays of Donald Barthelme

Edited by Kim Herzinger
With an Introduction by Thomas Pynchon

VINTAGE INTERNATIONAL
VINTAGE BOOKS
A DIVISION OF RANDOM HOUSE, INC. / NEW YORK

FIRST VINTAGE INTERNATIONAL EDITION, APRIL 1998

Some of the pieces that appear in this book were originally
published in *The Atlantic, Esquire, Harper's, Harper's
Bazaar,* the Houston *Post, Mademoiselle, The New York
Times, The New Yorker, Ontario Review,* and
The Village Voice.

The Library of Congress has cataloged the
Turtle Bay edition as follows:
Barthelme, Donald
The teachings of Don B. : the satires, parodies, fables,
illustrated stories, and plays of Donald Barthelme / edited
by Kim Herzinger; with an introduction
by Thomas Pynchon.
p. cm.
ISBN 0-679-40982-3
I. Herzinger, Kim A. II. Title.
PS3552.A76A6   1992
813'.54—dc20   92-53663

Vintage ISBN: 0-679-74119-4

Random House Web address: www.randomhouse.com

Printed in the United States of America
10 9 8 7 6 5 4 3 2 1

Preface

Donald Barthelme's work is uncategorizable. It's so notoriously uncategorizable, in fact, that its uncategorizability is almost the first thing we notice about it. Categories are a way of signifying meaning in advance, and Barthelme concedes nothing in advance; his work playfully resists being resolutely fixed. "They called for more structure," Barthelme once wrote, "so we brought in some big hairy four-by-fours from the back shed and nailed them into place with railroad spikes."

Barthelme himself was often asked how he distinguished between, say, a "story" and a "satire," or a "satire" and an "essay" —and equally often his answer was quite intentionally ambiguous. He simply did not concern himself overmuch with the kinds of rules that are supposed to govern such things. A piece of writing, he once said, is "an *itself*, if it's successful." Still, in 1974, Barthelme brought in some of the work from his back shed and published it in *Guilty Pleasures*, a book over which, he said in an interview, he "went to some trouble to label . . . non-fiction to distinguish it from the stories." It was, he admitted, "a somewhat difficult line to draw," but it was a reasonably firm line, nevertheless. "I think of it [*Guilty Pleasures*] as journalism. A certain part of it was written out of anger, obviously a very creative emotion, at the government. I just feel that [these pieces] ought to be thought of as distinct from the fiction."

These were pieces, he wrote in the book's short preface, which were "written on all sorts of occasions and in response to all sorts of stimuli and overstimuli." Most of *Guilty Pleasures* was made up of parodies ("a disreputable activity, ranking only a little higher on the scale of literary activity than plagiarism") and satires ("simple expressions of stunned wonder at the fullness and mysteriousness of our political life"). The remaining pieces had to do with "having one's coat pulled, frequently by five people in six directions. Some are brokeback fables and some are bastard reportage and some pretexts for the pleasure of cutting up and pasting together pictures, a secret vice gone public."

Barthelme's "satires, parodies, and fables" were the guiding notion for this book, and the reader will note that the terms *satire*, *parody*, and *fable* are all used in the introduction to *Guilty Pleasures*. The reader will also note that they are not quite as clearly defined as an editor hell-bent on guidance, not to mention a title, might wish. Still, these are robust terms with robust histories—a number of sprightly books, and a great many very dreary ones, have been written about their nature—and after all, Barthelme uses the terms himself. Happily, at least some of the pieces we wanted to put in this book were pretty clearly parodies and satires, recognizably so. These terms, we thought, would not disappoint. Unhappily, though, we had to admit that many pieces were both parody *and* satire, some were probably fables as well, some might reasonably be called stories, and some more would do perfectly well in a book of essays, thank you. Barthelme's work is chockablock with rambunctious items that do not so easily settle down inside even the wonderfully expandable frameworks suggested by satire, parody, and fable.

Nor does his helpful introduction to *Guilty Pleasures* entirely solve the problem of what to call the pieces in this book. Publishers, the editor considered, might balk at a book titled *The Satires, Parodies, Brokeback Fables, Bastard Reportage, and Secret Vices of Donald Barthelme*. And readers, turning immediately to the "Secret Vices" section, might be somewhat disappointed to find there none of the more well-publicized vices, but instead a series of ingenious prose pieces illustrated by an equally ingenious series of pictures. In a 1976 Pacifica Radio interview, Barthelme had occasion to call one of his pieces "an odd ox . . . a whatchacallit." This seemed, for a giddy moment, a way out of the quandary. But, somehow, a book titled *The Odd Oxen and Whatchacallits of*

Donald Barthelme did not seem to do justice to the quality of the work within.

Stirred, but weary, the editor gave up. The issue was decided, and this book is titled—or subtitled—*The Satires, Parodies, Fables, Illustrated Stories, and Plays of Donald Barthelme.* The editor means it when he says it, even though he may not be entirely confident that he knows what he means. He asks for generosity from those who hanker for precision. And anyway, he blames Barthelme. It's Barthelme, after all, who refuses to have us believe in what the world would have us believe. It's Barthelme who continually displays in his work an unlimited freedom of formal invention. It's Barthelme who fractures every rule. And it's Barthelme who shows us that the rules no longer obtain, or perhaps that they never obtained. And it's precisely this that makes him one of the most important and influential writers of our time. Blame *him.*

Deciding exactly what in Barthelme's work might legitimately be called a parody, satire, or fable—as opposed to a story, an essay, or a whatchacallit—was difficult enough. But that was by no means the only difficulty.

Readers have every reason to believe that a piece of writing comes full born from the mind of the author, each work being discrete from any other work, complete with a handsome title which, as it were, provides a kind of border around the piece, disallows leakage, and admits of no confusion whatsoever. But Barthelme's working methods were quite different indeed. First, he knew what all good writers know: nothing is written that might not someday be used elsewhere. In a number of cases, parts of a published piece, or parts of an otherwise unpublished piece, were to find homes quite distant from where they began. Second, Barthelme often worked by a kind of inspired juxtaposition—the cunning method of the collagist—revising, changing, recombining, and intercutting to create entirely new works from the refreshed fragments of the old. Third, some pieces were moved about almost wholly, the only major change being that they acquired entirely new frames in the process. And as we know, new frames tend to make new pictures. One of Barthelme's unsigned

"Notes and Comment" pieces, for instance, first appeared in *The New Yorker* in 1975. It appeared again, in very slightly altered form, in his limited-edition collection *Here in the Village* in 1978, and once again—slightly altered for context—in his essay "Not-Knowing," first published in 1985. It's a wonderful piece, a lovely piece, and it fits snugly inside every context Barthelme devised for it. But where, the bedeviled editor must ask, should we put it now? Though it could have found a perfectly happy home in this volume, you will not find it here. Don't despair, however. In a forthcoming volume of essays, you will have your chance to read it: twice.

The satires, parodies, fables, illustrated stories, and plays that do appear in this book are of four kinds: (1) unpublished work; (2) uncollected work; (3) work—other than the novels, of course —which did not appear in either of his two compendium collections, *Sixty Stories* and *Forty Stories*; and (4) work which, though later collected, first appeared in significantly different form. Editorial information will be kept to a minimum, but certain crucial information (the likely dates of composition for unpublished work, the dates of publication for uncollected work, the identification of variant texts, and so on) is included in the "Notes" at the back of the book. A number of the published and unpublished pieces in this book were not given titles by Barthelme. The first-line short titles we have adopted have no definitive status. These short titles exist only to provide a convenient way of identifying otherwise untitled pieces.

We hope, of course, that readers will smile upon the pieces collected here. Donald Barthelme was, to quote Robert Coover, "one of the great citizens of contemporary world letters." For those unfamiliar with his work, this book hopes to introduce them to some of the things that are so remarkable about it: its brilliant and sudden juxtaposition of modes, its accent and pace and intonation, its irreducibility, its problematic engagement with the world, its bereaved amusement, its power to influence an entire generation of writers who came after him. For those who are already familiar with Barthelme's work, this book is a kind of replenishment. And it will remind them, too, of what they have been missing.

Kim Herzinger

Acknowledgments

Thanks to Wynn Handman and the American Place Theatre; Lee G. Campbell of Joseph the Provider Books; Wylie, Aitken & Stone; Julie Grau; Thomas Pynchon; Wayne Alpern; Derek Bridges; and Angela Ball.

And particularly special thanks to Marion Knox Barthelme, Frederick Barthelme, and Steven Barthelme, without whom the book could not have been put together.

Contents

Contents

Contents

PLAYS

Introduction

Though to all appearances a gathering of odds and ends, what this volume in fact offers us is the full spectrum of vintage *Barthelmismo*—fictions thoughtfully concocted and comfortably beyond the reach of time, reactions less exempt from deadlines and rent payments to news of past moments that nonetheless remain our own, not to mention literary send-ups, intriguing recipes, magisterially extended metaphors, television programming that never was, strangely illuminated dreams, elegant ranting, debonair raving, and more, much more.

The do-it-yourself hypertextualist will get a chance to browse and recombine, often with striking results. Scattered about in here, for instance, are half a dozen or so pieces that, taken together, define a single vexed meditation upon the Watergate Affair of the seventies, which could profitably be consulted by future historians seeking to understand that Byzantine daytime drama. This is assuming that Barthelme got it by way of the Tube, right in the lateral geniculates like the rest of us, in which case readers might then also like to refer to "And Now Let's Hear It for the *Ed Sullivan Show!*" a good general rundown on Don. B.'s viewing procedures, as well as evidence of the radiant quality of his attention.

Trying to describe Barthelme's politics is as dodgy as trying to label his work, but Watergate sure did get him revved up. Nixon by then had already mutated into a desperate and impersonal force, no longer your traditionally human-type President, but now some faceless subgod of folly. Barthelme, perhaps as a species of anarchist curse, just calls him "the President." The rage behind it, provoked by the ongoing spectacle of national politics in the U.S. as presided over by *anybody*, is natural enough if you look at the regimes Barthelme happened to be working under. Among many sad consequences of his passing is that we won't know what he might have done with Bush as a subject, although "Kissing the President," in its consideration of Reagan, may give off premonitory hints.

Another combination of interest is the interchapter material from *Overnight to Many Distant Cities*, which furnishes an instance of Barthelme's way with dream material. One out of several humiliating features about writing fiction for a living is that here after all is just about everybody else, all along the capitalist spectrum from piano movers to systems analysts, cheerfully selling their bodies or body parts according to time-honored custom and usage, while it's only writers, out at the fringes of the entertainment sector, wretched and despised, who are obliged, more intimately and painfully, actually to sell their dreams, yes dreams these days you'll find are every bit as commoditized as any pork bellies there on the financial page. To be upbeat about it, though, in most cases it doesn't present much moral problem, since dreams seldom make it through into print with anything like the original production values anyway. Even if you do good recovery, learning to write legibly in the dark and so forth, there's still the matter of getting it down in words that can bring back even a little of the clarity and sweep, the intensity of emotion, the transcendent *weirdness* of the primary experience. So it's a safe bet that most writers' dreams, maybe even including the best ones, manage to stay untranslated and private after all.

Barthelme, however, happens to be one of a handful of American authors, there to make the rest of us look bad, who know instinctively how to stash the merchandise, bamboozle the inspectors, and smuggle their nocturnal contraband right on past the checkpoints of daylight "reality." What he called his "secret vice" of "cutting up and pasting together pictures" bears an analogy, at least, to what is supposed to go on in dreams, where images from the public domain are said likewise to combine in unique, private, with luck spiritually useful, ways. How exactly Barthelme then got this into print, or for that matter pictorial, form, kept the transitions flowing the way he did and so on, is way too mysterious for me, though out of guild solidarity I probably wouldn't share it even if I did know. The effect each time, at any rate, is to put us in the presence of something already eerily familiar . . . to *remind* us that we have lived in these visionary cities and haunted forests, that the ancient faces we gaze into are faces we know. . . .

Of course Barthelme could work in more daylit modes as well. The parodies of works that for one reason and another gave him the pip, though wicked, are straightforward enough. "Two Hours to Curtain" is a closely observed and affectionate piece of reporting. The radio plays and pieces like "The Joker's Greatest Triumph" suggest how much sheer fun he must have had writing dialogue. You can feel him sometimes getting lightheaded with it. It could be generational, the result of coming up during the "golden age" of radio drama, when speech, music, and sound effects had to fill the audience's attention and carry the whole show. I imagine him working on the Batman piece trying not to laugh too much at his own work because that might get in the way of maintaining the idiotically slow pulse he wanted, not at all his usual narrative tempo, which ran between frenzied and warp drive.

There are also pieces too free of form to be parody, too funny to be simple invective, that express Barthelme's deep annoyance with any number of selected offenders—the federal government, Thanksgiving, just about anything from California, not perhaps geographical so much as psychological California, with its reputation for granting asylum to, call them wishful thinkers, seeking to deny, in mostly unorthodox ways, the passage of time, and what time brings in the way of aging, the evils of history, the turns of Fortune. Like most writers who are serious about what they do, Barthelme could not afford any such luxuries, and so had little patience with anyone who appeared to him to be indulging them.

See, for example, "The Teachings of Don B." Though it has the look of a writerly reflex to some piece of industry gossip about Carlos Castaneda's deal with Simon & Schuster for the first Don Juan book, Barthelme is also here enjoying a surrender to annoyance with the parties involved, the book itself, and the culture of eternal youth that has allowed it to flourish. The operative text here would seem to be from II Corinthians, "For ye suffer fools gladly, seeing ye yourselves are wise." Wise satirical practice requires the sensitivity and skill of a *fugu* chef at controlling toxicity, that is, knowing how long to suffer, and how gladly, and when to give in to rage, and the pleasure of assaulting at last the fools in question. Barthelme's timing in this regard was flawless, though unfortunately he was prevented from becoming a world-class curmudgeon on the order of, say, Ambrose Bierce, by the stubborn counter-rhythms of what kept on being a hopeful and unbitter heart. Much of this journeyman impatience with idiocy concealed a tenderness and geniality which always shine through whenever he drops the irony, even for a minute. That, and, of course, his inescapable sadness. That elegiac voice—"The wives of the angry young man are now married to other people—doctors, mostly." That "mostly." You think of the music of Dietz and Schwartz, of Fred Astaire *singing* Dietz and Schwartz, just that combination of grace and disenchantment, darkish lyrics and minor modalities.

Melancholy. As any Elizabethan could tell you if they all weren't dead, melancholy is a far richer and more complex ailment than simple depression. There is a generous amplitude of possibility, chances for productive behavior, even what may be identified as a sense of humor. Barthelme's was a specifically urban melancholy, related to that look of immunity to joy or even surprise seen in the faces of cab drivers, bartenders, street dealers, city editors, a wearily taken vow to persist beneath the burdens of the day and the terrors of the night. Humor in these conditions leans toward the anti-transcendent—like jail humor and military and rodeo humor, it finds high amusement in failure and loss, and it celebrates survival one day, one disaster, to the next.

But behind Barthelme's own slick city-sophisticate disguise still lounged, alarmingly, this good old Dairy Queen regular in some conspicuous hat, around in whose backseat opened containers had been known to roll, harboring the mischievous daydreams of a Texas rounder, not to mention a lengthy stretch of DNA dedicated just to locating and enjoying various highly seasoned pork products. On the principle that you can take the boy out of the country but not vice versa, Houston, Texas, his hometown before New York, must have caused Barthelme some lively internal discomfort over the course of a love-hate affair with the place that went on, it seems, for most of his life. From what I remember of Houston at about that same time, it could have provoked the one emotion just as easily as the other, and in Texas-size quantities, too. The Astrodome was brand new in those days. Air conditioning in the city was ubiquitous. There were schemes afoot to put a dome over part of downtown and air-condition *it*, creating what today we would call a mall. Entire boulevards were dedicated to churches, side by side, one after another, allowing you to drop the family car in low and actually cruise places of worship. The nearest venue for dope, sex, and rock 'n' roll, then as now, was Austin. The new NASA space center out by Buffalo Bayou was hiring heavily, while from the marshlands around it, mosquitoes were busy spreading an encephalitis epidemic. Sir John Barbirolli had fashioned of the Houston symphony an exquisitely first-rate instrument, while teenage musical heresy focused on California surf culture—though the Gulf only had surf during hurricanes, all kinds of kids could still be observed driving around with some stick in some woody, flaunting boards that never caught a wave, as if trying to make it all be California. Anyplace but what it was.

Whatever psychological traces of Houston he may have retained, Barthelme fortunately also brought along his Southwestern food consciousness to New York, though the theory of Tex-Mex eats he found there must have alarmed him, based as it was on tomato sauce, and tasting like Italian food made with Tabasco. The recipes reprinted in this volume may thus have developed out of some nostalgic necessity.

Those recipes. That oxtail soup mix. That "burgoo," with the frozen ducks in it? A notable moment in chef psychopathology, to be sure—yet such is Barthelme's genius that even the most porkophobic or duck-intolerant among us is drooling, unashamed, by recipe's end. His ingredients tend to come from outside New York, back in the U.S., brand names always good for some evocation of his native region, mostly canned or otherwise preserved, food meant to sit on shelves or in freezers for months before being used, each meal, each can opened or dinner defrosted, being an occasion for sadness, because, like using a dream or a memory in a piece of writing, it's taking something back inside the passage of time that otherwise might have continued on, suspended, exempt. This is a cuisine of solitude, suggesting too many nights of unfamilied boredom and eating over the sink, a life-style that was certainly not for Don B. He disliked being alone, preferring company, however problematical, to no company. In cities such a willingness to socialize can lead a man up peculiar streets indeed, anything from all-out Uzi-toting misanthropy to a full Dickensian embrace of human diversity, foolishness and all. But to move in that direction, to open up instead of shut down, meant risking the possibility of finding spiritual dimensions sooner or later hiding inside a space he thought he owned and knew, and what would the next step have to be after that? Herbs, crystals, astrology? *California?*

Nevertheless, here are two illustrated stories, "The Photographs," about the scientific discovery of the soul, and "The Dassaud Prize," about a competitive search for God, and what are we to make of them? Two British scientists, after getting into another of those stupefyingly stretched-out exchanges, agree to destroy their photographs of the soul. Their French counterparts, failing to discover God, generate as a by-product this museumful of mad-inventor gear. In both stories reachings after the transfinite fall apart, into twit dialogue, into eccentric technological dreaming, reentangled with Earth and the earthbound. In a writer less attendant upon the given world, this might have been occasion for some cheap glee. But this being another luxury Barthelme couldn't afford, he was obliged to stick with reliable melancholy, a less dramatic mode but one he struggled for and came by honorably.

Not to try to make any case for Barthelme as any heavy-duty metaphysician. Heaven forfend. He was too connected to calendar dates and named streets, too engaged with the quotidian—like García Márquez's magician Melquíades in *One Hundred Years of Solitude*, "in spite of his immense wisdom and mysterious breadth, he had a human burden, an earthly condition that kept him involved in the small problems of daily life." Because his verifiable miracles are all literary in nature, Barthelme is probably not about to make saint anytime soon, either. But along with his published work, his other great gift to us is precisely his melancholy, presented, if we will but look, as praxis and example, a way to get us through, trading off time for spectacle, now and then even providing, as they used to sing at the end of *Hee Haw,* "a smile and a laugh or two." If this is not exactly a guide for the perplexed, it is still a good honest push back against the forces that favor tragedy, and who of us wouldn't like to have left something like that behind us?

All things, in any event, will be set right when the biopic or *Donald Barthelme Story* is aired at last. This will be a made-for-cable-TV miniseries starring Barthelme lookalike Luke Perry in the title role. Paul Newman, in his first small-screen appearance, will have a cameo as Norman Mailer, for which he will win an Emmy. In the picture, Barthelme will return, sometime in the final installment, to Houston. Neighbors from long ago will bring him casseroles, Kiri Te Kanawa and Willie Nelson will come sing medleys of country classics to him in a vividly lit Astrodome before a sellout crowd. Ravishing Texas tomatoes of all shapes and sizes, played by starlets who think they have to be kind to the second assistant director, will fling themselves upon the person of Don B., cooing, squealing, gaga. Bartenders in sorrowful-looking crossroads saloons, where the records on the jukebox are all from Barthelme's youth, will fix him perfect city drinks such as martinis and Singapore slings, and everything will be on the house.

He will go sit in out-of-the-way Mexican eateries scarfing all afternoon and evening on chef specials not available to the average customer, featuring chiles you need a Department of Energy permit even to plant, and so forth. He will get the key to the city and a ride on a fire truck. Reviewers who trashed his work years ago will now fly into town, paying the full fare out of their own pockets, to apologize abjectly. All his books will show up again on the best-seller lists. Mike Ovitz of CAA will call from Hollywood with high-budget movie plans for some story the author has forgotten he wrote, and Barthelme will put him on hold while he goes to the fridge for another beer.

As catastasis yields to catastrophe, shots of Barthelme are gradually replaced with shots of people talking about him, and shots of the city, parkland, sunsets, hospitals, and the like. The last we get to see of him, Barthelme is driving some gray primer–coated outlaw's dream of a Trans-Am, pulling onto some freeway, softly thundering away into the evening humidity, Lightnin' Hopkins on the soundtrack singing "Baby Please Don't Go," the camera pulling back into a helicopter shot, swooping upward as credits roll—production, technical, Houston and New York second units, dialogue coaches, duck wranglers. Lights beginning to come on all

across the crowded prairie. Album is available on Rounder Records. Studio logo. Two seconds of quiet, neutral darkness. Then a
promo for the news at ten.

Thomas Pynchon

Satires, Parodies,
Fables, and
Illustrated Stories

THE TEACHINGS OF DON B.:
A YANKEE WAY OF KNOWLEDGE

While doing anthropological fieldwork in Manhattan some years ago I met, on West Eleventh Street, a male Yankee of indeterminate age whose name, I was told, was Don B. I found him leaning against a building in a profound torpor—perhaps the profoundest torpor I have ever seen. He was a tallish man with an unconvincing beard and was dressed, in the fashion of the Village, in jeans and a blue work shirt. After we had been introduced, by a mutual acquaintance, I explained to him that I had been told he knew the secrets of certain hallucinogenic substances peculiar to Yankee culture and in which I was professionally interested. I expressed a wish to learn what he knew and asked if I might talk with him about the subject. He simply stared at me without replying, and then said, "No." However, taking note of the dismay which must have been plain on my face, he said that I might return, if I wished, in two years. In the meantime, he would think about my proposal. Then he closed his eyes again, and I left him.

I returned in the summer of 1968 and found Don B. still leaning against the same building. His torpor was now something very close to outright gloom, but he greeted me civilly enough. Again I asked him if he would consider taking me under instruction. He stared at me for a long time and then said, "Yes." But, he warned me, states of nonordinary reality could not be attained by just anybody, and if just anybody did, by accident, blunder into a state of nonordinary reality, the anybody might bloody well regret it.

3

Yankee culture was a fearsome thing, he told me, and not to be entered into lightly, but only with a prepared heart. Was I willing, he asked, to endure the pain, elation, shock, terror, and boredom of such an experience? Was I, for example, ticklish? I assured him that I was ready and was not ticklish, or not overmuch. He then led me into the building against which he had been leaning. He showed me into a small but poorly furnished apartment containing hundreds of books stacked randomly about. In the center of the room a fire was blazing brightly. Throwing a few more books on the fire, Don B. invited me to be seated, and we had the first of what proved to be a long series of conversations. The following material, reproduced from my field notes, has been edited somewhat to eliminate the dull parts, but in the main reflects accurately what took place during the period when I was Don B.'s apprentice.

In dealing with any system of world interpretation different from our own, it is necessary to make use of the technique of suspended judgment. This I have done, and I urge the reader to do so also.

June 11, 1968

We were sitting cross-legged on the floor of Don B.'s apartment, facing each other, with the fire, which was kept going even in summer, between us. I decided to ask Don B. about the fire, for it was markedly hot in the room.

"Why is the fire burning, Don B.? It's hot in here."

Don B. gazed at me for a time without answering. Then he said: "Fire burns because it is his nature to burn. Fire is a friend. But one must know how to treat him. He contains a thousand invisible *brillos* which, unleashed, can cause considerable harm to life and property. That is why we have fire engines. The fire engines throw water on Fire and drown the invisible *brillos*. They fear water."

"What is a *brillo*, Don B.?"

"A sort of devil who is invisible."

"But why doesn't your fire burn a hole in the floor?"

"Because I understand Fire and know his secrets," Don B. said. "When I was a boy in the city of Philadelphia, Fire seized many houses, shops, and other buildings and burned them to the

4

ground. But he never seized my house because I knew his secrets and he knew I knew his secrets. Therefore he stayed away."

"What *are* his secrets, Don B.?"

Don B. laughed uproariously.

"You are a fool," he said. "You are not a man of knowledge. Only a man of knowledge can understand secrets. Even if I told you Fire's secrets, they would be of no use to you."

"Can I become a man of knowledge, Don B.?"

Don B. fell silent. He stared at his knees for some moments. Then he gave me an intense look.

"Maybe," he said.

I went away filled with a powerful and deep sense of warmth.

June 13, 1968

We were sitting as before on the floor of Don B.'s apartment.

"What is a man of knowledge, Don B.?" I asked him.

"A man of knowledge," Don B. replied, "is one who knows. He not only knows, he knows that he knows. He has an ally to help him know."

"What does the ally do, Don B.?"

"The ally helps the man of knowledge know and also helps him know that he knows."

"Do you have an ally, Don B.?"

"Of course."

"Who is your ally, Don B.?"

"Turkey," he said, and laughed uproariously.

I went away filled with a sensation of not having heard him correctly.

June 17, 1968

I had brought Don B. some food. We sat on the floor eating fettucine on rye in silence. I had noticed that although Don B. as a rule ate very little, whenever there were two sandwiches on the floor he ate both halves of his and half of mine, which I thought a little strange.

Without warning he said: "You feel uncomfortable."

I admitted that I felt a bit uncomfortable.

"I knew that you felt uncomfortable," he said. "That is because you have not found your spot. Move around the room until you have found it."

"How do you mean, move around the room?"

"I mean, like sit in different places."

Don B. rose and left the apartment. I tried sitting in different places. What he had said made no sense to me. True, I had been slightly uncomfortable in the spot I had been sitting in. But no other place in the room seemed any better to me. I sat experimentally in various areas but could discover no spot that felt any better than any other spot. I was sweating and felt more uncomfortable than ever. An hour passed, then two hours. I was sitting as hard as I could, first in one place, then another. But no particular place seemed desirable or special. I wondered where Don B. was. Then I noticed that a particular spot near the south wall was exuding a sort of yellow luminosity. I painfully sat over toward it, sit by sit, a process which consumed some twelve minutes. Yes! It was true. In the spot occupied by the yellow luminosity I felt much more comfortable than I had felt in my original spot. The door opened and Don B. entered, smiling.

"Where have you been, Don B.?"

"I caught a flick. I see that you have found your spot."

"You were right, Don B. This spot is much better than my old spot."

"Of course. You were sitting too close to the fire, idiot."

"But Don B.! What is this yellow luminosity that seems to hover over this particular spot?"

"It's the lamp, dummy."

I looked up. Don B. was right. Immediately above my new spot was a light fixture containing two 150-watt bulbs. It was turned on.

I went away filled with a powerful sensation having to do with electricity.

June 18, 1968

Once again I had asked Don B. about the famous hallucinogenic substances used by the Yankees.

Without replying, he carefully placed another book on the fire. It was Elias Ashmole's *Theatrum chemicum Britannicum*.

"When I sneeze, the earth shakes," Don B. said, after a time.

I greeted this announcement with a certain amount of skepticism.

"Show me, Don B.," I said.

"The man of knowledge does not sneeze on command," he said. "He sneezes only when it is appropriate and right to do so, that is, when his *brillo* is inside his nose, tickling him."

"When is it appropriate and right to sneeze, Don B.?"

"It is appropriate and right to sneeze when your *brillo* is inside your nose, tickling it."

"Does each man have his own personal *brillo*, Don B.?"

"The man of knowledge both *has* a *brillo* and *is* a *brillo*. That is why he is able to sneeze so powerfully that when he sneezes, the earth shakes. *Brillo* is nose, arms, legs, liver—the whole shebang."

"But you said a *brillo* was a devil, Don B."

"Some people *like* devils."

"How does the man of knowledge find his personal *brillo*, Don B.?"

"Through the use of certain hallucinogenic substances peculiar to Yankee culture," Don B. said.

"Can I try them?"

Don B. gazed at me for a long time—an intense gaze. Then he said: "Maybe."

I departed with a strong sense of epistemological obfuscation.

June 20, 1968

"The four natural enemies of the man of knowledge," Don B. said to me, "are fear, sleep, sex, and the Internal Revenue Service."

I listened attentively.

"Before one can become a man of knowledge one must conquer all of these."

"Have you conquered the four natural enemies of the man of knowledge, Don B.?"

"All but the last," he said with a grimace. "Those sumbitches never give up."

"How does one conquer fear, Don B.?"

"One takes a frog and sews it to one's shoe," he said.

"The right or the left?"

Don B. gave me a pitying look.

7

"Well, you'd look mighty funny going down the street with only one frog sewed to your shoes, wouldn't you?" he said. "One frog on *each* shoe."

"How does having frogs sewed to your shoes help one conquer fear, Don B.?"

But Don B. had fallen asleep. I was torn inside. My most deeply held values, such as being kind to frogs, had been placed in question. I really did want to become a man of knowledge. But at such a cost?

June 21, 1968

Today Don B. looked at me for a long time. His gaze, usually so piercing, was suffused with a sort of wet irony.

"Xavier," he said, "there is something about you I like. I think it's your credulity. Belief is very important if one wishes to become a man of knowledge—to truly 'see.' I think you might possibly be able to 'see' someday. But 'seeing' is very difficult. Only after the most arduous preparation of the heart will you be able to 'see.' Even though you are not a Yankee, it may be that you will be able to prepare your heart adequately. I don't know. I'm not guaranteeing anything."

"How does one prepare the heart, Don B.?"

"One cleanses it with either a yellow warmth or a pink luminosity. I don't know which is right in your case. It varies with the individual. Each man must choose. So we will try both. But I must warn you that the experience is dangerous and sticky. Your life may hang on how you behave in the next hour. You must do everything exactly as I tell you. This isn't kid stuff, buddy."

I was filled with a sense of awe and dread. Could I, a Western man, enter into the darkest mysteries of the Yankees without putting myself and my most deeply held convictions in peril? A profound sadness overtook me, followed by an indescribable anguish. I suppressed them.

"All right, Don B.," I said. "If you really think I'm ready."

Don B. then rose and went to a cupboard. He opened it and removed two vessels which he placed on the floor, near the fire. He opened a second cupboard and produced two ordinary drinking glasses, which he also placed on the floor. Then he went into another room, returning with a sort of crock with a lid on it, a small round yellow object, and a knife. All of these he placed on the floor near the fire. He knelt alongside them and began a strange, rather eerie chant. I could not make out all of the words, but they included *town, pony,* and *feather*. I wondered if I was supposed to chant too, but dared not interrupt him to ask. I began chanting, tentatively, "town-pony-feather."

Abruptly, Don B. stopped chanting and began whittling at the small yellow object. Was it this, I wondered, that generated the "yellow warmth" he had spoken of? Soon there was a small pile of yellow-white chips before him. He then reached for one of the vessels he had taken from the cupboard and poured a colorless liquid, perhaps four ounces of it, into each of the drinking glasses. Then he crossed his eyes and sat with his eyes crossed for some moments. I crossed my eyes also. We sat thus for four minutes, our gazes missing each other but meeting, I felt, somewhere in the neutral space on either side of us. The sensation was strange, eerie.

Don B. uncrossed his eyes, blinked, smiled at me.

He reached for the second vessel and poured a second colorless liquid into each glass, but much less of it: about half an ounce per glass, I estimated. He then removed the top of the crock and took from it six small colorless objects, each perhaps an inch and one-half square, placing three of them in each glass. Next he picked up one of the yellow-white chips and rubbed it around the rim of each glass. Then he stirred the mixtures with his index finger and handed me a glass.

"Drink it down without stopping," he said, "for if you pause in the drinking of it the *brillo* which it summons, your personal *brillo*, will not appear. And the whole thing will be a bloody god-damn fiasco."

I did as Don B. bade me, and drained the glass in one gulp. Immediately a horrible trembling convulsed my limbs, while an overwhelming nausea retracted my brain. I flopped around on the floor a lot. I became aware of (left to right) a profound sadness, a yellow warmth, an indescribable anguish, and a pink luminosity. Don B. was watching me with a scornful smile on his face. I was sweating, my stomach was cramping, and I needed a cigarette. I saw, on my left, the profound sadness merging with the yellow warmth, and on my right, the indescribable anguish intermingling with the pink luminosity, and, suddenly, standing with one foot on the profound sadness/yellow warmth and the other on the indescribable anguish/pink luminosity, a gigantic figure half-human, half-animal, and a hundred feet tall (roughly). A truly monstrous thing! Never in the wildest fantasies of fiction had I encountered anything like it. I looked at it in complete, utter bewilderment. It was strange and eerie, and yet familiar. Then I realized with a shock of horror, terror, and eeriness that it was a colossal Publisher, and that it was moving toward me, wanted something from me. I fainted. When I revived, it took me to lunch at Lutèce and we settled on an advance in the low fifties, which I accepted even though I knew I was not yet, in the truest sense, a man of knowledge. But there would be other books, I reflected, to become a man of knowledge in, and if I got stuck I could always go back and see good old Don B.

I WROTE A LETTER...

I wrote a letter to the President of the moon, asked him if they had towaway zones up there. The cops had towed away my Honda and I didn't like it. Cost me seventy-five dollars to get it back, plus the mental health. You ever notice how the tow trucks pick on little tiny cars? You ever seen them hauling off a Chrysler Imperial? No, you haven't.

The President of the moon replied most courteously that the moon had no towaway zones whatsoever. Mental health on the moon, he added, cost only a dollar.

Well, I needed mental health real bad that week, so I wrote back saying I thought I could get there by the spring of '81, if the space shuttle fulfilled its porcelain promise, and to keep some mental health warm for me who needed it, and could I interest him in a bucket of ribs in red sauce? Which I would gladly carry on up there to him if he wished?

The President of the moon wrote back that he would be delighted to have a bucket of ribs in red sauce, and that his zip code, if I needed it, was 10011000000000.

I cabled him that I'd bring some six-packs of Rolling Rock beer to drink with the ribs in red sauce, and, by the way, what was the apartment situation up there?

It was bad, he replied by platitudinum plate, apartments were running about a dollar a year, he knew that was high but what could he do? These were four-bedroom apartments, he said, with three baths, library, billiard room, root cellar, and terrace overlooking the Sea of Prosperity. Maybe he could get me a rent abatement, he said, 'cause of me being a friend of the moon.

The moon began to sound like a pretty nice place. I sent a dollar to the Space Shuttle Hurry-Up Fund.

Drumming fiercely on a hollow log with a longitudinal slit tuned to moon frequencies, I asked him about employment, medical coverage, retirement benefits, tax shelterage, convenience cards, and Christmas Club accounts.

That's a roger, he moonbeamed back, a dollar covers it all, and if you don't have a dollar we'll *lend* you a dollar through the Greater Moon Development Mechanism.

What about war and peace? I inquired by means of curly little ALGOL circuits I had knitted myself on my Apple computer.

The President of the moon answered (by MIRV'd metaphor) that ticktacktoe was about as far as they'd got in that direction, and about as far as they would go, if he had anything to say about it.

I told him via flights of angels with special instructions that it looked to me like he had things pretty well in hand up there and would he by any chance consider being President of us? Part-time if need be?

No, he said (in a shower of used-car asteroids with blue-and-green bumper stickers), our Presidential campaigns seemed to damage the candidates, hurt them. They began hitting each other over the head with pneumatic Russians, or saying terminally silly things about the trees. He wouldn't mind being Dizzy Gillespie, he said.

CHALLENGE

In 1981, the superiority of the Japanese-made book review to the faltering domestic product, long a source of concern to industry insiders (*Publishers Weekly*, June 10, 1979, "Those Snazzy New Imports"), was dramatically endorsed by enthusiastic American consumers as Japan's U.S. market share rose to a stunning forty-seven percent. The sleek, space-efficient Japanese reviews were appearing everywhere, and it was clear that the big, clunky American reviews, whose basic design had not been rethought since the days of Orville Prescott, were in Trouble City.

The *soul* of the Japanese review, rooted in the concept of Ma, or space interfacing with time, was large, forthright, ultramodern, yet warm. It was a soul that consumers found agreeable, spread out all over the coffee table on a Sunday morning, and one that wore its technology lightly, like a plastic raincoat. At the same time, bench tests of the new Japanese reviews disclosed a ferocious efficiency.

The Nakamichi Model 500, for instance, was capable of deconstructing a book of average length in seven seconds, with 0.5 percent distortion, signal-to-noise ratio of 124 db, and a damping factor of 60—a technological feat well beyond the capacity of any U.S. review. American notices tended to be handwritten, typically by either John Kenneth Galbraith or Joyce Carol Oates; the new Japanese reviews, on the other hand, were produced by teams of computer-directed, white-gowned specialists between bouts of singing the company song ("Forward, Nakamichi, Forever"). And there were, in the imports, numerous refinements that the plodding, bulbous American reviews could not hope to match. In the Sanyo Model 350, "highs," or undue enthusiasm, were suppressed by a special microprocessor unit, which could itself sing the company song ("Greatness, Sanyo, Is Possible"). In March of 1981 Yamaha introduced the ultimate in politesse—a review with a sensational "muting" or self-canceling feature (although in fairness it must be noted that this was based on original research done in this country by Lehmann-Haupt and others). Nikko's Model 770 came equipped with a three-foot clip-on extension probe that actually *reached out and touched the reader's heartstrings*, aided by dual LED heartstring meters.

There were, of course, variations in the Japanese product. Close readers ("review nuts") could discern a mushiness in the midrange in some Mitsubishi reviews; the upper registers of a Yamaha review were, in some models, unpleasantly shrill; Subaru's notices were thought to be "charitable." (Sansui's use of industrial robots in book-review assembly was not in itself considered innovative; *The New York Review of Books* had been using robots, usually British, for years.) Still, feature for feature and dollar for dollar, the Japanese entry was a brushed-chrome nifty and the native effort sad, drab knotty pine.

Nor was the export challenge confined to the American market. In England, *The Times Literary Supplement*, never known for liberality in the matter of reviewers' pay—"I would *accept* birdseed," one Brit-crit famously declared—converted instantly to an all-Nippon mode, the Japanese having savvily modified basic models to permit maundering, a fave reviewer tactic in Albion. The imports were cost-effective—that is to say, cheap. An English novelist, renowned for his ability to turn out two lengthy *Sunday Observer* pieces an hour while writing a symphony with his toes, said for attribution, *"It's just bloody unfair!"*—a plaint voiced again and again by his colleagues worldwide. From the *Irish Times* through the *Corriere della Sera* and *Le Monde* to Stockholm's mighty *Aftonbladet*, there was capitulation after capitulation, and big yen flowed toward the Ginza.

In this country, perilously high levels of reviewer unemployment were reached. The Kirkus Service closed down plants in New

Rochelle, New York, and Lordstown, Ohio. *Publishers Weekly*, already under pressure from the Department of Labor for its exclusive employment of thirteen-year-old girls, laid off its entire work force, using blue bubble gum as severance pay. *Book World, The Washington Post's* lit. sup., wavered, and then fell; as of the issue of September 18, it was printed on rice paper and read back to front. The *Saturday Review's* splendid quarterbrow pages looked like so many plates of sushi, and only *The New York Times Book Review*, where the editor-san brooded in his glass-walled office while frightened subeditors practiced the tea ceremony, held out.

The National Book Critics Circle, under the leadership of Fremont-Smith, although stoutly maintaining in public its belief in global freedom of expression, made private representations to the President demanding savage import quotas, hinting that its members would have a thing or two to say about the Reagan memoirs (a projected $8 million blockbuster for S&S) when he got around to writing them. A noted *Times* daily appraiser announced that he would henceforth devote himself exclusively to his flower-arranging classes at the New School, and a celebrated *Newsweek* critic was observed entering the building wearing a beautifully folded black obi over his Paul Stuart worsteds.

Inevitably, in December, the *TBR* too caved in, the contract going to giant Hitachi Industries of Osaka. As dejected *Times*men stuffed their attaché cases with clips of old reviews and half-consumed packages of Figurines, Hitachi's Managing Director I. Yamaguchi was asked by media reps for the secret of his company's success. "Ma knows best," he said.

THREE GREAT MEALS

I n this article I am going to tell you how to make three great meals using standard ingredients. By "standard ingredients" I mean things that can be found in any supermarket from one end of the country to the other. I am going to name names and tell you what brands I use, not because I am in the pay of these particular brands or have any fiduciary relation to them but because they are the ones I use daily and ones that I have found work well, day in and day out. In each case you will notice that the meal is geared to the person who does not have too much time to screw around but at the same time wants extra-good results, something a little better than what you would get if you just used these fine products straight, without informed guidance or nuance.

It is true that all of these great meals fall roughly under the rubric "Southern Cooking," but I stress that the ingredients have nationwide distribution, for the most part, and that because something has its origins in the South doesn't automatically mean that it can be dismissed as "low-rent" or beneath contempt. An open mind toward the cuisines of various regions is the first hallmark of the educable palate.

A GREAT BREAKFAST

For the Great Breakfast we assume that, the night before, you have gone out and bought 8–10 pieces of Popeye's Fried Chicken at the drive-in window of your local Popeye's, together with 6–8 Popeye's Biscuits. Now I am not sure that Popeye's is entirely national, but it is widely found throughout the South which makes it national enough for our purposes. Colonel Sanders' may be substituted if you wish. The average family will have eaten about seven of the chicken pieces and maybe four of the biscuits during the original meal leaving you with a wealth of residue for the Great Breakfast.

Upon awakening, take one package McCormick Chicken Gravy Mix and place it in a saucepan, adding one-half can of Swanson's Clear Chicken Broth. This is the first subtlety. The directions for the gravy mix suggest cold water; by adding Swanson's Chicken Broth you get a gravy that is far richer. (You also double your expense, but as the Gravy Mix is typically about 63 cents a package and the Broth about 49 cents a can, it's not that much.)

Next, chop a fresh onion very fine—very *very* fine, about two tablespoons' worth. Throw this in the gravy. You may then add a splash of Soave Bolla white wine and raise heat to boil off the alcohol. If your religious convictions do not permit the use of alcohol in your breakfast it may be omitted, but what do you do when you get to turtle soup, leave out the sherry? While the gravy is simmering, take the leftover Popeye's Biscuits and split them, placing them in a small container in a 425-degree oven for approximately eight minutes.

Now, strip chicken from leftover Popeye's pieces and add to gravy, being careful to not include the heavy crispy skin that was your motivation for getting the Popeye's Chicken in the first place. Then remove biscuits from oven, ladle gravy over them, and sprinkle with Spice Islands thyme, taking care to crush thyme between thumb and forefinger to release flavor. The result is a chicken-with-dumplings that cannot be equaled this side of that tin-roofed place on a dirt road outside of Talladega, Alabama, that we've all heard about but no one has ever found. The masterstroke here is of course the onion.

AN UNUSUAL LUNCH

This kind of lunch is possible when the green-skinned tomatillo is in season. Luckily the green-skinned tomatillo is always in season in the canned version put out by Herdez, which also includes chilies. Take a can of Gebhardt Tamales and place in a small ovengoing vessel. Layer with chopped onion. Add one can Herdez Salsa Verde Tomatillos. Cover with Kraft Shredded Sharp Cheddar, which is available in a resealable plastic bag for about $2.09 for 10 oz. Use about one third of the bag to top the dish, spreading the cheese smoothly around with your hand. Bake in 425-degree oven for fifteen minutes. In the more developed parts of the country there will be locally produced tamales (usually differentiated as to "Hot" or "Mild") made by gifted indigenous personnel and these can be substituted for the Gebhardt variety. Renown and Ro*Tel brands of tomatoes and chilies can also be used; both are excellent, although not green. This lunch has a strong Mexican flavor due to the use of ingredients associated with Mexico; although it is not in any sense authentic, it is unusual.

SUPERB DINNER FOR SIXTY

You probably did not know that a superb dinner for sixty could be made out of canned goods, but that is true. Begin with five Smok-A-Roma Fully Cooked Boneless Hams. Remove hams from wrappers and cut in chunks, each chunk roughly the size of a Bic cigarette lighter. Set aside. Next take thirty 15-oz. cans of Trappey's Black Eye Peas Flavored with Slab Bacon, open, and set aside. Next brown thirty pounds of Oscar Mayer Little Smokies, which are very good bite-sized smoked sausages. Tearing open the packages is tiresome but you can usually get children to do this for you. In the same fat, make a roux by stirring in ten pounds of Gold Medal All-Purpose Flour. This gives you approximately twelve pounds of roux (flour plus oil). Set aside.

Next, into some gallons of water in huge immense pots on four six-burner stoves pour any number of cans of Progresso Peeled Tomatoes Italian Style with Basil (Pomidoro Pelati Tipo Italiano con Basilico). If you use the larger cans you have fewer cans to open. Add forty-eight cloves of chopped Elephant Garlic, which is sold in little net bags from Frieda of California and has a subtle explosiveness that is piquant.

By now you will be slightly confused as you look around you at the mighty forces you have mustered but everything is easier than it looks. You must understand that we don't like to get this involved either but maybe it's your daughter's wedding or something and you have the choice of giving the whole problem over to some unreliable caterer who'll just supply some pink froufrou on lettuce leaves at a horrible price per head or doing it yourself with your accustomed élan and goodwill. Place a half pound of the roux into each pot and paddle it around in there until the liquid has achieved a rich dark-brown color, then add the ham, sausages, and Black Eye Peas. Simmer for some time; you are doing just fine.

Pork is the motif which has up to now dominated the mix, and the pork has to have a contrasting flavor. The only thing to do is to slug in five Maple Leaf Farms Frozen Ducklings. Defrost and cut up ducks, brown quickly in Lou Ana 100% Pure and Natural Peanut Oil, home office, Opelousas, La., place in pots and let simmer for one hour. Salt (Morton), pepper (Lawry's), and parsley your twenty-four pots all to hell, and you are ready to serve. About twenty pounds of sliced onions would be a good addition, although they probably should have gone in earlier. If you want something to call this superb meal you could probably call it a burgoo. (I would like to acknowledge input for this recipe from the Arkansas Department of Corrections, Food Services Division.)

For other excellent recipes involving American canned goods, my 64-page leaflet is available upon request. But I am not trying to sell the leaflet, only to stress an appropriate respect and love for the American canned good, which is not, and never will be, Japanese.

LANGUISHING, HALF-DEEP
IN SUMMER...

Languishing, half-deep in summer, soul-sick and under-friended, I decided to find love. So I zipped over to the new-suit store and bought me a Giorgio Armani rig, unbacked, and a little skinny nothing tie to go with it, and some face bronzer by Daunt. Thinking: O mistress mine, where are you hiding? Are you at the Whitney Museum, cheek to cheek with the George Segal retrospective? Are you at Crazy Eddie's, bent over the Grover Washington, Jr., bin? Are you at Paragon Sporting Goods, in the killer-knife area? Have you got your thumb stuck in a dark-green avocado at Balducci's fruit and produce? Are you riding a Japanese ten-speed the wrong way down Sixth Avenue, with friends? With a whistle in your mouth? Whistling, whistling, wildly whistling?

So I answered an ad in the back pages of a literary review—Box 222, to be precise—and got me a pretty, lively, successful, vibrant prof. female, fluent French, German, witty affectionate caring, backgammon, racquetball. She was vibrating visibly when we met, at One Fifth in the bar, but I cooled her out with about half a gallon of kir; she was indeed pretty, lively, witty, and her name was Mindy Sue.

She asked if it had been raining in my part of the city, and I said no, the suit was supposed to look that way, it was an unbacked Giorgio Armani. We looked at my credit cards for a while and then she showed me hers, shyly—her American Express, her Avis, her Bergdorf's. We discussed backgammon, racquetball, three

20

hundred films, and the urban crisis. Then I said, "Mindy Sue, you are a pretty, lively, successful female, fluent in French and German. You are a professional woman but also *sportif*. You care buckets, I can see that. How did you get yourself in this terrible predicament? How did you become a four-line seventy-five-cents-a-word advertisement in the back pages of *The New York Review of Books*?"

"Pete," she said, "there are thousands of us. The true urban crisis, from my angle of vision, is marriage. All the good men are married, and most of the bad. There is nothing much left except lames, kiddies, and poor people. What can I do? You think I *like* describing myself as 'cultivated, sensuous'?"

I said that hadn't been in the ad.

"Whoops," she said. "Must have been the *Saturday Review*. Or maybe the *Chronicle of Higher Education*. Sometimes I have trouble keeping track."

I said she seemed to have a lot of lines out.

"Well some of these dealies pull and some don't," she answered, splashing a little kir behind her ears. "One is looking for a certain type of person, right? One stuffs one's message into the bottle and hopes for the best. You should see what springs from *semiotexte*. Or *praxis 4*. Let me tell you, if a journal runs its logo in lower case, what you get is lower depths. With mauve teeth, usually."

Ghastly, I said.

Mindy Sue looked a bit fierce—matter of lowering the lovely eyebrows. "I have also," she said, "responded to some of these items. Myself. 'Dynamic, attractive professor seeks supplemental relationship with superior fox, to 40.' It was piggy of me. Like that cutoff point? Like it? Like that 'supplemental'? Well, I was punished. He took me to a joint so tacky that when I ordered Cherries Jubilee the captain said 'We don't flame for one.' Can you hear that? 'We don't flame for one'?"

I said something to the effect that the course of periodical love was seldom smooth, and that some comfort could be derived from the excellent editorial matter—the parsley, as it were, in these particular meat marts.

"Well, I bring it on my own damn self," said Mindy Sue. "I could sit home and talk to myself in my fluent French and German, I suppose. I could be witty, affectionate, caring with the cat. I could go to the George Segal retrospective at the Whitney and think about the human condition, or plaster. I have a ten-speed Japanese bicycle and a whistle. Nobody's *forcing* me to insert myself in the back pages of the damn *New York Review of Books*—"

She seemed distraught; I beamed support at her through my newly bronzed façade.

"But *I will not give up!*" she said, pounding on the table with her small fist and making the dead Salems dance in their ashtray. "I will persevere. I will check out handsome, cerebral, overachieving prof. male, young 42, likes music, ballet, stamps & coins. I will investigate earthy, outgoing, tall semiretired humanist idealist, sailing, tennis, good coffee. I will encounter, tentatively, dentist, 28, sincere, intelligent. I will invest an evening in warm, bright, NY mensch, assertive but not hostile booklover, walks, talks, concerts. *I have to try.*"

I bought her a wurst and an anisette, and told her she was brave.

THE PALACE

I was standing in line at the bank (Chase Manhattan Fourteenth Street) last Friday, and I happened to notice the amount of the check the short Puerto Rican woman in front of me was cashing: $84.06. I looked away very quickly, but the check was yellow and I noticed that there were a lot of white and black and Puerto Rican women in line holding in their hands the same yellow paycheck. And I thought, $84.06, that's not much for a week's work. Then I tried to remember what the federal minimum wage was, and remembered, and tried to multiply $1.60 by forty hours and got it wrong, and more women were coming into the bank now with these yellow checks in their hands (it was lunchtime), and I began running down the purchasing power of $84.06. It's a single session with a $50-an-hour analyst, with $34.06 left over for coffee, cakes, and the rent. And a lady I know has informed me that her panty hose cost $2.50 the pair, and a kennel owner I know has offered me a purebred Rhodesian Ridgeback for $350, and you can buy a Pontiac Firebird for $4,385. And a house in the country . . .

But you can get a pretty good tennis racket for $84.06, and all of a sudden I flashed on a scene in which all these ladies, white, black, and Puerto Rican, were zipping into Abercrombie's or somewhere and lashing out their $84.06s for brand-new tennis racquets. And for a minute, there in the bank line, every yellow check became in my mind a good-quality tennis racquet, all these ladies were waving good-quality tennis racquets, and what else was there to do with these tennis racquets but *beat me to death with them*? What if the Revolution occurred to all these women simultaneously? What if they put it together, figured it out, got hold of the real numbers, all at once, and then, armed with their death-dealing Bancrofts or Wilsons, and me armed only with a little card that says I'm a member of the ACLU, came after me? Because my check wasn't yellow and it wasn't for $84.06, and although I am for the Revolution in principle, I haven't done much about it lately in a practical way. So in order not to think about this distressing situation I thought about the palace.

The palace is quite a wonderful place, full of Eames chairs and Barcelona chairs and Pollock paintings and David Smith sculptures and other high-class cultural grid coordinates. The palace was partly designed by Breuer, but then Mies came over one day while the thing was still a-building and said something about how wouldn't it be nice if the travertine that covers the west wall ran *this* way instead of *that* way (waving his hands in the air, which is how architects do their thinking), and Breuer, who is the most modest of men, said, "Mies, just for fun, why don't *you* do part of it and *I'll* do part of it and we'll see what happens?" Well, Mies liked to play, too, so he agreed, and then when Corbu visited the site *he* wanted to get in on it, and, in fact, the entire east wing is Corbu's. And then Nervi and Aalto and Neutra and Saarinen and Louis Kahn and all sorts of other people, all geniuses, got interested, contributed bits, ideas, little pieces, because none of them had ever done a palace before—I mean a real, honest-to-God palace, as opposed to a corporate headquarters. The king came out to the site every day wearing a blue hard hat and was just beside himself. I have never seen a king, even a limited constitutional monarch, take so much pleasure in anything. The wonderful part was that the whole place *worked*, it came together beautifully, none of the architects tried to upstage each other—the palace appears to be the product of a single hand. Kahn's dark-red brick towers look amazing and lovely against Mies's exposed steel (in this case, Cor-Ten, which rusts to a handsome reddish brown, rather than his usual black-painted steel—just one instance of the courtesy and tact and sweetness that prevailed). Aalto used dark woods instead of light, Le Corbusier did not insist on pilotis, and everyone wondered what Wright would have done if he had been around to participate, and Venturi jumped up and down and clapped his hands in glee and sent a telegram to Paolo Soleri, out there in the desert, and ordered forty dozen wind bells and wondered if Soleri would be interested in doing the grand ballroom. Soleri was enchanted with the idea of doing a grand ballroom, and the next day the model arrived by air express, together with a blueprint forty feet long and so splendid in conception that everybody agreed it gave new meaning to the words *grand* and *ballroom*. And the throne room, done by Simon Rodia, who did the Watts Towers, is as gaudy as Gaudí, and the royal kitchens, by Edward Durell Stone, make you want to get in there and cook your heart out.

The royal tennis courts extend for miles in every direction—grass courts set in glades and dells (each glade and dell the work of a great-grandson of Frederick Law Olmsted himself), and I suddenly shouted, right out loud, right there in line at Chase Manhattan Fourteenth Street, "Tennis, everyone?" And everyone shouted back, "Yes, yes, *tennis!*" And we all set out, the white and black and Puerto Rican women with their tennis racquets, and the clerks and tellers, too, with their racquets, and even the bank officers, in their dark suits, with their racquets, in a long straggle, or friendly mob, in the direction of the palace. The palace exists; we have only to get there—that is, walk hard enough. That is a beautiful idea of which I have always been very fond. The truth is that the palace does not exist but the serfs do.

MR. FOOLFARM'S JOURNAL

Mr. Foolfarm, the well-known Generalist, was not in again today. He had hauled Himself to Washington on the Shuttle, to see his Ambassadorship. The post, as Plenipotentiary to North Minerva (the handsome and vivacious South Pacific atoll), was awarded him not in Consequence of his campaign contribution of $1.95, as malicious Tongues have whispered, but rather for his lifetime of service to the Nation, as well as his great talents at Stroking and Mental Reservation. He is also known to excel at Face-Slapping, holding the world Title for same at 34 hours 20 minutes (Kiev, USSR, 1961).

Mr. Foolfarm was not in again today. He is in Washington, the Capital of the Country, advising an Important Person about Hangout. It had been suggested to the Important Person that he Let It All Hang Out, but Mr. Foolfarm is not entirely Sanguine as to the Consequences of this Policy. The noted Generalist has, it is said, offered a Bouquet of Options, including Partial Hangout, Semipartial Hangout, Semipartial Reversible Hangout, More or Less Total Hangout, and Absolutely Final Weighted Plus-or-Minus Hangout. The Important Person is giving these Choices the consideration they Deserve.

———

Mr. Foolfarm, the Omnidirectional Thinker, was not in again today. He is in Washington, the Capital of the Country, learning to play Tennis. By fierce perusal of the Newspapers, he has learned that if he is ever put away in one of the better government Nicks, he will have to be Able to at least get the Ball back over the net, or else suffer social Obloquy. Golf he has already mastered.

It was noticed that the lights burned late at Mr. Foolfarm's house last evening, and again today he is not in it. Reliable information has it that he is in Washington, the Seat of Government, advising the Revenue Service as to What Must Be Done. They are said to be furiously grateful. The celebrated Glossarist is urging that a Pie Chart be added to the first page of the Form, so that the joyous Ratepayer will be enabled to indicate *pristinae virtutis memores* how he wants his Mopus dissipated. Thus if the citizen wishes to pay less for War, for example, he will be able to skimp the War slice of the pie appropriately; and if he wishes to obtain more Booze, he will be able to sweeten the Booze slice. Mr. Foolfarm has Provided (lest he be thought a glistering Ninny) that not more than 12 percent of the people's wishes thus expressed be heeded. The remaining 78 percent of the decision-making process is to be reserved to the Same Old Crowd. The Crowd has proposed Mr. Foolfarm for the National Medal and a bank charter.

Mr. Foolfarm, the esteemed Longhead, fled his digs in Velvet Street at near midnight last evening, so as not to be at home again today. He is in Washington, the Country's Capital, for the purpose of declining with thanks an appointment as Attorney General. "There are my probably pressing duties in North Minerva," he said in a prepared statement shaped very like a Waffle, "and besides, there is something yukky about that job. Do you understand me? Y*u*k*k*y." He is expected to urge that the position be abolished and that an institutional-size can of Drāno be substituted.

———

Mr. Foolfarm's health is reported to be not of the Best, and it is thought that yesterday's Tender of the Attorney Generalship may be the Cause. Or it may be the alarming Dispatches from North Minerva, where the battle against the Eyelash Maggot is not Going Well. In any case, he is today away in Washington, where he is advising the Vice President, Mr. Ford, as to certain provisions of the Hatch Act. Mr. Foolfarm has suggested that the Vice President not count his Chickens until they are Hatched. The Vice President is alleged to have responded with Paroxysms of Geniality.

"Ich dien," Mr. Foolfarm said simply, and turned away. With these words, the famed Moonshee once again left home and fireside for Washington to deal with the new Crisis. It appears that Occidental Petroleum's profits have Increased 716 percent for the first Quarter, and that the other oil companies have also done Handsomely, a fact which has occasioned Concern in some Quarters. Mr. Foolfarm's proposal is that the Government award a Bonus of 125 percent of Profits to any Company whose Gleanings have produced same in a given Time Frame. "Profit should be rewarded," said Mr. Foolfarm, "for without profit, who would want to do all that moiling in the earth, *mon cher?*" Maggots chuckled dementedly in the grass at this remark (the phrase is the late Brian O'Nolan's), but they were our maggots thanks be to the living God and not the terrible Eyelash Maggot which has wreaked such Havoc in North Minerva.

Mr. Foolfarm is today in Washington for the publication of his long-awaited Novel. It is a Very Advanced Work in which three wispy Characters, identified only as "P," "E," and "H," wander about in a sort of Epistemological Hell, trying to discover what they are to Say. Sample dialogue:

P—What did I do then?
E—You understood that inaudible had unintelligible.
P—When did I understand that?
E—You understood that on the morning of the unintelligible.

P—Oh, I see. I understood that because inaudible had informed me that unintelligible.

H—Right, right. But if you understood that, at that point, then we'll have to give them the tamale grande. There's no other way.

P—The what?

H—The big tamale.

P—Oh, I see.

E—We could give them huevos rancheros.

H—Or maybe chicken mole.

E—I would just like to kind of throw this out, as a suggestion, but what about nopales con queso?

P—What?

E—Nopales con queso.

P—What is that in English?

E—Cactus.

H—They'd never bite. No, I think it's going to have to be something like frijoles refritos.

P—How do we do that?

H—You mash up a lot of beans and then fry them with, you know, your various spices.

P—But won't that look like expletive deleted?

H—It will look like you at least knew that unintelligible before inaudible and had the guts to be unintelligible.

P—I've never been afraid to be unintelligible.

E—We've never been afraid to be unintelligible.

P—That's right. I've always told everyone around here to be unintelligible.

E—And we have! We have! That's what we've got to put across.

H—Honesty is the best inaudible. Always.

P—When have I ever failed to be unintelligible?

E—You've never failed to be unintelligible.

P—What?

E—Unintelligible.

P—Oh, I see.

H—So you were inaudible then, on that date, and now you are unintelligible.

P—That's right! That's right! So that's what we'll say. And just remember one thing. What is it?

E—What is what?

P—The one thing that you're to remember.

E—I forget. Or maybe it's inaudible.

P—It *is* inaudible! *The only thing we have to inaudible is inaudible itself.*

H—That's right.

P—OK, boys. Thank you and get a good night's unintelligible.

Mr. Foolfarm was so saddened by a reading of his own Work that he called a Press Conference and declared himself Inoperative, and has been silent as a Parsnip ever since.

NATURAL HISTORY

Animalisticism, or the practice of placing too much faith in animals or in the intuitions or perceptions derived from the contemplation of same, has deviled human beings since 902 B.C., or maybe even earlier. Not to be confused with *animalitarianism*, the term used by Lovejoy for the belief that animals are happier than we are, animalisticism seems to have particularly plagued some of the world's notables. Herewith, from the Disposall of history, some examples.

The original canvas of *La Gioconda* (1503–05?) showed, according to Cassola, an octopus hurriedly departing the picture plane, on the right side. During the Frisbian Wars (1661–70) the octopus was either scraped off, or fell off. Winckelmann asserts that the octopus, in Leonardo's iconography, represents either virility or uncollectible debts. In either case the animal was clearly not trustworthy.

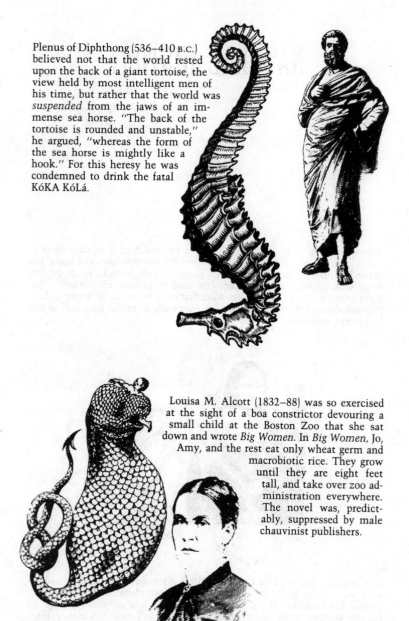

Plenus of Diphthong (536–410 B.C.) believed not that the world rested upon the back of a giant tortoise, the view held by most intelligent men of his time, but rather that the world was *suspended* from the jaws of an immense sea horse. "The back of the tortoise is rounded and unstable," he argued, "whereas the form of the sea horse is mightly like a hook." For this heresy he was condemned to drink the fatal KóKA KóLá.

Louisa M. Alcott (1832–88) was so exercised at the sight of a boa constrictor devouring a small child at the Boston Zoo that she sat down and wrote *Big Women*. In *Big Women*, Jo, Amy, and the rest eat only wheat germ and macrobiotic rice. They grow until they are eight feet tall, and take over zoo administration everywhere. The novel was, predictably, suppressed by male chauvinist publishers.

The last original idea had by Archduke Maximilian of Austria, during his brief tenure as Emperor of Mexico (1864–67), was the importation of sixty-four African rhinos, which he envisioned using, much as present-day armor is used, against the forces of Benito Juárez. The rhinos, however, almost immediately went over to the enemy and were barbecued at Querétaro, Mexico, on June 19, 1867, the same day Maximilian was executed. They were delicious.

The turbot was the immediate cause of the return from Elba. Overhearing one day a guard singing "Nobody Knows the Turbot I've Seen," Napoleon at once poignantly recalled the turbot in champagne served at the palace. The Hundred Days followed swiftly. Here is a recipe for Turbot Napoleon: Marinate fish in champagne and stock for two hours. Add two Tb finely minced shallots, dill, and a whiff of grapeshot. Simmer for eight to twelve minutes.

The explorer Sebastian Cabot (1474?–1557) brought back from America a dancing bear. This animal radically misled him when he came to write his treatise on the bears of America, which do not dance, mostly.

Robert E. Lee regarded a porcupine. "The fox knows many things, but the porcupine knows one big thing," he reflected. Lee quickly ordered porcupine quills distributed to all of the men in his army. But the notoriously inept Confederate quartermaster department neglected to provide instructions for their use. The soldiers used the quills to write letters and clean their fingernails. The South lost the war.

The Brontë sisters, Charlotte and Emily, firmly believed that all of their books were inspired by a cat. That is, they considered that the cat, Tabitha, acted as a sort of spirit control or medium. Emily could not write when the cat was staying with Charlotte, and Charlotte could not write when the cat was staying with Emily. The death of Tabitha (1843) was followed by a period of dryness broken only when Anne Brontë appeared with a basket of clairvoyant penguins.

There are, on the other hand, many examples in our daily lives of people being bucked up or otherwise nourished by thoughts of the common rabbit. The foot of the rabbit, especially the left hind foot, has brought the promise of good fortune to thousands. The rabbit ball and the rabbit punch have enlivened the sports in which they are found and no television set is complete without a set of rabbit ears atop it. The Welsh rabbit is especially tasty although not rabbit. The timidity of the rabbit has provided a useful lesson for the overbold, and the rabbit's enthusiasm for procreation a vivid simile for the Cassandras of Zero Population Growth. Gentlemen and ladies, the rabbit! Long may he waver!

THE JOKER'S GREATEST
TRIUMPH

Fredric went over to his friend Bruce Wayne's house about every Tuesday night. Bruce would be typically sitting in his study drinking a glass of something. Fredric would come in and sit down and look around the study in which there were many trophies of past exploits.

"Well Fredric what have you been doing? Anything?"

"No Bruce things have been just sort of rocking along."

"Well this is Tuesday night and usually there's some action on Tuesday night."

"I know Bruce or otherwise I wouldn't pick Tuesday night to come over."

"You want me to turn on the radio Fredric? Usually there's something interesting on the radio or maybe you'd like a little music from my hi-fi?"

Bruce Wayne's radio was a special short-wave model with many extra features. When Bruce turned it on there was a squealing noise and then they were listening to Tokyo or somewhere. Above the radio on the wall hung a trophy from an exploit: a long African spear with a spearhead made of tin.

"Tell me Bruce what is it you're drinking there?" Fredric asked.

"I'm sorry Fredric it's tomato juice. Can I get you a glass?"

"Does it have anything in it or is it just plain tomato juice?"

"It's tomato juice with a little vodka."

"Yes I wouldn't mind a glass," Fredric said. "Not too heavy on the vodka please."

While Bruce went out to the kitchen to make the drink, Fredric got up and went over to examine the African spear more closely. It was he saw tipped with a rusty darkish substance, probably some rare exotic poison he thought.

"What is the stuff on the end of this African spear?" he asked when Bruce came back into the room.

"I must have left the other bottle of vodka in the Batmobile," Bruce said. "Oh that's curare, deadliest of the South American poisons," he affirmed. "It attacks the motor nerves. Be careful there and don't scratch yourself."

"That's okay I'll just drink this tomato juice straight," Fredric said settling himself in his chair and looking out of the window. "Oh-oh there's the bat symbol spotlighted against the sky. This must mean a call from Commissioner Gordon at headquarters."

Bruce looked out of the window. A long beam of yellowish light culminating in a perfect bat symbol lanced the evening sky.

"I told you Tuesday night was usually a good night," Bruce Wayne said. He put his vodka-and-tomato-juice down on the piano. "Hold on a minute while I change will you?"

"Sure, take your time," Fredric said. "By the way is Robin still at Andover?"

"Yes," Bruce said. "He'll be home for Thanksgiving, I think. He's having a little trouble with his French."

"Well I didn't mean to interrupt you," Fredric said. "Go ahead and change. I'll just look at this magazine."

After Bruce had changed they both went out to the garage where the Batmobile and the Batplane waited.

Batman was humming a tune which Fredric recognized as being the *Warsaw Concerto*. "Which one shall we take?" he said. "It's always hard to decide on a vague and indeterminate kind of assignment like this."

"Let's flip," Fredric suggested.

"Do you have a quarter?" Batman asked.

"No but I have a dime. That should be okay," Fredric said. They flipped, heads for the Batmobile, tails for the Batplane. The coin came up heads.

"Well," Batman said as they climbed into the comfortable Batmobile, "at least you can have some vodka now. It's under the seat."

"I hate to drink it straight," Fredric said.

"Press that button there on the dashboard," Batman said. Fredric pressed the button and a panel on the dashboard slid back to reveal a little bar, with ice, glasses, water, soda, quinine, lemons, limes etc.

"Thanks," Fredric said. "Can I mix you one?"

"Not while I'm working," Batman said. "Is there enough quinine water? I forgot to get some when I went to the liquor store last night."

"Plenty," Fredric said. He enjoyed his vodka tonic as Batman wheeled the great Batmobile expertly through the dark streets of Gotham City.

In Commissioner Gordon's office at Police Headquarters the Commissioner said: "Glad you finally got here Batman. Who is this with you?"

"This is my friend Fredric Brown," Batman said. "Fredric, Commissioner Gordon." The two men shook hands and Batman said: "Now Commissioner, what is this all about?"

"This!" Commissioner Gordon said. He placed a small ship model on the desk before him. "The package came by messenger, addressed to you, Batman! I'm afraid your old enemy, The Joker, is on the loose again!"

Batman hummed a peculiar melody which Fredric recognized as the *Cornish Rhapsody* which is on the other side of the *Warsaw Concerto.* "Hmmmmm!" Batman said. "This sounds to me like another one of The Joker's challenges to a duel of wits!"

"Flying Dutchman!" Fredric exclaimed, reading the name painted on the bow of the model ship. "The name of a famous old ghost vessel? What can it mean!"

"A cleverly disguised clue!" Batman said. "The 'Flying Dutchman' meant here is probably the Dutch jewel merchant Hendrik van Voort who is flying to Gotham City tonight with a delivery of precious gems!"

"Good thinking Batman!" Commissioner Gordon said. "I probably never would have figured it out in a thousand years!"

"Well we'll have to hurry to get out to the airport!" Batman said. "What's the best way to get there from here Commissioner?"

"Well if I were you I'd go out 34th Street until you hit the War Memorial, then take a right on Memorial Drive until it connects with Gotham Parkway! After you're on the Parkway it's clear sailing!" he indicated.

"Wait a minute!" Batman said. "Wouldn't it be quicker to get on the Dugan Expressway where it comes in there at 11th Street and then take the North Loop out to the Richardson Freeway? Don't you think that would save time?"

"Well I come to work that way!" the Commissioner said. "But they're putting in another two lanes on the North Loop, so that you have to detour down Strand, then cut over to 99th to get back on the Expressway! Takes you about two miles out of your way!" he said.

"Okay!" Batman said. "We'll go out 34th! Thanks Commissioner and don't worry about anything! Come on Fredric!"

"Oh by the way," Commissioner Gordon said. "How's Robin doing at Exeter?"

"It's not Exeter it's Andover," Batman said. "He's doing very well. Having a little trouble with his French."

"I had a little trouble with it myself," the Commissioner said jovially. *"Où est mon livre?"*

"Où est ton livre?" Batman said.

"Où est son livre?" the Commissioner said pointing at Fredric.

"Tout cela s'est passé en dix-neuf cent vingt-quatre," Fredric said.

"Well we'd better creep Commissioner," Batman said. "The Joker as you know is a pretty slippery customer. Come on Fredric."

"Glad to have met you Commissioner," Fredric said.

"Me too," the Commissioner said, shaking Fredric's hand. "This is a fine-appearing young man Batman. Where did you find him?"

"He's just a friend," Batman said smiling under his mask. "We get together usually on Tuesday nights and have a few."

"What do you do Fredric? I mean how do you make your living?"

"I sell *Grit*, a newspaper which has most of its circulation concentrated in rural areas," Fredric said. "However I sell it right here in Gotham City. Many of today's leaders sold *Grit* during their boyhoods."

"Okay," said Commissioner Gordon, ushering them out of his office. "Good luck. *Téléphonez-moi un de ces jours.*"

"Righto," Batman said, and they hurried down the street to the Batmobile, which was parked in a truck zone.

"Can we stop for a minute on the way?" Fredric asked. "I'm out of cigarettes."

"There are some Viceroys in the glove compartment," Batman said pushing a button. A panel on the dashboard slid back to reveal a fresh carton of Viceroys.

"I usually prefer Kents," Fredric said, "but Viceroys are tasty too."

"They're all about the same I find," Batman said. "Most of the alleged differences in cigarettes are just advertising as far as I'm concerned."

"I wouldn't be surprised if you were right about that," Fredric said. The Batmobile sped down the dark streets of Gotham City toward Gotham Airport.

"Turn on the radio," Batman suggested. "Maybe we can catch the news or something."

Fredric turned on the radio but there was nothing unusual on it.

At Gotham Airport the jewel merchant Hendrik van Voort was just dismounting from his KLM jet when the Batmobile wheeled onto the landing strip, waved through the gates by respectful airport police in gray uniforms.

"Well everything seems to be okay," Batman said. "There's the armored car waiting to take Mr. van Voort to his destination."

"That's a new kind of armored car isn't it?" Fredric asked.

Without a word Batman leaped through the open door of the armored car and grappled with the shadowy figure inside.

HA HA HA HA HA HA HA HA HA HA HA HA HA HA HA HA HA HA HA!

"That's The Joker's laugh!" Fredric reflected. "The man inside the armored car must be the grinning clown of crime himself!"

"Batman! I thought that clue I sent you would leave you *completely at sea!*"

"No, Joker! I'm afraid this leaves your plans *up in the air!*"

"But not for long Batman! I'm going to bring you *down to earth!*"

With a swift movement, The Joker crashed the armored car into the side of the Terminal Building!

CRASH!

"Great Scott!" Fredric said to himself. "Batman is stunned! He's helpless!"

"You foiled my plans Batman," The Joker said, "but before the police get here, I'm going to lift that mask of yours and find out who you *really are*! HA HA HA HA HA HA HA HA HA HA HA HA HA HA HA HA HA HA HA HA HA HA HA!"

Fredric watched, horror-stricken. "Great Scott! The Joker has unmasked Batman! Now he knows that Batman is really *Bruce Wayne*!"

At this moment Robin, who was supposed to be at Andover, many miles away, landed the Batplane on the airstrip and came racing toward the wrecked armored car! But The Joker, alerted, grasped a cable lowered by a hovering helicopter and was quickly lifted skyward! Robin paused at the armored car and put the mask back on Batman's face!

"Hello Robin!" Fredric called. "I thought you were at Andover!"

"I was but I got a sudden feeling Batman needed me so I flew here in the Batplane," Robin said. "How've you been?"

"Fine," Fredric said. "But we left the Batplane in the garage, back at the Bat-Cave. I don't understand."

"We have two of everything," Robin explained. "Although it's not generally known."

With Fredric's aid Robin carried the stunned Batman to the waiting Batmobile. "You drive the Batmobile back to the Bat-Cave and I'll follow in the Batplane," Robin said. "All right?"

"Check," Fredric said. "Don't you think we ought to give him a little brandy or something?"

"That's a good idea," Robin said. "Press that button there on the dashboard. That's the brandy button."

Fredric pressed the button and a panel slid back, revealing a bottle of B & B and the appropriate number of glasses.

"This is pretty tasty," Fredric said, tasting the B & B. "How much is it a fifth?"

"Around eight dollars," Robin said. "There, that seems to be restoring him to his senses."

"Great Scott," Batman said, "what happened?"

"The Joker crashed the armored car and you were stunned," Fredric explained.

"Hi Robin what are you doing here? I thought you were up at school," Batman said.

"I was," Robin said. "Are you okay now? Can you drive home okay?"

"I think so," Batman said. "What happened to The Joker?"

"He got away," Fredric said, "but not before lifting your mask while you lay stunned in the wreckage of the armored car."

"Yes Batman," Robin said seriously, "I think he learned your real identity."

"Great Scott!" Batman said. "If he reveals it to the whole world it will mean the end of my career as a crime fighter! Well, it's a problem."

They drove seriously back to the Bat-Cave, thinking about the problem. Later, in Bruce Wayne's study, Bruce Wayne, Fredric, and Robin, who was now dressed in the conservative Andover clothes of Dick Grayson, Bruce Wayne's ward, mulled the whole thing over between them.

"What makes The Joker tick I wonder?" Fredric said. "I mean, what are his real motivations?"

"Consider him at any level of conduct," Bruce said slowly, "in the home, on the street, in interpersonal relations, in jail—always there is an extraordinary contradiction. He is dirty and compulsively neat, aloof and desperately gregarious, enthusiastic and sullen, generous and stingy, a snappy dresser and a scarecrow, a gentleman and a boor, given to extremes of happiness and despair, singularly well able to apply himself and capable of frittering away a lifetime in trivial pursuits, decorous and unseemly, kind and cruel, tolerant yet open to the most outrageous varieties of bigotry, a great friend and an implacable enemy, a lover and an abominator of women, sweet-spoken and foul-mouthed, a rake and a puritan, swelling with hubris and haunted by inferiority, outcast and social climber, felon and philanthropist, barbarian and patron of the arts, enamored of novelty and solidly conservative, philosopher and fool, Republican and Democrat, large of soul and unbearably petty, distant and brimming with friendly impulses, an inveterate liar and astonishingly strict with petty cash, adventurous and timid, imaginative and stolid, malignly destructive and a planter of trees on Arbor Day—I tell you frankly, the man is a mess."

"That's extremely well said Bruce," Fredric stated. "I think you've given really a very thoughtful analysis."

"I was paraphrasing what Mark Schorer said about Sinclair Lewis," Bruce replied.

"Well it's very brilliant just the same," Fredric noted. "I guess I'd better go home now."

"We could all use a little sleep," Bruce Wayne said. "By the way Fredric how are the *Grit* sales coming along? Are you getting many subscriptions?"

"Yes quite a few Bruce," Fredric said. "I've been doing particularly well in the wealthier sections of Gotham City although the strength of *Grit* is usually found in rural areas. By the way Dick if you want to borrow my language records to help you with your French you can come by Saturday."

"Thanks Fredric I'll do that," Dick said.

"Okay Bruce," Fredric said, "I'll see you next Tuesday night probably unless something comes up."

THE AUTHOR

My deranged mother has written another book. This one is called *The Bough* and is even worse than the others. I refer not to its quality—it exhibits the usual "coruscating wit" and "penetrating social observation"—but to the extent to which it utilizes, as a kind of mulch pile, the lives of her children.

This one, as I say, is even worse than the others (two American Book Award nominations and a Literary Guild alternate). My poor brother Sampson, who appears as "Rafe," is found, in the first chapter, performing a laparoscopy upon a patient who had been under the impression she was paying for quite another procedure. My brother is a very busy and popular doctor, and a hiatus in his office staffing was responsible for this understandable if lamentable mixup. What the book does not say is that the laparoscopy disclosed a fair amount of endometriosis which was then dealt with in a highly skilled and professional manner, thus averting considerable patient disgruntlement. Mother never puts anything good about any of us into her books.

"Rafe" 's relations with "Molly" (read Callie, Sam's wife) are, as you might imagine, not spared. Some time ago Sam and Callie had a little disagreement about his conduct during the Miami OB-GYN meeting when he was missing for some hours during a presentation on ultrasound and she learned that he had been out drinking with a bunch of heavily armed survivalists who liked to shoot up lifesize plywood cutouts of Gorbachev with their (more or less illegal) Ingram M-11s which they can fire one-handed with a can of Stroh's in the other. Girl survivalists were also present. OK, so my brother Sam is a gun nut. Why tell everybody in the world? Intervention is what surgeons are all about. How my mother gleans these details is beyond me, as none of us has spoken to her since 1974, when *Fumed Oak* was published.

My mother's treatment of my sister Virginia—"Alabama" in the new book (Mother's masks are clear glass)—is flatly vicious. Virginia has had some tough times of late, what with the accident and the fallout from the accident. In *The Bough* "Alabama" has a blood alcohol reading of 0.18 percent immediately after the crash, and that happens to be the right number, as many of Virginia's friends have recognized. What is truly reprehensible is the (painfully accurate) analysis of my sister's character. Virginia did her dissertation on Emerson; so does "Alabama." That certain passages in "Alabama" 's dissertation offer striking parallels to recent work by Joel Porte (Harvard University Press) and Eric Cheyfitz (Johns Hopkins University Press) is announced for the first time in *Bough*; I had not thought Mother that much of a scholar. The line in the book "They shouldn't let me go into a bar without training wheels on" is pure Virginia.

My other brother, Denis (the "good brother" in the book), has asked his lawyers to look into the legal aspects. They have told him that suing one's mother is an awkward business at best and the appearance of filial impiety more or less cancels, for jurors, any merit such a suit might possess. They also pointed out, very reasonably, that the public nature of such an action, involving a well-known author, would tend to call attention to some of the very things we are not anxious to emphasize: for example, Denis's practice of purchasing U.S. Army morphine Syrettes from disaffected Medical Corps master sergeants and the ingenious places he finds to hide them in the office (hollowed-out cigars, his computer's surge suppressor) and the consequences of this for his brokerage business, all finely detailed in *The Bough*. I must say I have never read a more telling account of the *jouissance* produced by high-grade morphine. What busy little bee brought her this news?

The Bough is No. 9 this week on the *Los Angeles Times* list. Thus does Stamford provide titillation for Santa Barbara, by way of Mother's bee-loud glade in Old Lyme. Somehow she uncovered the specifics of my "theft" of several inconsequential medicine bundles (cloth, painted wood, feathers) from the Native American

Institute, where I am the former curator-at-large. I say "theft" because I wish to be as hard on myself as possible in this matter; others might call it "creative deaccessioning," and the Ghost Dance material (drum charts, dance notation) received in exchange, which the board would never have realized the value of, will be my monument. Yes, the finder's fee charged to the transaction was quite substantial, in the high six figures, as Mother does not fail to note, but Willie Leaping Deer and I earned every penny of it. No one who fully understands the Ghost Dance, whose object was to render the participants impervious to the encroachments of the white man (rifle bullets included), would have hesitated for a moment. "Mark" has a ridiculous affair with a Dakota shaman of ambiguous sex, and none of that is true except the trance scene; furthermore, the chanting on that occasion involved no intoxicants save *Pinafore*, which I was teaching Wokodah and which he greatly enjoyed.

It is not that we, my mother's children, lead or claim to lead exemplary lives. But couldn't she widen her horizons just a bit?

"Mother, why do you do this to me?" I asked her recently.

Mother is handsome still, and bears a carefully cultivated resemblance to Virginia Woolf.

"What?" she said. "Do what?"

I was holding up a copy of *The Bough*. "This," I said, more or less pointing it at her.

"But you're *mine*," she said.

I WAS GRATIFIED THIS WEEK...

I was gratified this week to learn that I am a Human Resource. I learned this from a letter I received from the American Bicentennial Research Institute, Inc., of Dallas, Texas. The letter began:

> The American Bicentennial Research Institute takes pleasure in bringing to your attention that you [my name inserted here] have been selected to appear as a reference source in its LIBRARY OF HUMAN RESOURCES. . . . The expressed aim of the Institute is to recognize and methodically classify those persons or groups of persons who have . . . As a part of this effort, The American Bicentennial Research Institute is preparing for publication THE LIBRARY OF HUMAN RESOURCES, a unified compilation of microfiche directories intended to serve as . . . As your inclusion in THE LIBRARY OF HUMAN RESOURCES is by virtue of your value as an outstanding individual at the close of the First Bicentennium of the United States of America, we have prepared for you a beautiful parchment certificate, personalized with your name. . . .

The beautiful parchment certificate would cost me, I learned, fifteen dollars, and I could order one (but only one) duplicate beautiful parchment certificate for ten dollars additional.

Well, *of course* I was thrilled to be certified as a Human Resource, even though I hadn't done anything particularly resourceful lately except send Ramsey Clark a campaign contribution in the amount of $101.00. A Human Resource—it was very like, and possibly better than, being named a Historic District or a National Treasure, and all I had to do was mail my twenty-five dollars to 6116 North Central Expressway, Dallas, Texas. Then I noticed at the bottom of the letter a line printed in the same elegant script of the letterhead and reading, "Not Affiliated with the United States Government." This puzzled me. Was it the case that the American Bicentennial Research Institute, Inc., was in some way *displeased* with the United States Government? Had the ABRI seceded from the U.S. Govt.? And at such a moment, too—a moment when we should all join hands bicentennially and have a party? And was I, perhaps, in some way to blame? (I accept blame from any quarter, just like praise.) Had the issue between the ABRI and the U.S. been precisely my nomination to the high status of Human Resource, with the ABRI championing my candidacy and the U.S. saying, "Well, look, if you're going to let this sort of person in, this sort of person that we, as a government, view as rather an underachiever, human-resourcewise . . ." Worried to flinders now by the whole affair, I took my twenty-five dollars and invested it in cans of chicken noodle soup, which is appreciating, I notice at my local market, at the rate of something like thirteen per cent a year—a sort of government bond with a considerably higher return than the regular ones. I shall greet 1976 certificateless but with faith in America intact. Where else can one profit either by being bullcentennialish on soup or by bullcentenniuming on parchment?

WHEN I DIDN'T WIN...

When I didn't win the forty-one million dollars in the New York State Lottery last week, I had to change my plans a bit. I had gone as far as to just sort of tentatively write out a few checks. (I didn't sign them, of course, lest one might accidentally get into the mail prematurely—I was prudent.) But now that the results are in I'm kind of just sitting here looking at the checks. And studying them, I think they represent a moderately sound set of decisions—nothing spectacularly wonderful but not the worst I ever made. In short, I didn't lose my head, or anything. I handled the whole thing pretty well, it seems to me, without a lawyer or a financial adviser, or even a stern, thrifty spouse.

The thirty-five thousand dollars to Audio Horizons for the pair of Infinity Reference Standard speakers was the main personal item, except for the five hundred and fifty dollars to Lucchese, of San Antonio, for a new pair of boots, and the twenty-three dollars and eighty-four cents to Balducci's, in the Village, for two pounds of oyster mushrooms. If you sauté the oyster mushrooms in butter and strew them wantonly over your pasta, people think you're a superb cook, but oyster mushrooms are a shade on the dear side, so I don't buy them very often. Nobody (to my knowledge) makes better-looking cowboy boots than Mr. Lucchese, and the speakers have twelve midranges each, incomparable bass, and highs that could be bounced off the space shuttle. Self-indulgence, yes, but, proportionately, perhaps not overmuch.

All the people I saw quoted in the newspapers said that if they won they were going to build a new house for their mothers. Well, my mother already has a pretty-good house, in Decatur, Illinois, and I don't think she wants a new one. She might want a new husband, because my father has been extremely cranky lately, especially since she made him stop wearing his John Deere gimme hat in public places, but there's not much I can do about that. I thought it might be nice, though, if she could have a chat with A. J. Ayer, the British philosopher, whom she's been a fan of ever since she read *Language, Truth and Logic*, published in 1936. So there's a check here made out to Sir Alfred Jules Ayer, with the amount unspecified, because I didn't know what his fee for this sort of one-on-one encounter might be. I really regret that this won't happen. Professor Ayer would probably have had a smashing time with Mother—maybe he'd even have learned a thing or two.

And all the people quoted in the newspapers were also going to send money to Africa for famine relief if they won. I've already sent twenty-five bucks; I more or less felt off the hook there. But some kind of damn philanthropy is indicated when you're a Max Winner, I figured—it would mitigate the guilt, for one thing. So I wrote twenty checks for five hundred thousand dollars each, dating them 1985, 1986, 1987, and so on, to a wheat farmer I know in Montana, together with a covering letter instructing him to send wheat, in whatever tonnage the money would buy, and carefully packaged, to Africa. I don't think the crisis will be resolved in twenty years. My friend is a young guy but very reliable. This disembarrassed me of about half my fortune, after taxes, and I felt —well, *lighter*.

Parenthetically, large numbers do not frighten the modern citizen. I've noticed that. For instance, the number of dogs worldwide is thought to be between a hundred and twenty and a hundred and fifty million. Quite a few dogs. The number of people on earth, as of the most recent figures, is something like four billion seven hundred sixty-six million three hundred and twenty-four thousand. The national debt is running right around a trillion eight hundred billion. The notion of forty-one mil didn't scare me. I mean, it was a problem, but superable.

There were some small, trivial items among my thirty-two unsigned checks: a few dollars for Bill, so that he can get a new transmission for that Chevy (his transmission junked out in July;

he's the man who gave me a thirty-mile tow when my radiator blew in Maine a couple of years ago), and a neat one thousand for the National Endowment for the Arts, earmarked for a struggling young country fiddler of promise. On Wednesday night, I watched the Lotto machine make the plastic balls bounce and bubble on television and checked the numbers as they appeared on the screen. My ticket, when I compared it with the numbers on the screen, was not what you'd call handsome—it was downright meager. But I was sane, even serene.

RETURN

I went on the Azalea Trail, and shot one, right through the heart. I took the dead azalea home and put it in my freezer, and all at once I was seized by a deep and fearful melancholy. Had I done something wrong? I had been long away from Texas, living in the wicked, sinful cities of the East—perhaps I no longer understood Texas ways, perhaps the roar and clatter of New York City had permanently damaged the delicate tissues of my flabellum. Had I misunderstood the Azalea Trail?

But I put my melancholy aside and went vigorously about the business of getting connected. I got myself connected to Southwestern Bell, and Entex, and the Light Company, and cable TV, long lines binding me once again into the community. I subscribed to two of our great city newspapers, the American one and the Canadian one, and I bought an Old Smoky barbecue pit.

I set out to sail Buffalo Bayou on a four-by-eight sheet of three-quarter-inch plywood powered by eight mighty Weed Eaters and I saw many strange and wonderful things. I saw an egret and then another egret and a turtle and a refrigerator without a door on it and a heron and a possum and an upside-down '52 Pontiac. And I said to myself, This blessed stream contains many strange and wonderful things. It was getting dark now, and the moon had risen, and I saw a wise old owl sitting in a tree. So I throttled back my eight powerful Weed Eaters and spoke to the owl, saying, "How's by you, boychick?"

And then I looked closely and saw that it wasn't a wise old owl at all; it was Philip Johnson, out hunting for new clients, by the light of the moon. So I congratulated him on all his great and tall new buildings, and we gazed together at the glowing tower of the city, all the great and tall new buildings glowing like the wondrous towers of Oz, we looked at them and were content.

But then my melancholy came upon me with doubled force, and I decided to take additional measures. So I joined the First Baptist Church of Aldine, the First Baptist Church of Alvin, the First Baptist Church of Friendswood, the First Baptist Church of Golden Acres, the First Baptist Church of Jacinto City, and the First Baptist Church of the Woodlands. Then I started in on the Methodists. Before I had finished, I was a member in good standing of some two hundred twenty congregations, and had been appointed to a number of important committees. I was on the Old Clothes Committee here, and the Potato Salad Committee there, vice-chairman of the Fellowship of Song Committee at another place, and treasurer of the Total Immersion Committee at yet another place. It felt fine, being connected.

But by this time I was a little tired of being good, you can be good just so long and then you get a little tired of it. So I decided to be bad, and went out to find some Totally Nude Live Girls. And found some, right there on South Main, acres and acres of them. Totally Nude Live Girls. And I must tell you that they were lovely, rarely had I seen Totally Nude Live Girls quite so lovely, so I sat down, and took off my shoes, and began to talk to them.

It was a slow afternoon and there must have been forty or sixty Totally Nude Live Girls in that bar, and they all began to confide in me, telling me their hopes and fears, their visions of the future, and their regrets about the particolored past. One Totally Nude Live Girl told me that she was from Secaucus, New Jersey, and had only been a Totally Nude Live Girl for a month, but it was better than being a mailman, which is what she had been in Secaucus, New Jersey, because of the dogs scaring you all the time, she knew she was supposed to like dogs but she really didn't, and so on. She was very nice. I liked her.

———

We were drinking, me and the forty or sixty Totally Nude Live Girls, martinis and margaritas and one thing and another, buckets and buckets of them, there was loveliness in every direction, as far as the eye could see, and with a rush the melancholy came upon me once again, because nothing can make you so melancholy, sick in the heart, as forty to sixty excited, confiding, lovely, and partially drunk Totally Nude Live Girls. So with regret I put my shoes on and left them, promising to write.

That was what I was, I remembered, a writer—a strange fate but not uncongenial. I remembered that years ago, as a raw youth, I had worked for the Houston newspaper that is now the Canadian one. This was shortly after the Civil War. The newspaper building was populated with terrifying city editors whose gaze could cut brass, and ferocious copy desk men whose contempt could make a boy of twenty wish that his mother and father had never met. I loved working there. They paid us in pretzels, of course—I got about forty pretzels a week, and then, when I got back from the Spanish-American War, I got a generous raise, to fifty. Pretzels.

When I was hired they showed me my desk, an old beat-up scarred wooden desk, and they told me that it had been O. Henry's desk when O. Henry worked for the paper, as he had at one time. And I readily believed it. I could see the place where O. Henry had savagely stabbed the desk with his pen in pursuit of a slimy adjective just out of reach, and a kind of bashed-in-looking place where O. Henry had beaten his poor genius head on the desk in frustration over not being able to capture that noun leaping like a fawn just out of reach . . . So I sat down at the desk and I too began to chase those devils, the dancy nouns and come-hither adjectives, what joy.

But I had no time to dwell upon these precious memories. I had been long away from Texas and had to reacculturate, fast. So I joined the YMCA, the AAA, the American Legion, the Art League, the Fern Society, the Canary Club, the Turnverein, the AFL-CIO, the Great Books Council, the Clean Air Caucus, the Loyal Order of Moose Number 2106, Planned Parenthood, the Gay Coalition, the On Leong Merchants' Association, the Mothers of Twins Club, and Mensa. These new associations greatly enriched my life. I was caught up in a whirl of activity, so to say, zipping over to the Fern Society to inspect a comely new frond one day and to the Canary Club to look at a bold new Meistersinger the next, protesting outrages with my brothers of the Gay Coalition in the morning and cuddling nurselings with my fellow mothers of the Twins Club in the afternoon, and thinking the long long thoughts of Mensa all the while.

Yet the melancholy hung about me like an unchampionship season and I realized that I needed professional help. So I went off to consult a true expert in unhappiness, the Hunchback of the Galleria. I found the Hunchback up by the running track, watching with fascination the tiny, graceful skaters inscribing ampersands on the ice far below. "Hunchback," I said to him, "what is wrong with me? Am I laboring under some kind of a curse? Can it be that the deep and fearful malaise which informs all my days is the result of my having shot that damned azalea?"

"Woe," said the Hunchback, "woe unto him who—"

"Hunchback," I said, "what is this woe-unto-him-who business? Can you give me a straight answer, or not?"

"Woe," said the Hunchback, "woe unto him who, or, take another case, woe unto *her* who—"

He could see that I was becoming a little exasperated, so he said, in the wisest possible tones, "Why are you being so hard on yourself?" and then was off, swinging on a rope through the great cathedrallike spaces of the Galleria, and I thought I heard bells ringing, but maybe I didn't. In fine, I obtained no satisfaction, any ordinary shrink could have said to me, "Why are you being so hard on yourself?" and many have, I was disappointed.

I was disappointed, so I took myself to the Opera to cheer myself up. It was a grand evening, with a lot of flash and glitter, there were Cadillacs and Rolls-Royces and pumpkins and Mercedes-Benzes pulling up to the glistening façade of the Opera. I parked my mule and rushed inside, all of us were in a high state of pleasurable tension because we were going to the Opera, going to grasp that core experience of culture which is the Opera, that irreducible minimum of irrefrangible soul stuff which the Opera is.

And as I made my way to my seat in Row GG I saw a caped and masked figure lurking in the shadows. My God! I thought, It's the Phantom of the Opera! But it was only Philip Johnson, seeking new clients in the corridors of the Opera, and I said to him,

"Noble architect! Can you design for me some kind of an azalea that I can plant somewhere on the surface of this wondrous city and thus redeem, in some measure, the hasty and ill-considered act of azaleacide that I would not have committed had I not lingered too long in the wicked, sinful cities of the East and gotten my values screwed up?" And the great architect whipped from his sleeve his magic Eberhard Faber 2B pencil and waved it in the air, and sketched a most beautiful stainless steel azalea nine hundred feet high. My melancholy fell away from me, and I was content. And some day, God and the Gerald D. Hines Interests willing, you'll see this nine-hundred-foot-high stainless steel azalea, taking its place with the city's other great and tall monuments in the garden of the creative imagination.

AT LAST, IT IS TIME...

At last, it is time to speak the truth about Thanksgiving. The truth is this: it is not a really great holiday. Consider the imagery. Dried cornhusks hanging on the door! Terrible wine! Cranberry jelly in little bowls of extremely doubtful provenance which everyone is required to handle with the greatest of care! Consider the participants, the merrymakers. Men and women (also children) who have survived passably well through the years, mainly as a result of living at considerable distances from their dear parents and beloved siblings, who on this feast of feasts must apparently forgather (as if beckoned by an aberrant Fairy Godmother), usually by circuitous routes, through heavy traffic, at a common meeting place, where the very moods, distempers, and obtrusive personal habits that have kept them happily apart since adulthood are then and there encouraged to slowly ferment beneath the cornhusks, and gradually rise with the aid of the terrible wine, and finally burst forth out of control under the stimulus of the cranberry jelly! No, it is a mockery of a holiday. For instance: *Thank you, O Lord, for what we are about to receive.* This is surely not a gala concept. There are no presents, unless one counts Aunt Bertha's sweet rolls a present, which no one does. There is precious little in the way of costumery: miniature plastic turkeys and those witless Pilgrim hats. There is no sex. Indeed, Thanksgiving is the one day of the year (a fact known to everybody) when all thoughts of sex completely vanish, evaporating from apartments, houses, condominiums, and mobile homes like steam from a bathroom mirror.

Consider also the nowhereness of the time of the year. The last week or so in November. It is obviously not yet winter: winter, with its death-dealing blizzards and its girls in tiny skirts pirouetting on the ice. On the other hand, it is certainly not much use to anyone as fall: no golden leaves or Oktoberfests, and so forth. Instead, it is a no-man's-land between the seasons. In the cold and sobersides northern half of the country, it is a vaguely unsettling interregnum of long, mournful walks beneath leafless trees: the long, mournful walks following the midday repast with the dread inevitability of pie following turkey, and the leafless trees looming or standing about like eyesores, and the ground either as hard as iron or slightly mushy, and the light snow always beginning to fall when one is halfway to the old green gate—flecks of cold, watery stuff plopping between neck and collar, for the reason that, it being not yet winter, one has forgotten or not chosen to bring along a muffler. It is a corollary to the long, mournful Thanksgiving walk that the absence of this muffler is quickly noticed and that four weeks or so later, at Christmastime, instead of the Sony Betamax one had secretly hoped that the children might have chipped in together to purchase, one receives another muffler— by then the thirty-third. Thirty-three mufflers! Some walk! Of course, things are more fun in the warm and loony southern part of the country. No snow there of any kind. No need of mufflers. Also, no long, mournful walks, because in the warm and loony southern part of the country everybody drives. So everybody drives over to Uncle Jasper's house to watch the Cougars play the Gators, a not entirely unimportant conflict, which will determine whether the Gators get a bowl bid or must take another postseason exhibition tour of North Korea. But no sooner do the Cougars kick off (an astonishing end-over-end squiggly thing that floats lazily above the arena before plummeting down toward K. C. McCoy and catching him on the helmet) than Auntie Em starts hustling turkey. Soon Cousin May is slamming around the bowls and platters, and Cousin Bernice is oohing and ahing about "all the fixin's," and Uncle Bob is making low, insincere sounds of appreciation: "Yummy, yummy, Auntie Em, I'll have me some more of these delicious yams!" Delicious yams? Uncle Bob's eyes roll wildly in his head. Billy Joe Quaglino throws his long bomb in the middle of Grandpa Morris saying grace, Grandpa Morris speaking so low nobody can hear him—which is just as well, since he is reciting what he can remember of his last union contract; and then, just as J. B. (Speedy) Snood begins his ninety-two-yard punt return, Auntie Em starts dealing second helpings of her famous stuffing to everyone, as if she were pushing a controlled substance, which it well might be, since there are no easily recognizable ingredients visible to the naked eye.

Consider for a moment the Thanksgiving meal itself. It has become a sort of refuge for endangered species of starch: sweet potatoes, cauliflower, pumpkin, mince (whatever "mince" is), those blessed yams. Bowls of luridly colored yams, with no taste at all, lying torpid under a lava flow of marshmallow! And then the sacred turkey. One might as well try to construct a holiday repast around a fish—say, a nice piece of boiled haddock. After all, turkey tastes very similar to haddock: same consistency, same quite remarkable absence of flavor. But then, if the Thanksgiving pièce de résistance were a nice piece of boiled haddock instead of turkey, there wouldn't be all that fun for Dad when Mom hands him the sterling silver, bone-handled carving set (a wedding present from her parents and not sharpened since) and then everyone stands around pretending not to watch while he saws and tears away at the bird as if he were trying to burrow his way into or out of some grotesque, fowllike prison.

What of the good side to Thanksgiving? you ask. There is always a good side to everything. Not to Thanksgiving. There is only a bad side and then a worse side. For instance, Grandmother's best linen tablecloth is a bad side: the fact that it is produced each year, in the manner of a red flag being produced before a bull, and then is always spilled upon by whichever child is doing poorest at school that term and so is in need of greatest reassurance. Thus: "Oh, my God, *Veronica*, you just spilled grape juice [or "plum wine" or "tar"] on Grandmother's best linen tablecloth!" But now comes worse. For at this point Cousin Bill, the one who lost all Cousin Edwina's money on the car dealership three years ago and has apparently been drinking steadily since Halloween, bizarrely chooses to say, "Seems to me those old glasses are *always* falling over." To which Auntie Meg is heard to add, "Somehow I don't remember *receivin'* any of those old glasses." To which Uncle Fred replies, "That's because you and George decided to go on vacation to *Hawaii* in the summer Grandpa Sam was dying." Now Grandmother is sobbing, though not so uncontrollably that she cannot refrain from murmuring, "I think that volcano painting I threw away by mistake got sent me from Hawaii, heaven knows why." But the gods are merciful, even the Pilgrim-hatted god of cornhusks and soggy stuffing, and there is an end to everything, even to Thanksgiving. Indeed, there is a grandeur to the feelings of finality and doom which usually settle on a house after the Thanksgiving celebration is over, for with the completion of Thanksgiving Day the year itself has been properly terminated—shot through the cranium with a high-velocity candied yam. At this calendrical nadir, all energy on the planet has gone, all fun has fled, all the terrible wine has been drunk.

But then, overnight, life once again begins to stir, emerging, even by the next morning, in the form of Japanese window displays and Taiwanese Christmas lighting, from the primeval ooze of the nation's department stores. Thus, a new year dawns, bringing with it immediate and cheering possibilities of extended consumer debt, office-party flirtations, good—or, at least, mediocre—wine, and visions of cheapskate excursion fares to Montego Bay. It is worth noting, perhaps, that this true new year always starts with the same mute, powerful mythic ceremony: the surreptitious tossing out, in the early morning, of all those horrid aluminum-foil packages of yams and cauliflower and stuffing and red, gummy cranberry substance which have been squeezed into the refrigerator as if a reenactment of the siege of Paris were expected. Soon afterward, the phoenix of Christmas can be observed as it slowly rises, beating its drumsticks, once again goggle-eyed with hope and unrealistic expectations.

THE INAUGURATION

Now that another splendid and charming and wise President has been elected, it is, in our judgment, not a moment too soon to begin worrying about the inauguration. The main point to be held in mind is that we want the pomp to be bang-up, and not marred by flaws. Many of these, in human form, can be minimized by the proper authorities ahead of time, if properly identified, before they begin to flaw everything. Some examples follow.

Some people have a vicious and unnatural and disproportionate dedication to peace, which they don't hesitate to display in the public streets, very often at times when everybody else is trying to be happy, such as at an inauguration. They should under no circumstances be allowed to ride, or even feed, the elephants.

There are individuals who programmatically go against the current, even if that current is the main stream. They are likely to be wearing peculiar-looking clothes. They may even go so far as to offer you a dangerous drug. Be alert. We don't want any of these individuals at the inauguration.

Honest doubt is not, at present, an indictable offense. But it does damage and compromise the mood of joyous rejoicing and new creativity we wish to prevail, on this occasion. Honest doubt is difficult to stifle and shades rather quickly into dishonest doubt, which, if the doubter is doubting with others, is known as conspiracy.

Some people are never satisfied, no matter what. They wear bitter black mourning and utter loud ululations, at conspicuous places along the line of march. Perhaps some large plants can be placed around them, so that other people can't see them.

Villains are a particular problem. It always makes an inauguration look tacky and déclassé if too many well-known villains are hanging about—this is especially true of the reviewing stand, the ball, and the private dinners. But before the villains are rounded up and put away, it is necessary to determine to which party they belong. They may be our villains.

Worshipful admiration is permitted, and even encouraged. *Too many* of the *same kind* of worshipful admirers *together in the same place* is bad planning.

The large contributor is a potential embarrassment. Careful thought is mandatory here. On the one hand he is very touchy about his placement and handling, and on the other, we don't want people to think that . . . He should be positioned not too close to the throne, and not too far away.

Yes, a display of armed might contributes to pomp—is pomp, in a sense— but it can be easily, easily misinterpreted. We recommend that not more than two divisions be employed, and that these not be our best divisions, but rather sort of sloppy and amateurish-looking—stouthearted men, but maybe not entirely persuaded. Not more than three dozen generals, please.

THE ART OF BASEBALL

Art is, at an important level, play, as theoreticians from Huizinga to Roger Caillois have pointed out. Art is a game in which it is possible to win, to lose, or to fight one's way to an exhausting, desperate tie. So it is not surprising that a number of this century's most famous artists were also, at odd moments in their careers, baseball players. As a kind of antidote to their labors in the studio or at the writing desk, these giant figures typically played for a season or two and then returned, refreshed, to their artistic pursuits. Curiously, they have left little trace in orthodox histories of the game. It is as if baseball's chroniclers were *frightened* by these apparitions from another world, whose contributions to the sport were, very often, of a kind to provoke the denial mechanism familiar to readers of psychology texts.

Recent research has, however, turned up some notable instances of the magical combination of art and baseball, a number of which are adduced here.

T. S. ELIOT, SHORTSTOP

T. S. Eliot's *The Waste Land* is without doubt the most thoroughly studied, carefully annotated, and nitpickingedly commented-upon poem in the language. What has been missed (in a series of misreadings so horrendous as to be without parallel in the annals of quality lit. scholarship in this country) is that the poem is essentially about the St. Louis Browns of 1922, a team for which Eliot, back from Britain in that year, briefly starred at short.

Eliot, it will be recalled, had been living in the United Kingdom since 1914 (he became a citizen in 1927). After the publication of *Poems* (1920), he felt that some creative impetus, some vital impulse, had leaked from his work. His solution was to return to the St. Louis of his youth and enlist for a hitch with the Browns, a fateful choice for poetry, as we shall see. The Browns played him at shortstop, and he astonished fans and teammates alike by presenting himself on the field wearing not only the standard St. Louis regalia but also a black bowler hat, to which he had added, in proper English fashion, a rolled umbrella of the same hue. These eccentricities were tolerated because young Tom never failed to render a heads-up performance; his sector of the diamond was, during his tenure, safe as houses.

But if the poet was brilliant, the Browns of 1922 were not, a circumstance that decisively influenced the major Eliot work to come. The internal evidence is overwhelming, as open-minded consideration of the following citations will demonstrate.

Item. The poem's very first line, "April is the cruellest month." was originally "*August* is the cruellest month." The allusion is to the dreadful set of games the Browns dropped to the Yanks, in St. Louis, in August 1922, a setback that effectively removed them from serious league competition. Ezra Pound, whose magisterial editing of the poem wrought it into the great cultural artifact that it is, successfully argued that everybody, not only in St. Louis but in the larger world as well, knew that August was a terrible month and that its use made the work far too accessible.

Item: The line (in Part I) "Here is the man with three staves" is beyond cavil a foreshadowing of the movement toward the batter's box of the awesome Babe Ruth—one can almost see the Bambino twirling a trio of bats as he stumbles plateward. Ruth had been suspended for the first month of the season (by Judge Kenesaw Mountain Landis, the first Commissioner of Baseball) for illegal barnstorming, but saw action against St. Louis, and the anxiety he inspired is everywhere present in the poem.

Item: The line, in Part III, "I Tiresias, though blind . . . can see" is transparently umpire-related.

Item: Also in Part III, the lines

While I was fishing in the dull canal
On a winter evening round behind the gashouse

predict the Gashouse Gang of the mid-thirties, while the Fisher King himself is obviously George Sisler, the Browns' heavy hitter (averaging over .400 that season), who felt that his exertions were imperfectly backed by his mates—the poignant

Fishing, with the arid plain behind me

makes this abundantly clear.

Item: The line in Part V, "And bats with baby faces in the violet light," is a direct response to a game that has gone into extra innings—into a hallucinatory twilight rife with peril. Would *you* throw a ball (at ninety miles an hour) at a bat with the face of a baby? No, you'd hesitate, and in fact, hesitation, here as elsewhere, is key in the Eliotic canon.

One could go on, but why? The case is proved.

DJANGO

Few of us know more than one person named Django. It is, therefore, a virtual certainty that the Django who pitched for the Cardinals in the 1931 World Series (against the Philadelphia Athletics) was the three-fingered French gypsy jazz guitarist Django Reinhardt, star of innumerable Hot Club of France discs in which he was paired with his still-living colleague, the elegant Stéphane Grappelli.

Rumors of the time suggested that the Cards, scared to death of a Philly lineup that included Lefty Grove, Jimmie Foxx, and Mickey Cochrane, had smuggled the great Frenchman into the country inside a giant éclair used as a centerpiece for the daily luncheon buffet on the Cunard ship *Queen Mary*, then sailing from Le Havre on a twice-a-month schedule. Be that as it may, the redoubtable jazzman was a compelling presence on the field. "He put a lot of French on the ball," recalls one contemporary observer. Django's tridigital grip had much the same effect as that of any number of pitcher's dodges usually deemed illegal—chewing gum on the (then) horsehide, scarring the surface of the ball with the cutting edge of a saber concealed in the pantaloons. It was deadly to the hapless would-be hitter; the ball leaped upward two to four inches as it crossed the plate. St. Louis's Pepper Martin, one of the heroes of the Series and a son of the sovereign state of Oklahoma, summed it up this way: "It was like having the Terrible Williamsons fix your road." The reference was to a tribe of gypsies of the period who roamed Texas, Oklahoma, and Arkansas in a fleet of decrepit vehicles contracting to repair roadways—their asphalt tended to disappear in a light rain.

Memories of Django's days on the mound may be discerned in his tunes "Whiff," "Forkball," and "Pepper," all available on Vox 3084.

SONTAG AT FIRST

The distinguished novelist and critic Susan Sontag sparkled for Chicago for a single season, that of 1959. Sontag played college ball under trying circumstances at the University of Chicago, a school noted for many years for not having a football team—it's often forgotten that the place didn't have a baseball team, too. Undeterred, Sontag and a group of similarly baseball-mad graduate students formed the notorious Grind League, which played its games in the vast heating tunnels under the university's South Side campus. A White Sox scout, trying to ransom his son from the Physics Department, where the boy had unwisely lingered for thirteen years on the track of unnilhexium (an artificial radioactive transuranium element not actually produced until 1974, at Berkeley, as it happened), opened the wrong door one night and blundered into a game. Transfixed by the dark-haired beauty's luminous activities at first, he inked her to a Sox pact immediately.

Plagued as she was by baseball's shameless (and continuing) prejudice against women on the field, Sontag was forced to appear with her hair firmly pinned up under her cap, and not under her own name: she is listed on the rosters of the time as S. Sunday. Fans remember with particular clarity that her stance in the infield was that of one thinking, fist deeply buried in the right cheek, little sidelong glances at the man at bat—the picture of one dreaming of Gregory Bateson and the double bind she intended to place on said man at bat were he so fortunate as to make it to Sack No. 1.

In later years, her well-known essay on "Firstness" incorporated her Windy City experience. The 1959 Sox went to the Series with high hopes, three handy outfielders, Jim Landis, Jim Rivera, and Al Smith, and such standouts as Luis "Base Thief of Baghdad" Aparicio, but lost to the Dodgers in six games. "Firstness," its twin themes excellence and loss, is an extended meditation on *being* first, first obstacle to the runner's progress (involvement in the agon in a negative, life-denying manner), while, paradoxically, granted the first opportunity to lift one's group (and by extension, mankind) toward apotheosis.

A footnote to the above: at the 1967 International PEN Conference at Bled, Yugoslavia, Sontag was observed autographing a worn first baseman's glove for Yurio Kawabata, the celebrated Japanese rare-glove dealer.

TWO DUTCHMEN

Willem "Big Bill" de Kooning swings perhaps the biggest brush in the contemporary art world, and his hard-charging, go-for-broke style at the easel has long been a matter of wonderment and green envy among his colleagues. How much his tour with the Dodgers influenced the Dutch master is a question oft debated, in Manhattan brasseries and East Hampton gin mills alike. This is one of those mysteries which resist the closest critical attention. Did the painter learn at least a part of his ferocious attack during his time with Brooklyn, or did he bring same to Ebbets Field already fully formed? What sticks in memory, in any case, is an amazing duel with a countryman and fellow painter in August 1939.

It was the year Piet Mondrian, another Netherlander, was taking a sabbatical from the purity of his severely geometric canvases to pitch for Cincinnati. The great Neoplasticist had insisted on designing his own uniform, a splendor of large red and blue and yellow rectangles immaculately placed against stark white. When de Kooning's moment at the plate came round, the two artists glared at each other in friendly fashion across the 18.4 meters separating them.

"Piet," yelled de Kooning, anent the uniform, "the red, it's too close to the yellow."

"Bill," Mondrian shouted back, "how would you know?"

"A child could see it," de Kooning answered, choking his bat.

"Bill," Mondrian announced calmly and clearly, "that's my space you're leaning all over." And he dusted the Rotterdamer's breastbone with a pay-attention pitch that sent Big Bill reeling backward into the Reds' catcher, Ernie Lombardi.

On the next pitch, Mondrian went through his windup (a spectacular affair, given the uniform) and released a perfect strike. De Kooning took a mighty cut and missed. Mondrian's third pitch was low, but within the parameters; de Kooning let it pass him by for a second strike. The doughty Abstract Expressionist was by now visibly irritated, and he rapped the plate with his stick in a way that could not be mistaken for amiability. Mondrian's next pitch was squarely on the invisible line dividing inside from outside, and de Kooning stepped into it with a set of shoulders made massive by decades of paint hurling. The ball rose in the air like a mortar shell, and Kurt Schwitters,* the Cincinnati centerfielder, went back, back, back for it, thrust up his arm, and lost it by a good twelve feet. De Kooning trotted round the bases to extravagant applause, and Mondrian, long after the other players had left the park, was discovered with a tape, in the fading light of an Ohio evening, measuring the diamond in an attempt to prove that the diamond, not his sense of where to place what, had been at fault.

PASSION

Finally, it must be kept in mind that the traffic between art and baseball is not a one-way street. Gifted athletes venture onto the terrain of the artist almost as often as the reverse is the case. A memorable instance: in 1977 the multitalented Billy Martin exhibited, at the posh Pace Gallery on Manhattan's Fifty-seventh Street, a startling series of junked refrigerator doors smashed into likenesses of his patron, George Steinbrenner. The critics gave Martin high marks for surface tension, structural integrity, originality in choice of materials, and use of the sledge, but most of all for passion, without which neither art nor baseball would signify at all.

---

* Schwitters, the German collagist, spent much of his early career in Switzerland and learned his baseball in Basel, where it is called Baselball.

GAMES ARE THE ENEMIES OF BEAUTY, TRUTH, AND SLEEP, AMANDA SAID

I was playing Password, Twister, Breakthru, Bonanza, Stratego, Squander, and Gambit. And Quinto, Phlounder, Broker, Tactics, and Stocks & Bonds. All at once. On the floor. It was my move. When I play alone, it is always my move. That is reasonable. I kneel first on one side of the board, then the other. I think a bit. I examine my move to make sure it is the correct move. I congratulate myself. Then I hobble to the next board, on my knees.

The floor of my study is covered with game boards, and there are boards in the bedroom, the kitchen, the bath. Conestoga, the Game of the Oregon Trail. Gettysburg, Stalingrad, Midway, D-Day, U-Boat, Bismarck, and Waterloo. Le Mans. Management, Verdict, and Dispatcher. Merger, the Game of Stock Manipulation in the Automobile Industry. Qubic, the 3-D Tic Tac Toe Game. My move. It is my move when I depart for the office in the morning and my move when I return at night. I move before, during, and after dinner, hobbling from board to board. It is my move when I go to bed and my move when I awake.

I extended an arm in its yellow vinyl smoking jacket. I moved. Then I hobbled around to the other side of the board to evaluate the move from the point of view of my opponent. A foolish move. Now I was in a position to destroy myself. Should I destroy myself?

Then the bell rang. It was Amanda. She was in tears. "Amanda," I said. "What is it?" She was wearing a tent dress, two-ply brown

73

canvas with a tent-peg trim. Her eyes were full of sparklers and tears.

"Oh, Hector," she said. "You are the only one who can help me. Something awful—"

"Is it the same old thing?"

"No," she said. "It is a new thing. It is the worst thing you can imagine."

"Come," I said. "Stay with me. Take this buffalo robe and wrap it around your tent dress. And have a shot of this apricot brandy, and sit down here in this comfortable chair in front of the thermostat."

"I was playing Afrika Korps," she said. "You know Afrika Korps. A re-creation of the famed exploits of Field Marshal Rommel. You command the actual units and introduce the original divisions, brigades, and regiments at the actual time of their arrival, according to the actual historical situation."

"I know. One is given an opportunity to display one's generalship, strategic grasp, and tactical sense."

"Right," Amanda said, knocking back a bit of the brandy. "Well, when I came home this evening—Hector, I can't describe it! An entire Army Group had mixed itself up with the pieces from my Water Polo game. And the battleships from Midway have drifted into the Verdict box, and all the stock shares from Merger, the Game of Stock Manipulation in the Automobile Industry, are scrambled up with the counters from Depression, and—Hector, why am I playing all these *games*? Card games, word games, board games, educational games, and games people play? What is it, Hector? Is there something strange about me? Am I some kind of a creepy nut freak? I seem to spend all my time—"

I took her hand with its four-inch orange, yellow, and blue papier-mâché Fish & Game Commission ring.

"Amanda," I said. "You are not alone. Everyone is playing these games. Everyone I know." I took her to the window and opened it. We stuck our heads out into the papier-mâché night. "Listen, Amanda."

She listened. "What is that sort of funny thrimp-thrimp sound? Thrimp thrimp thrimp thrimp thrimp thrimp?"

"That is the sound made by the nation's terrific and gigantic electronic computers pulsing," I said. "Of which there are now perhaps thirty-five thousand in use, from sea to shining sea. It is estimated that there will be eighty-five thousand of them in use by 1975. And a substantial portion of these computers are playing games, Amanda, even as you and I. The businessmen are playing Daddy Warbucks games, the Lost Horse game for example, in order to establish patterns that will enable them to mangle the competition. The military men are playing war games, Escalation for example, in order to test the efficacy of alternate responses to the provocations of the enemy. And to make new enemies, for all I know. The scientists are playing scientific games, and some people are playing plain old checkers. And Marshall McLuhan says that games are dramatic modes of our psychological lives, providing release for particular tensions in social groups. And Huizinga says that the play element in culture serves a civilizing function, combining an agonistic principle of competitiveness with a ludic principle, or pure play. And Shub in his *Game Theory and Related Approaches to Social Behavior . . .*"

"Yes," Amanda said, "but what about me? My head is full of Diplomacy, and my heart is full of Careers. And my hands are full of Hoodwink, and my bank account is full of Monopoly money. I'm exhausted, Hector. I'm *tired* of playing games. I want—"

"I know," I said. "Relax, Amanda. We can lick this thing. Just trust me."

"What do you propose?" she asked, her brilliant aqua eyes full of fondness and eye shadow. "What?"

"New games," I said. "New games, Amanda, to set the turkey of mental excitement flying through the thin air of intellectual irresponsibility."

"New games?" I noticed that the blood had run out of her face. But I could not see where it had gone. "You mean people can make up their own games? Isn't that . . . hubris?"

"Have another brandy," I said. "Have another brandy, and we will play Contretemps, the Game of Social Embarrassment. And Cofferdam, and Double Boiler, and Hubris too, if you like. Listen to the names of these glorious new games—Leftwards, Gearbox, Dentist's Appointment, and Stroke. We will invent them together, dear friend."

"How is this game played? Contretemps or whatever it is?"

"I'm glad you asked me that question," I said, "because I know the answer. One starts with a situation, a social situation. One with a potential for embarrassment. One in which one is a bit out of one's depth, so to say. Then the potential is actualized. Imagine for instance that you are attending a lavish reception at the Court of St. James's. You have just converted your holdings in sterling, which were vast, into Siamese baht. In consequence, the Queen's allowance has been cut. You notice that she is wearing last year's tiara. You step up to be presented. You notice that she is staring at you with a funny expression on her face."

"Not bad," Amanda said. "Give me another one."

"Okay. A more elaborate one. You are attending a lavish reception at the Court of St. James's. Present also is Lord Snowdon, husband of Princess Margaret and famous photographer. The editor of the *Sunday Times* color—that should be colour—magazine is there too. Lord Snowdon has been on assignment for the magazine. He is doing a picture story on—"

"The Stones."

"Very good. He is doing a picture story on the Stones. Lord Snowdon is showing his prints to the editor. You are looking over their shoulders. As it happens, you too have recently taken some colour shots of the Stones. With your old box camera."

"Your old box camera that was your great-grandmother's that you found in an old trunk in the attic and that is held together with masking tape," Amanda said.

"Superb. Whereas Lord Snowdon has been shooting with a pair of matched Hasselblads with four-thousand-dollar lenses. You regard Lord Snowdon's pictures over the editor's shoulder. Then you reach into your reticule and withdraw your own pictures. 'These are terrible,' you say, 'but I thought you might just . . .' The editor gazes intently at your photographs. He drops Lord Snowdon's photographs on the floor. 'By God,' the editor says. 'You mean you . . . with your great-grandmother's camera held together with masking tape . . .' Lord Snowdon is staring at you with a funny expression on his face."

"*Quelle horreur!*" Amanda murmured.

"That is Contretemps," I said. "The situations tend to get more and more elaborate and horrible. A particularly good game for self-punishment, if that is what you crave. The situation in which you are in the studio of a famous artist, one who paints pitiful little girls with big eyes, and your own child, come to have her portrait done, refuses to open her eyes at all—that one is rather stimulating, I must say. And there are others. You are on the operating table. You are draped with a white sheet. You have borrowed a kidney from a friend. Now it is time to return it. The doctor—"

"More games," Amanda said. "More games and more brandy."

"We could play Broadway Flop," I said. "The Game of Ill-Conceived Musical Comedy. One attempts to construct the particular work least likely to get out of New Haven alive. A Lionel Bart musical based on *The Waste Land*, for example. Titled *Wasteland!* At the finale, Albert and Lil decide to leave Rats' Alley and make a new start in America. Or we could play Bag, the History of Jazz Game. The object of the game is to bring jazz up the river from New Orleans. Conflict provided by evil commercial-music interests who want to stop the spread of the New Thing. The evil commercial-music interests represented on the board by—"

"Squares," Amanda said triumphantly, and I gathered her into my arms. Then we played Famous Last Words, the Game of Deathbed Utterances, locked in a lovers' embrace on the fire escape. People down below stood agape, hanging upon the tense exchange between us.

"*It is enough,*" I said.

"Immanuel Kant," she said.

"*If there is no question, there is no answer.*"

"Gertrude Stein."

"*This is a fickle and faithless generation.*"

"Captain Kidd."

"*Bertie.*"

"Queen Victoria."

"*I do not understand what I have to do.*"

"Leo Tolstoy."

"*Hang on to the Matchless; it will make millions again.*"

"I can't remember, I can't remember!"

"Tabor, the Silver King," I said. "Didn't you see *The Ballad of Baby Doe?*"

"These games are marvelous," Amanda said. "I like them especially because they are so meaningless and boring, and trivial. These qualities, once regarded as less than desirable, are now everywhere enthroned as the key elements in our psychological lives, as reflected in the art of the period as well as—"

"Yes," I said. Then we played:

Crise du Cinéma, in which one improves existing films by supplying new casting and variant endings (Doris Day for Ingrid Bergman in *For Whom the Bell Tolls*; after El Sordo's band is wiped out, Maria persuades Robert Jordan to settle with her in a nice suburb of Barcelona).

Zen Zen (pointless answers are given to simple questions. "Where is the Administration Building?" "Ha-ha. Your hat is falling off." Blows are exchanged).

Break the Ball (an accumulation of balls from ball games—footballs, baseballs, basketballs, tennis balls, cricket balls—is demolished, using a twelve-pound sledge).

"What comes after Break the Ball?" Amanda asked.

"After the Ball Is Over. A fine game played with an empty punchbowl and four hundred overcoats. You attempt to find your overcoat in the pile of overcoats. You are forbidden to use your hands, feet, or teeth. Or anybody else's hands, feet, or teeth."

"Games are the enemies of beauty, truth, and sleep," Amanda said. The brandy was almost gone.

"There remains one more game."

"What is it?"

"Ennui," I said. "The easiest of all. No rules, no boards, no equipment."

"What is Ennui?" Amanda asked, setting it up for me.

"Ennui is the absence of games," I said, "the modern world at its most vulnerable." But she had folded her tent dress and silently stolen away.

AN HESITATION ON THE BANK
OF THE DELAWARE

Well, General Washington, sir, we are just about ready to croff the Delaware. The men are ready. Their morale is good. The boats are prepared. Shall I give the word?"

"Just a moment, Major Kinsolving. A dispatch rider is due, carrying word of the ftate of the heating plant in my houfe in Virginia. It's been acting awfully cranky. And another dispatch rider is due, bringing news of the well that is being dug at my estate at Fig Island, off the Carolinas. We have gone down forty-three feet and not yet got water. And I await ftill another messenger, carrying intelligence of my summer home in Georgia. We've been having a few problems with the fenestration. Rude boys have been breaking windows by throwing giant crayfish at them. It's moft annoying."

"But, General, unless we launch the boats pretty shortly, the attack will lose the element of furprife. Dawn is faft approaching. Although I admit nobody likes to have his carpets littered with wet, muddy giant crayfish."

"And then there is the matter of the mosquito nets for my tiny little retreat and hideaway in the Louisiana Territory. The mosquitoes down there are fomething fierce, Kinsolving."

"You certainly have a lot of houfes, General. Although I'm not being critical. I understand. Everybody understands. The four million pounds that these houfes have coft the infant Republic doesn't bother us a bit. Even though most of us have had to sell our cow to pay for them. We didn't need a cow anyway. A cow

79

was, for most of us, an unnecessary luxury. The fecurity of your mind and person is, of courfe, paramount."

"You do understand, Kinsolving. You showed that when you picked out the wallpaper for my houfe in Angle, Vermont. That was nice wallpaper."

"No more than you deserve, General, you being the Father of Our Country and all. No man can lead the patriots into battle without solid-silver wallpaper in his houfe. Or one of his houfes. The General Fervices Administration howled, of courfe."

"Is the General Fervices Administration standing on the bank of this river, preparing to launch one of the decifive battles of the war? No. No, it is not. But to business. My boat. Is the hand-carved rosewood seat in place?"

"It is, General. The Fecret Fervice installed it. Although, I might point out that you're fupposed to be ftanding up. Wrapped in your cloak against the icy winds. A ftern and determined expression on your vifage."

"A good bunch of boys, the Fecret Fervice. What about the beaten-gold boat bottom?"

"Done and done. The gold beaters have finished their arduous labor."

"And the costly Oriental rugf in place, on the farther shore?"

"Yef."

"And the golf courfe?"

"Eighteen holes, General, each hole and approach beautifully landscaped by private contributions extracted from a grateful and nearly beggared citizenry. You have a foursome scheduled with Cornwallis and the other soon-to-be-defeated Limey generals at three-thirty fharp."

"Very good, Kinsolving. To the boats, then. But wait! I just remembered. What about the houfe for my horfe? Have the funds been appropriated?"

"Sir, I regret to tell you that there can be no houfe for your horfe. Both the Houfe Appropriations Committee and the Horfe Appropriations Committee bounced it back."

"No houfe for my horfe?"

"The Continental Congress resolved that your famous plainneff and modefty would be ill ferved were it known that a houfe for your horfe was paid for from the public purfe."

"No houfe for my poor horfe! Oh, vile! My horfe, houfeless!

Suddenly I feel infecure, Kinsolving—terribly, terribly infecure. Tell the army to get out of the boats. And send the Congress a ftatement: one river crossing under hazardous conditions, two thousand pounds, payable in advance. We don't budge until we get the fhillings."

"Two thousand pounds! The exact cost of the houfe for your horfe!"

"I trust the gentlemen in Philadelphia will get the meffage. If the young nation is to endure, the serenity of my head is crucial, Kinsolving, absolutely crucial. And it takes a heap of houfing to make a head at home."

I HAVE FOR SOME TIME...

I have for some time longed to "leak" something to a national magazine, and now, at last, I have a burst pipe which might interest you. This is good stuff, so pay attention. The president's energy bill has been having a rough time in the Senate, as you know, and the president has had some angry words for "narrow, special-interest attacks on ... the national energy plan." Who is he talking about, exactly? The true gen, from a guy I know who is very, *very* close to Jody Powell, the president's press secretary, is this: *The plot to wreck the energy bill is the work of none other than China's notorious Gang of Four, which has half the Senate by the throat!* Yes, it's Chiang Ch'ing and her pals, up to their old tricks. Well, I was flabbergasted, as I assume you are, but the notion took on more credibility when my source listed for me the names of the particular senators around whose Adam's apples the Gang's tendrils restlessly wrap, unwrap, and rewrap. (I can't reveal them here, because of the libel laws.) What a Gang! They have already rented an office on H Street and applied for a Blue Cross group policy. How did the Gang get from mainland China to the continental U.S.? The answer, for students of Comparative Disinformation, is ridiculously simple: they had standby seats on the Bell & Howell plane.

THE GREAT DEBATE

The exhilarating Ford-Carter debates in September 1976 were such a significant—many say decisive—factor in that year's presidential campaign that the historian's urge to get them down on paper as soon as, or even sooner than, possible will be readily understood. Such an exercise in Preemptive History will be derided by those members of the profession still shackled to more traditional procedures, but for those ancients a fig, I say, a fig. The first of the prime-time debates (September 8) was set in a Denver studio and reached an estimated thirty-two million people. Both candidates wore blue suits, wine-dark ties, and a certain amount of unbleached flour. In addition, President Ford wore two left shoes and Governor Carter spent the entire hour tossing from hand to hand a bale of alfalfa. Herewith the transcript:

MR. FORD: Well, I would just like to welcome Governor Carter —I mean former Governor Carter—to the studio here tonight and to America, our America. I have been following with interest his various appearances around the country and in a general way listening with interest to some of the things he has been saying in his various public appearances, and I would just like to say here that in my opinion he has done very well, extraordinarily well, for someone who was at the beginning of the campaign only a dim little cloud on the horizon—a cloud no bigger than a little wee dark cloud, you might say.

MR. CARTER: He who hath Love in his heart hath in his heart Love.

MR. FORD: What I would like to put in front of the American people tonight are some of our programs and achievements which affect in one way or another each and every American—when I say "our" I mean of course programs and achievements generated by my Administration, and by that I don't mean only the President but the whole team. One of the most important of these is, I think, our new initiative in international relations—that is, the relations between the various nations of the world who relate to each other and to themselves. In phasing out the outmoded concept of détente and offering what I think and hope is a very creative new approach—what I have called *faerdigskranskelse*, which is Finnish for "dynamic tension"—or rather I didn't call it that, Secretary Kissinger called it that, and because he called it that I just naturally, as who wouldn't, began calling it that—in conceiving this new concept, and I know it's hard to pronounce but most new things are a little difficult to pronounce at first until you get the hang of it. Say after me: *"Faerdigskranskelse."*

MR. CARTER: He who hath faerdigskranskelse in his heart hath no room in his heart for Love.

MR. FORD: And I think this new concept will also satisfy those critics of our policies who feel, honestly and sincerely, that we have not been in the past sufficiently rigid in our international posture, in our dealings with those who call themselves, rightly or wrongly, enemies of freedom, and I think this will go a long way toward correcting that. Faerdigskranskelse plain and simple, or, in English, dynamic tension.

In addition to this new initiative in the international area, we have sent to the Congress proposals for five new initiatives in the domestic area. Now, as you know, we have been working very hard on the problem of unemployment, which means, very simply, that there are individuals in this country today who do not have employment, or jobs. These individuals, and it's been running and will continue to run for the foreseeable future at about seven and a bit percent, and what we have done on that is to send to the Congress proposals that will, in the event that Congress sees fit to implement them, permit a crash program, nationwide —a very important and I think creative program that is fiscally responsible, fiscally sound—to develop something that is very much needed in America: an artificial peanut butter. This is also, I may say, directly related to the problem of hunger in this country, because, as you know, most of the children, the young children, in this country have as a mainstay of their diet peanut-butter sandwiches, very often peanut-butter-and-jelly, and the development of a new low-cost peanut butter that they could put on their bread when they come home from school or even take to school with them for their lunches would be of inestimable value to the mothers and fathers who are now paying what we consider ridiculously high prices for the so-called organic product, and we hope to put three to four million people to work in that program.

MR. CARTER: He who tampereth with peanut futures not only hath not Love in his heart but tampereth also with God's grand design and insulteth also the memory of that great American George Washington Carver, who I always include on my Great Americans list when I am north of the thirty-ninth parallel.

MR. FORD: Now, our other four new initiatives in the domestic area, the first of these—actually, the second if you think of the one I just spoke about as the first—the second one has involved giving the bottom half of the country, what has become known as the Sun Belt, to Governor Reagan to be President of, or, as I think he calls it, Shah of. I think that's working out very well, and we will continue to enjoy very good relations with that part of the country, especially if our current negotiations to pay them an additional one-hundred-and-twenty-five-percent-per-barrel royalty at the wellhead are successful, as I think they will be.

MR. CARTER: If a man hath the entire Sun Belt and two Disneylands also and hath not Love, then it may be said he hath the moola but heedeth not the call of the mullah, which is Love.

MR. FORD: Moving along, because I see by the clock that we don't have very much more time for these very important matters, I want to point out that since I have been President we have achieved a nine percent reduction in—I think the figure is nine percent or approaches nine percent—a nine percent reduction in the No Frills Fare to the Miami/Ft. Lauderdale area, to sixty-six dollars, which is five dollars and sixty-seven cents, roughly, for every man, woman, and child in America who happens to be traveling to that area. And I think we can promise similar reductions in the near future for travel to other points our citizens might be interested in traveling to. This rate does not apply, by the way, during these periods: southbound, April 12 through 22, and May 27. Northbound, April 19 through 29, and May 31 through June 1.

MR. CARTER: In every person there is something fine and pure and noble and good and he that sayeth that there is not in every person something fine and pure and noble and good fiddleth with the truth, but I will never fiddle with the truth, on my honor as a nuclear physicith.

MR. FORD: Let me make one further point tonight, and I know that it is an important point that all of you are vitally interested in. Certain individuals in this government, your government— not in the present Administration, because we wouldn't permit this sort of thing in the present Administration, but in former or bygone Administrations—certain individuals in these former Administrations have from the best and highest motives frequently, such as patriotism, which is usually defined as love of one's country—

MR. CARTER: Love of God, Love of country, Love of home, Love of wife, Love of children, Love of aunts and uncles, Love of cousins, Love of second cousins twice removed, Love of neighbor, Love of nature, Love of Love—he that hath not these things in his heart hath in his heart those things which are not these things.

MR. FORD: These individuals, with the best will in the world, have in the past from time to time initiated certain actions which might be construed, from the most favorable point of view, as revolting. This is not to say that they were not, and are not, in many cases, dedicated public servants, who . . . I refer to the—and of course it's been well publicized in the media, to a fare-thee-well—to these plans and initiatives developed by certain of our agencies, agencies of your government, for the—and I would like to underline the fact that none of these plans or initiatives were initiated, to my knowledge, by the present Administration or any of the Administrations which preceded it; in fact, they seem to have been, and especially the plan involving Prime Minister Wilson or former Prime Minister Wilson and the banjo strings—boy, somebody was really off the wall there—and I want to assure you that this Administration has taken the firmest possible measures to insure that this type of activity will never happen again, if it ever, in fact, happened in the first place. And therefore I would like to leave you tonight, if I may, with one thought—

MR. CARTER: God is Love and Love God, and the two are One, so that when a man sayeth unto you Gove, he meaneth that God is Love and Love God. Therefore when such a man comes before us saying Gove, Gove, Gove, we must raise up that man and exalt him in the simplicity of our hearts and the simplicity of our minds and the purity of our . . . of our purity.

MR. FORD: Swine flu very much.

MR. CARTER: Gove.

SNAP SNAP

uch a claim is ridiculous," Quynh snapped . . . (*Time*, June 4)
. . . Rusk snapped, "I don't know how one draws the
line . . ." (*Time*, June 4)

Snapped Canadian Heavyweight George Chuvalo: "It's a phony,
a real phony." (*Time*, June 4)

Harvard Law School Professor Charles Haar snapped . . . (*Time*,
June 4)

"We're not playing Mickey Mouse with this thing," snapped
Christopher Kraft, *Gemini 4*'s mission director. (*Time*, June 11)

Barry [Goldwater] snapped: "Frankly, I don't know enough
about John Lindsay to give you the time of day." (*Newsweek*,
June 14)

. . . snapped London's *Economist*. (*Newsweek*, June 14)

"I don't have to wait for revelation to know that I am the natural head in Nigeria," snaps [Mormon Anie Dick] Obot . . . (*Time*,
June 18)

"Ridiculous!" snapped Hollywood's Peter Lawford . . . (*Newsweek*, June 21)

"Goddammit, Bundy," snapped the President, "I've told you
that when I want you I'll call you." (*Time*, June 25)

"Adolescent," snapped Author Ralph Ellison. (*Time*, June 25)

Snapped [Walter] Hallstein: "The obstinate maintaining of di-
visive internal antagonisms could make Europe the Balkans of the
world." (*Time*, June 25)

Americans are "abominable," [Lord] Russell snapped . . . (*Time*, June 25)

"Oh, you have, have you?" snapped [Professor Daniel] Berman. (*Time*, July 2)

[Algerian Official Spokesman Si] Slimane snapped . . . (*Time*, July 2)

[Peking Foreign Minister] Chen Yi snapped: "That's not serious." (*Newsweek*, July 12)

Snapped one MP: "Philip is a very highly paid civil servant . . . who is expected to keep his nose out of politics." (*Time*, July 16)

Snapped Kenya's Foreign Minister Joseph Murumbi . . . (*Newsweek*, July 19)

In another speech he [Ludwig Erhard] snapped that . . . (*Time*, July 23)

Snapped Spahn: "First, I'm a pitcher. Then I'm a coach." (*Time*, July 23)

"A complete diplomatic sellout," snapped a conservative. (*Newsweek*, July 26)

[Robert] Kennedy snapped: "I'm shocked . . . " (*Newsweek*, July 26)

"I want you," snapped the President. "Bring Mrs. Goldberg right over to the office." (*Time*, July 30)

The difficulty is with my style. That much is clear. My style pure, unadulterated mouse. Mouse all the way. Gray movements along the baseboards of corridors of power. When what is wanted is mouse*trap* style. Snap-snap. Trigger-quick. Incisive. Decisive. Snapper knows what's what. Lashes out. Got the facts. Tip of the tongue. Snap-snap.

Twenty-three years in Bureau of Hatcheries and what to show for it? Nothing. Not a thing. Since the day in 1944 when they entrusted me with the pike. *Clitterhouse*, they said, *a chance to show what you can do*. And then decades of neglect. A GS-10 with no hope of 11. Not even allowed a framed photograph of the President for my wall. Make do with framed photograph of little beagle. Because I am soft-spoken. Because I am slow to anger. Because I mull, think through. What has it got me? Watery sauerkraut in the cafeteria every Wednesday. Eyes-only memos passing me by. The pike respects me, perhaps. How is one to know?

Perhaps even now it is not too late. Change style. Learn to snap. Leave government service, plunge into jungles of commerce. Then one day surface in the pages of *Time*, for instance, where I am seen to be doing my job with spectacular competence:

> For shareholders of giant U.S. Python, long one of the hemisphere's three top-rated producers of industrial snake musculature, there was good news last week: engorgement of two-hundred-year-old Pantages Plantfood, Inc., flourishing Chilean phosphorus concern. Acquisition of Pantages will give Python, already active in Christmas cards, calorie counters, and cut glass, a stranglehold on the booming international fishmeal market, solidly enhance its sly sidestep into rubber overshoes (through fast-climbing International Buckle, Java-based subsidiary whose 1964 year-end profits totaled $2.5 million). Behind the move was U.S. Python's shrewd, snappish Charles Clitterhouse III, forty-four, who came to Python three years ago after a hitch with Midwest Trace & Bit. Clitterhouse, a loner who scorns computers ("window dressing!" he snapped on one occasion) and programs the entire Python operation in his head, has guided the once-ailing colossus back to health with an unorthodox combination of brains, drive, and peevishness. "Asperity," he snaps, "is the key to greater profits in the current economic climate," and stencils the company motto ("Mala Gratia") on Python trucks, water coolers, and junior executives. An exotic who lives in a bank vault with his three wives, one child, Clitterhouse relaxes on rare days off by trading tartnesses with a few close friends, snapping Polaroid photos of company installations. "Let the other guy be civil," snaps he, "I'll . . ."

But this is fantasy, Clitterhouse. The problem remains. How to impinge upon consciousness of superiors? How to reach hearing aids of the mighty? Cry and warn. And urge. The newsweeklies a cacophony of crying and warning, and urging. Not just snapping. Rounded Top Person style includes snapping, crying, warning, urging. Vigor. The raised voice. No murmurers need apply.

Consider the month of June. Syrian Strongman Amin Hafez cried that Egyptian Strongman Gamal Abdel Nasser was soft on Israel. "Cried Hafez: 'What is he waiting for?'" (*Time*, June 11) Brazilian Politico Carlos Lacerda cried that Brazilian Economics Minister Roberto Campos was soft in the head. "'Campos,' cried

Lacerda, is 'a mental weakling . . . ' " (*Time*, June 11) Dominican Insurgent Colonel Francisco Caamaño Deñó cried that elections for his strife-torn country were out of the question. " 'First,' cried Caamaño, 'the revolution's goal must be fulfilled. After that we can talk about elections.' " (*Time*, June 11) Cuban Strongman Fidel Castro cried that this was a decisive year. " 'This was a decisive year,' cried Castro." (*Time*, June 18) Strongman Castro cried again (*Time*, June 25), discussing whereabouts of Henchman Che Guevera. " 'If the Americans are puzzled,' cried Castro . . . , 'let them remain puzzled.' " Strongman Castro nearly always cries in newsweeklies. Sometimes roars. Has been heard to snort. But mostly cries.

Others cry too. Humorist Harry Hershfield cried (*Time*, June 25). "O.K., cried Hershfield, so maybe [New York City Council President and Mayoral Candidate and Strongman Paul R.] Screvane is of Italian-Irish descent and married to Limerick-born Bridie McKessy—but 'he has a Jewish heart.' " An extended cry. Dominican Politico Rafael Tavera cried ("There will not be peace until the last invader is destroyed and the last Yankee property is seized"). An army general cried ("I thought you were going to play all the instruments, Mr. President"). Theodore Roosevelt cried ("By Jove! I'll have to do something for that young man"). Marcel Carné cried ("*Parties!*"). British Bridge Expert Ralph Swimer cried. Joseph Tronzo, sports editor of Beaver Falls, Pa., *News-Tribune*, cried. An old lady cried. Old pensioners cried. A Ferrari mechanic cried.

And there were warnings. Conservative French Novelist Michel de Saint Pierre warned ("We encounter Marxist infiltration at every step in our Christian lives"). Caamaño warned. Campos warned. Many economists warned. Meller & Co.'s John Amico warned darkly ("Smart money is leaving the market"). One Washington policymaker warned. And urgings. Sargent Shriver urged. The President urged. Senator Fulbright urged.

Clitterhouse, do you get the message? Pay attention to speech. Basically, you're not a bad fellow, but you have this terrible habit of . . . *saying* everything. Don't *say*. Snap, cry, urge, warn. Otherwise you stand in grave danger of being thought a relic of nineteenth century, a muted cough along the tapped wire of history.

Consider July. July, in newsweeklies, a shrill, clamorous, fateful month, cantanker, distemper everywhere, snappings, cryings, urgings, warnings. French Foreign Minister Couve de Murville cried ("Too much has been asked of France!"). Disc Jockey Murray the K cried ("Sarge, baby, you're a real swinger"). Missouri Democrat Paul Jones cried ("This is the damnedest thing I've seen in all my life"). Critics of India's Prime Minister Shastri cried ("sellout"). Painter Marc Chagall cried ("Divorce!"). British Deputy Prime Minister George Brown cried. Canadian Opposition Leader John Diefenbaker cried. Roger Rappenceau cried. Pakistan's President Ayub took up the cry. The Democrats cried. Walter Hallstein cried. Painter Bernard Buffet cried twice, once in *Time* ("*Au secours!*" July 16), once in *Newsweek* (something to the effect that a Swede was cutting up his refrigerator, July 19). Philosopher George Picht warned. British Chancellor of the Exchequer James Callaghan ("among others") warned. The President warned. White House and State Department spokesmen warned. The pastor of Cologne's powerful St. Ursula's Church warned. Brookfield (Ill.) Zoo authorities warned. Dodger Physician Dr. Robert Kerlan warned. CORE's James Farmer warned. U Thant warned. Robert Kennedy warned. Boumedienne warned. Papandreou warned. The government of Sarawak urged. *Clitterhouse, can you hear me? Open wide, Clitterhouse, open wide!*

MING

We had a conversation the other day with Ming the Merciless, one of the preeminent villains of modern times, whose half-century-long struggle with his opposite number, Flash Gordon, has helped generations of Americans conceptualize the fearsome enchantments of space. We caught up with the veteran malefactor at the Volney, where he greeted us in a turquoise-and-gold dressing gown, a black skullcap setting off his striking yellowish pallor. We immediately put our foot in it by addressing him as "Mr. Ming."

"I don't want to be stuffy," he said pleasantly, "but that's Emperor Ming, if you don't mind. I'm here working in a show we call *Defenders of the Earth*. It's a TV deal for children, and you can catch it locally at 7:30 in the morning on Channel 5. It's basically me against three other legendary figures, Flash Gordon, the Phantom, and Mandrake the Magician. I am, as ever, the threat, the heavy."

After noting that the Emperor was created by Alex Raymond in 1932, we asked him if he would hazard a comparison between the page and the small screen.

"They're very different. The first difference is not animation, as you might think, but the quality of the draftsmanship. I mean it's wonderful to be able to lift your arms and have death-dealing rays emanate from your fingertips and the rays actually pulsating right there on the screen—all that stuff is great. But you pay a price. The draftsmanship, the way the costumes hang, the way the swords clash, the way the castles tower, was just flat better in the old days. TV has very high costs, as you know, and they cut corners. You don't have a guy sitting at his drawing board inking in those extra lines, giving you those extra little frissons—

"Being merciless, while not exactly easy, is finally a job like any other. It's theater. It's got nothing to do with my private life. Still, sometimes when I used to yell at my kids, I wondered if I was maybe . . . putting a little too much into it. They're grown now, so the question is moot. They seem OK. Roderick is at Harvard and Betsy is married and has a couple of kids of her own."

We suggested that he had a lot on his plate in *Defenders of the Earth*—his opponents include not only Flash, the Phantom, Mandrake and Lothar, but also assorted sons and daughters of these distinguished folk.

"There used to be just Flash, Dale and Dr. Zarkhov. There's a tendency now to gang superheroes—you get a bit more dramatic impact by having three or more together, each one with his own shtick, Flash with his all-purpose machismo, Mandrake with his hypnotic powers, the Phantom with his rather vague African magic, all that. I rather like having three of them contending with one of me. Makes me feel I haven't lost my touch altogether. On the other hand, it's not what you'd call fair, is it? Strictly speaking?"

We said that we had noted that the show credits two clinical psychologists as consultants.

"That's right. They're both very good, give us a lot of input. We're trying to explore issues, within the context of entertainment. For instance, we recently did a show which centered on the drug problem. Flash's son, Rick, was a user, just dabbling, of course, but when my robots or whatever were putting the pressure on pretty good, and he was manning the defenses, he clutched because he was in a dope fog. There's a pretty strong message for young people there, I think."

We then inquired as to the Emperor's view of the President's Strategic Defense Initiative, something we felt he was uniquely qualified to comment upon.

"Of course, just because someone has been knocking about the galaxies for fifty some-odd years doesn't make that person an expert," he said. "Still, I can tell you this: SDI is a dumb idea. Look, we can't even do airplanes right. I was making some personal appearances in the Denver area last summer and I don't want to tell you how many hours I sat on the tarmac at the Denver airport, inside the plane with two hundred other people, waiting for these clowns to get the equipment in order. Two guys who appeared to be all of twenty with their screwdrivers inside the panels in the roof of the cockpit—the cockpit door was open—and I said to myself, Where are the old mechanics? Sent a chill down my spine, believe me.

"The general point is, I've always been a technology freak, as everybody knows, but this SDI thing just hasn't been thought through. I don't want it in space. Space is already full of our junk. The *Times* had a piece the other day that said we're monitoring something like seven thousand man-made objects the size of base-balls or larger in space, and there are an estimated forty thousand smaller objects floating out there, any one of them capable of inflicting mortal hurt on a satellite or an astronaut. They're talk-ing now about slowing down some of these objects with clouds of foam, which would cause them to reenter the atmosphere and be incinerated. Well, lots of luck, guys.

"Next, who knows what effect these laser beams and whatnot will have on the ozone layer, just for starters? They'll tell you the ozone layer can't possibly be affected, but you'll remember that just a few short years ago Agent Orange was said to be harmless to people, so we dumped God knows how much of it all over Vietnam and Cambodia. That's recent science we're talking about, science not twenty years old. You get an if-we-can-we-will situation. Scientists make their careers out of working on these things, and the question of whether or not it should be done flies out of the window. I know people tend to grow more conservative as they grow older, but frankly, this stuff scares the hell out of me. I may be merciless, but I'm not a damned fool."

DONALD BARTHELME'S
FINE HOMEMADE SOUPS

My fine homemade soups are interesting, economical, and tasty. To make them, one proceeds in the following way:

FINE HOMEMADE LEEK SOUP

Take one package Knorr Leek Soupmix. Prepare as directed. Take two live leeks. Chop leeks into quarter-inch rounds. Throw into Soupmix. Throw in ½ cup Tribuno Dry Vermouth. Throw in chopped parsley. Throw in some amount of salt and a heavy bit of freshly ground pepper. Eat with good-quality French bread, dipped repeatedly in soup.

FINE HOMEMADE MUSHROOM SOUP

Take one package Knorr Mushroom Soupmix. Prepare as directed. Take four large mushrooms. Slice. Throw into Soupmix. Throw in ½ cup Tribuno Dry Vermouth, parsley, salt, pepper. Stick bread as above into soup at intervals. Buttering bread enhances taste of the whole.

FINE HOMEMADE CHICKEN SOUP

Take Knorr Chicken Soupmix, prepare as directed, throw in leftover chicken, duck, or goose as available. Add enhancements as above.

FINE HOMEMADE OXTAIL SOUP

Take Knorr Oxtail Soupmix, decant into same any leftover meat (sliced or diced) from the old refrigerator. Follow above strategies to the letter. The result will make you happy. Knorr's Oxtail is also good as a basic gravy maker and constituent of a fine fake cassoulet about which we can talk at another time. Knorr is a very good Swiss outfit whose products can be found in both major and minor cities. The point here is not to be afraid of the potential soup but to approach it with the attitude that you know what's best for it. And you do. The rawness of the vegetables refreshes the civilization of the Soupmixes. And there are opportunities for mercy—if your ox does not wish to part with his tail, for example, to dress up your fine Oxtail Soup, you can use commercial products from our great American supermarkets, which will be almost as good. *These fine homemade recipes work!* Use them with furious enthusiasm.

ADVENTURE

Christine's had been a typical Metz childhood. But now she was ready for
something . . . larger. Entering the great city, the city of her dreams, she was
ready for anything. She was ready for evil itself, if that was what came her
way, and she had heard that it often did, in great cities. What new demands
would the city make on her? What dark unknown strands in her nature
would be unwound? With whom would these strands entangle?

"So this is grandeur!" Christine exclaimed. She
drank in the great city with all of her senses.

98

The gorgeousness of the architecture struck her dreaming eye with the force of a hundred blows. Even the telephone booths were—"They make our old Metz telephone booths look like—like shoe boxes! What would Yves say, if he could see me now?"

Back in Metz, Yves continued to devote himself to the billiard table.

Lounging in the Public Gardens, Christine became
aware of a stern and expressive gaze that seemed to
penetrate to the inmost recesses of her perturbed
heart.

The gaze was that of Henri Mohrt, the well-known dealer. Without hesitation she took his arm. Soon they were viewing his combined sculpture and
furniture store on the Rue du Bac.

Henri offered to "put her up" on the couch in the spare room. Christine slept dreamlessly as he watched through the night.

Life with Henri was not simple. Christine had to learn to eat many new foods: (1) Enameled Eggplant Climbing a Mound of Diced Buffalo, (2) Mother Crayfish Surrounded by Her Young, Electric Sauce, (3) Brained Chocolate-covered Turtle with Pineapple Shell, and (4) Shocked Pork Chops in Individual Strega-soaked Muslin Bags.

If she did not like one of these dishes, Henri would fly into a terrible rage. But this was his only major fault. Her nights vibrated with the strange music of his urgent whispers.

Meanwhile, in Metz, what must be described in all candour as a stroke of ill fortune had befallen Yves.

To finance his billiard losses. Yves had rustled a flock of ducks—12,000 head. His sentence was two years. One day in the gallery, Christine told Henri that she was returning to Metz. She would marry Yves, she said, as soon as his time was served. But she would never forget Henri and the life they had lived together in the radiant city.

The very sculptures seemed to express loss, resignation, and dubiousness.

"I hope you are making the right decision," Henri said, "because if you are not, you will not be happy."

Henri's farewell gift was a handsome rug.

"Is there never again to be . . . adventure?"

HELIOTROPE

It is April, and Heliotrope, the Open University of San Francisco, is once again turning toward the sun of felt needs and marigold-yellow fulfillments. Heliotrope is a real university, and lives at 21 Columbus Avenue, San Francisco, California, 94111. Marigold yellow is one of the colors of Heliotrope's April bulletin, on the cover of which three competition bicyclists, crash-helmeted, are bent low over their handlebars, pedaling madly toward Awareness. Come, let us join them. For too long have we tarried in the dismal sunless cities of the East. Come. Let us go, then, love, and enlist ourselves in Course D-16, Awareness and Weight Loss Workshop, designed for the unsuccessful dieter: "Each participant will have an opportunity to tailor-make a weight-loss program incorporating their food cravings, life-style needs, and principles of sound nutrition. Transactional Analysis will be used as a framework for understanding the personal motivations that contribute to overeating problems." Come. Your food cravings have long been a puzzlement (that time you ordered Blue Whale Stuffed with Ford Pinto), and as for your life-style— But I am not being critical; it is the East, the East, the Unreal City, to which I attach the blame. That, and the stuffy rigid hierarchical closed universities which infest it and us. Let us leave all that behind, shoulder our backpacks, and return to basics at Heliotrope, the Open University of San Francisco. We can take Basic Astrology, D-20: "Instructress is student of the vast harmonious order of the universe." And so can we be, if only we can shed our narrow paranoid pale untogether judgmental Valium-popping

Eastern ways. Required for the course: a birth certificate or correct
knowledge of time (hour, minute), month, day, year of birth. Or
we can take Basic Bridge (D-21), Basic Macramé (D-22), Basic Silk-
screening (D-24), Basic Herb Gardening (D-111), or Basic Turkish
(D-29): "Mellow low-key course." We are sour and high-key; that
is part of what ails us—how could we not have known? We have
been frittering. Let us fritter no more. Or we have been seeking
answers. That is a mistake. "When an answer is found, it is not
the end but only a beginning." Why didn't *we* think of that? The
Open University offers us beginnings and beginnings and beginnings, and what do we want more than beginnings? Come. We
can begin Alpha & Theta Brain Wave Training (D-8), Belly Dance
(D-30), Bicycle Repair and Maintenance (D-31), Common Medical
Problems (D-38), or Divorce Before & After (D-47). "If you are
thinking about divorce, if you have recently been divorced, or if
you are thinking of remarriage, this is an opportunity to clarify
your feelings and to share your experience with assistance from a
trained professional." Who among us is not thinking about divorce, except for a few tiny-minded stick-in-the-muds who don't
count? Come, love, and we will think about it together at the
Open University, with assistance from a trained professional. Heliotrope, you will notice, does not offer us any untrained profes-
sionals—Heaven forfend! And if we can't clarify our feelings,
perhaps we can clarify our butter, by taking Vegetarian & Natural
Foods Cooking, D-102. And if these resplendent opportunities are
not enough we can dip a toe into D-60, Happiness and Freedom;
D-65, Hypnosis with Color; D-81, Outdoor Meditation, Intensive;
D-100, Tide Pool Life; D-135, Two-Stroke Motorcycle Maintenance; D-136, Introduction to Gambling; or D-91, Stained Glass.
Come, dearly beloved, hung-up, rarefied, Con Ed–haunted man-
darin that you are, let us pick up our water beds and gimp off into
the sunrise, to Heliotrope, the Open University of San Francisco.
There is even a course in Love (D-71): "We cover self love, romantic love, humanitarian love, and spiritual love." Perhaps they
know something that we do not. Ah, happy Heliotrope, with its
Kung Fu, Tai Chi Chuan, Tap Dancing, Group Bioenergetic Re-
education, and Gestalt for Women Over 35! Come. You, dear
friend, can teach a course in Paying the Telephone Bill, and I will
teach one in Napping, and we will both, at long last, be avenged
upon that fancy-Dan Lionel Trilling.

THE ANGRY YOUNG MAN

Four thousand pieces of second-class mail! Four thousand pieces of second-class mail enriched with certain letters of historical importance and literary forgeries of great cunning! These cover the goatskin rug. The goatskin rug covers the lazy dog. The angry young man, using the new fiberglass pole, makes his run, jumps! He is aloft, he is up in the air, he has cleared the lazy dog, the goatskin rug, the four thousand pieces of second-class mail! A new earth record for the lazy dog's back jump!

What a wonderful thing it is to be angry! To be young.

WHAT THE DICTIONARY SAYS

an'gry young' man, 1. (*often cap.*) one of a group of British writers since the late 1950's whose works reflect strong dissatisfaction with, frustration by, and rebellion against tradition and society. **2.** any author writing in this manner. **3.** any frustrated, rebellious person. Also, *referring to a woman*, **an'gry young/ wom'an.**

—Random House Dictionary of the English Language

HIS OPINION OF THE QUEEN

"She's as comely as a cow in a cage."

HIS CLOTHING

Brown corduroy pants, black turtleneck sweater, work shoes, coonskin cap, glass of porter in right hand. Or, dark-blue suit, black shoes, white shirt, maroon tie—this worn when receiving the OBE or other honors.

OPINION OF THE PRESENT SITUATION

"What is your opinion of the present situation?"

"Well, it's better than sleeping with a dead policeman."

BEFORE THE MIRROR

The dark muscle of the angry young man, surrounded as it is by the light muscle, flexes.

"Mirror, mirror, on the wall, who's the most baddest angry young man of all?"

ATTITUDE TOWARD THE REVOLUTION

"Well, it can't happen here, can it? I mean, Daddy won't allow it, will he? Daddy and his pals, and the posh papers, the whole rotten lot of them? I mean, it's just a lot of cock, now, isn't it?"

TAXES PAID INLAND REVENUE FOR THE YEAR 1959

£2,850.

THE ANGRY YOUNG MAN MEETS THE
ANGRY YOUNG WOMAN

"Tom!"

"Helen!"

"How've you been? Angry?"

"Rabid."

"Good girl. Tea?"

"Yes thanks I'd love some."

MOMENT OF SELF-DOUBT IN THE PSYCHIC LIFE OF THE
ANGRY YOUNG MAN

"Is there any point in being an angry *old* man?"

THE ALBERT HALL LECTURE

"Yes. Well. My subject tonight is cooking before marriage. It has been my observation, and I'm not alone in this, other people have made the same observation, a blind man could see it, that the young people today are doing a bloody great lot of *cooking together before marriage*. Cooking together, shamelessly, night after night, and God knows I'm no prude but the sight of these young . . . *lovebirds* . . . without so much as a by-your-leave, without so much as the shred of a marriage contract between them, well it's a bit much now isn't it . . . wallowing in . . . *spices* . . . rosemary . . . saffron . . ."

PASSING OF TIME IN THE LIFE OF THE ANGRY YOUNG MAN

L(%¢, L(%&, L(%*, L(%(, L(¢), L(¢L, L(¢@, L(¢#, L(¢$, L(¢%, L(¢¢, L(¢&, L(¢*, L(¢(, L(&), L(&L, L(&@, L(&#, L(&$

CHARACTERISTICS OF THE ANGRY YOUNG BOOK

The angry young book should be a good true book of a familiar and reliable pattern. It should concern itself with human emotions of standard issue plus at least one (1) nonstandard emotion for seasoning and piquancy. It should extend to a good number of pages and said pages should hold a full body of printing both recto and verso, the lines so arranged as to come out even at the right-hand margin, save at the termination of paragraphs and the like. It should have a good true spine to which the pages are attached by sewing and a strong glue, and no page should fly out of the whole save by prior arrangement, as when the author is especially angry. The same should reflect strong dissatisfaction with, frustration by, and rebellion against tradition and society. The book should, ideally, burn the hands—a third-degree burn.

CURRENT MANIFESTATIONS OF THE "KITCHEN SINK" SCHOOL OF BRITISH PAINTING, THOUGHT AT ONE TIME TO BE ANALOGOUS TO THE WORK OF THE ANGRY YOUNG MEN

There are none.

THE ANGRY YOUNG MAN ATTENDS THE ANNUAL MEETING

At the Annual Meeting, voices are raised in anger. The hall is crawling with coonskin caps, which are waved, or dropped, or flung. Large wheyfaced angry young men grapple with small wiry angry young men—the faces of the latter are made of string. The chairman calls for order but in vain; order is not wanted here. Skiffle bands engage in cutting contests. The floor is black with spilled porter and bile. Individual angry young men stand at various points with their backs to the crowd playing trumpets or cornets—each is playing a different tune. Other angry young men are refusing to speak to other angry young men. The flag is trampled, spat upon, urinated upon, used as a bar rag. Harrod's is burned in effigy as it is every year (but some angry young men are seen snatching candied yummies from the flames).

Nevertheless, important theoretical questions are raised:

1. Is fresh ever-renewed soaring searing good-quality anger possible?
2. How long, expressed in decades, can true anger be maintained without modulating into, say, pique?
3. Was it *originally* pique, made to seem anger by skilled dramaturgy?
4. What can be learned by studies of the shelf life of the average volcano?
5. Can anger be institutionalized, can it avoid being institutionalized, and what is the place in all this of the cup of tea?
6. Does the boiling point of the cup of tea vary from corrupt society to corrupt society?

WHEREABOUTS OF THE WIVES OF THE ANGRY YOUNG MAN

The wives of the angry young man are now married to other people—doctors, mostly.

THE MOVEMENT OF HISTORY

The movement of history is heavy, and slow. The movement of history always takes place *behind one's back*. As your gaze is fixed upon something immediately in front of you—the object of your anger, for example—history makes a slight, almost imperceptible slither, or shudder, in a direction of its own choice. The distinguishing mark of this direction is that it is not the one that you had anticipated. How history manages this is not known. Because history is made of the will of all individuals taken together, because these oceans of individuals are mostly, or always, in conflict, the movement of history is at one and the same time tightly bound, and outrageous. The problem may be diagrammed in the following way:

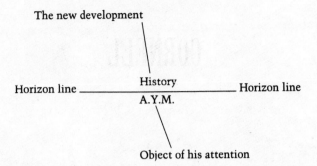

Study of the previous behavior of history does not prepare one for these shifts, which are discomfiting in the extreme. Nothing prepares you.

ULTIMATE MEANING OF THE ANGRY YOUNG MAN

The ultimate meaning of the angry young man is not known. What is known is the shape of his greatest fear—that all of his efforts, from learning to speak to learning to write, to write well, to write badly, to write angrily, from learning to despise to learning to abominate, to abominate well, to abominate badly, to abominate abominably, to rant, to fulminate, to shout down the sea, to age, to age gracefully, to age awkwardly, to age at all, to think, to regret, to list himself in the newspapers under "Lost and Found," might culminate precisely in this: a roaring, raging, crazy mad passionate bibliography.

CORNELL

I put a name in an envelope, and sealed the envelope; and put
that envelope in another envelope with a spittlebug and some
quantity of boric acid; and put that envelope in a still larger
envelope which contained also a woman tearing her gloves to
tatters; and put that envelope in the mail to Fichtelgebirge. At the
Fichtelgebirge Post Office I asked if there was mail for me, with a
mysterious smile the clerk said, "Yes," I hurried with the envelope to London, arriving with snow, and put the envelope in the
Victoria and Albert Museum, bowing to the curators in the Envelope Room, the wallpaper hanging down in thick strips. I put the
Victoria and Albert Museum in a still larger envelope which I
placed in the program of the Royal Danish Ballet, in the form of
an advertisement for museums, boric acid, wallpaper. I put the
program of the Royal Danish Ballet into the North Sea for two
weeks. Then, I retrieved it, it was hanging down in thick strips, I
sent it to a machine-*vask* on H. C. Andersens Boulevard, everything came out square and neat, I was overjoyed. I put the square,
neat package in a safe place, and put the safe place in a vault
designed by Caspar David Friedrich, German romantic landscape
painter of the last century. I slipped the vault into a history of art
(Insel Verlag, Frankfurt, 1975). But, in a convent library on the
side of a hill near a principal city of Montana, it fell out of the
history of art into a wastebasket, a thing I could not have predicted. I bound the wastebasket in stone, with a matchwood
shroud covering the stone, and placed it in the care of Charles the

112

Good, Charles the Bold, and Charles the Fair. They stand juggling cork balls before the many-times-encased envelope, whispering names which are not the right one. I put the three kings into a new blue suit; it walked away from me very confidently.

I AM, AT THE MOMENT...

I am, at the moment, seated. On a stump in the forest, listening. Ireland and Scotland are remote, Wales is not near. I will rise, soon, to hold the ladder for you.

Tombs are scattered through the tall white beanwoods. They are made of perfectly ordinary gray stone. Chandeliers, at night, scatter light over the tombs, little houses in which I sleep with the already-beautiful, and they with me. The already-beautiful saunter through the forest carrying plump red hams, already cooked. The already-beautiful do not, as a rule, run.

Holding the ladder I watch you glue additional chandeliers to appropriate limbs. You are tiring, you have worked very hard. Iced beanwater will refresh you, and these wallets made of ham. I have set bronze statues of alert, crouching Indian boys around the periphery of the forest, for ornamentation. For ornamentation. Each alert, crouching Indian boy is accompanied by a large, bronze, wolflike dog, finely polished.

I have been meaning to speak to you. I have many pages of notes, instructions, quarrels. On weighty matters I will speak without notes, freely and passionately, as if inspired, at night, in a rage, slapping myself, great tremendous slaps to the brow which will fell me to the earth. The already-beautiful will stand and watch, in a circle, cradling, each, an animal in mothering arms— green monkey, meadow mouse, tucotuco.

That one has her hips exposed, for study. I make careful notes. You snatch the notebook from my hands. The pockets of your

114

smock swing heavily with the lights of chandeliers. Your light-by-light, bean-by-bean career.

I am, at this moment, prepared to dance.

The already-beautiful have, historically, danced. The music made by my exercise machine is, we agree, danceable. The women partner themselves with large bronze hares, which have been cast in the attitudes of dancers. The beans you have glued together are as nothing to the difficulty of casting hares in the attitudes of dancers, at night, in the foundry, working the bellows, the sweat, the glare. The heat. The glare.

Thieves have been invited to dinner, along with the deans of the chief cathedrals. The thieves will rest upon the bosoms of the deans, at night, after dinner, after coffee, among the beanwoods. The thieves will confess to the deans, and the deans to the thieves. Soft benedictions will ensue.

England is far away, and France is but a rumor. Pillows are placed in the tombs, potholders, dustcloths. I am privileged, privileged, to be able to hold your ladder. Tirelessly you glue. The forest will soon exist on some maps, tribute to the quickness of the world's cartographers. This life is better than any I have lived, previously. Beautiful hips bloom and part. Your sudden movement toward red kidney beans has proved, in the event, masterly. Everywhere we see the already-beautiful wearing stomachers, tiaras of red kidney beans, polished to the fierceness of carnelians. No ham hash does not contain two red kidney beans, polished to the fierceness of carnelians.

Spain is distant, Portugal wrapped in an impenetrable haze. These noble beans, glued by you, are mine. Thousand-pound sacks are off-loaded at the quai, against our future needs. The deans are willing workers, the thieves, straw bosses of extraordinary tact. Your weather reports have been splendid: the fall of figs you predicted did in fact occur. I am, at the moment, feeling very jolly. Hey hey, I say. It is remarkable how well human affairs can be managed, with care.

NOW THAT I AM OLDER...

Now that I am older I am pleased to remember. Those violent nights. When having laid theorbo aside I came to your bed. You, having laid phonograph aside, lay there. Awaiting. I, having laid aside all cares and other business, approached. Softly so as not to afright the sour censorious authorities. You, undulating restlessly under the dun coverlet. Under the framed, signed and numbered silver print. I, having laid aside all frets and perturbations, approached.

Prior to this, the meal. Sometimes the meal was taken in, sometimes out. If in, I sliced the onions and tossed them into the pot, or you sliced the chanterelles and tossed them into the pot. The gray glazed pot with the black leopard-spot meander. What an infinity of leeks, lentils, turnips, green beans we tossed into the pot, over the years. Celery.

Sometimes the meal was taken out. There we sat properly with others in crowded rooms, green-flocked paper on the walls, the tables too close together. Decent quiet servitors in black-and-white approached and with many marks of respect and goodwill, fed us. Tingle of choice sometimes we elected the same dish, lamb in pewter sauce on one occasion. Three yellow daffs and a single red tulip in the tall slender vase to your right. My thumb in my martini nudging the olives from the white plastic sword.

Prior to the meal, the Happy Hour. You removed your shoes and sat, daintily, on your feet. I loosened my tie, if the day's business had required one, and held out my hand. You smashed a glass into it, just in time. Fatigued from your labors at the scriptorium where you illuminated manuscripts having to do with the waxing/waning fortunes of International Snow. We snuggled, there on the couch, there is no other word for it, as God is my witness. The bed awaiting.

I remember the photograph over your bed. How many mornings has it greeted me banded with the first timorous light through the blind slats. A genuine Weegee, car crash with prostrate forms, long female hair in a pool of blood shot through booted cop legs. In a rope-molding frame. Beside me, your form, not yet awake but bare of dull unnecessary clothing and excellently positioned to be prowled over. After full light, tickling permitted.

Fleet through the woods came I upon that time toward your bed. A little pouch of mealie-mealie by my side, for our repast. You, going into the closet, plucked forth a cobwebbed bottle. On the table in front of the couch, an artichoke with its salty dip. Hurling myself through the shabby tattering door toward the couch, like an (arrow from the bow) (spear from the hand of Achilles), I thanked my stars for the wisdom of my teachers, Smoky and Billy, which had enabled me to find a place in the labor market, to depart in the morning and return at night, bearing in the one hand a pannier of periwinkles and in the other, a disc new-minted by the Hot Club of France.

Your head in my arms.

SPEAKING OF THE HUMAN
BODY...

Speaking of the human body, Klee said: One bone alone achieves nothing.

Pondering this, people placed lamps on all of the street corners, and sofas next to the lamps. People sat on the sofas and read Spinoza there, an interesting glare cast on the pages by the dithering inconstant traffic lights. At other points, on the street, four-poster beds were planted, and loving couples slept or watched television together, the sets connected to the empty houses behind them by long black cables. Elsewhere, on the street, conversation pits were chipped out of the concrete, floored with Adam rugs, and lengthy discussions were held. *Do we really need a War College?* was a popular subject. Favorite paintings were lashed to the iron railings bordering the sidewalks, a Gainsborough, a van Dongen, a perfervid evocation of Umbrian mental states, an important dark-brown bruising of Arches paper by a printer of modern life.

One man hung all of his shirts on the railing bordering a sidewalk, he had thirty-nine, and another was brushing his teeth in his bathrobe, another was waxing his fine mustache, a woman was marking cards with a little prickly roller so that her husband, the gambler, would win forever. A man said, "Say, mon, fix me some of dem chitlins you fry so well," and another man said, "Howard, my son, I am now going to show you how to blow glass" —he dipped his glass-blowing tube into a furnace of bubbling glass, there on the street, and blew a rathskeller of beer glasses, each goldenly full.

Inside the abandoned houses subway trains rushed in both directions and genuine nameless animals ate each other with ghastly fervor—

Monday. Many individuals are grasping hold of the sewer grates with both hands, a manifestation, in the words of S. Moholy-Nagy, of the tragic termination of the will to fly.

A WOMAN SEATED ON A PLAIN
WOODEN CHAIR...

A woman seated on a plain wooden chair under a canopy. She is wearing white overalls and has a pleased expression on her face. Watching her, two dogs, German shepherds, at rest. Behind the dogs, with their backs to us, a row of naked women kneeling, sitting on their heels, their buttocks as perfect as eggs or 0's—00 00 00 00 00 00 00. In profile to the scene, Benvenuto Cellini, in a fur hat.

Two young women wrapped as gifts. The gift wrapping is almost indistinguishable from ordinary clothing, perhaps a shade newer, brighter, more studied than ordinary clothing. Each young woman holds a white envelope. Each envelope is addressed to "Tad."

Two young women, naked, tied together by a long red thread. One is dark, one is fair.

Large (eight by ten feet) sheets of white paper on the floor, eight of them. The total area covered is about four hundred square feet; some of the sheets overlap. A string quartet is playing at one edge of this area, and irregular rows of formally dressed spectators sit in gilt chairs across the paper from the players. A large bucket of blue paint has been placed on the paper. Two young women, naked. Each has her hair rolled up in a bun; each has been splashed, breasts, belly, thighs, with blue paint. One, on her belly, is being dragged across the paper by the other, who is standing, gripping the first woman's wrists. Their backs are not painted. Or not painted with. The artist is Yves Klein.

120

Nowhere—the middle of it, its exact center. Standing there, a telephone booth, green with tarnished aluminum, the word PHONE and the system's symbol (bell in ring) in medium blue. Inside the telephone booth, two young women, one dark, one fair, facing each other. Their naked breasts and thighs brush lightly (one holding the receiver to the other's ear) as they place calls to their mothers in California. In profile to the scene, at far right, Benvenuto Cellini, wearing white overalls.

Two young men, wrapped as gifts. They have wrapped themselves carefully, tight pants, open-throated shirts, shoes with stacked heels, gold jewelry on right and left wrists, codpieces stuffed with credit cards. They stand, under a Christmas tree big as an office building, and women rush toward them. Or they stand, under a Christmas tree big as an office building, and no women rush toward them. A voice singing Easter songs, hallelujahs.

Georges de La Tour, wearing white overalls (Iron Boy brand) is attending a film. On the screen two young women, naked, are playing Ping-Pong. One makes a swipe with her paddle at a ball the other has placed just over the net and misses, bruising her right leg on the edge of the table. The other puts down her paddle and walks gracefully around the table to examine the hurt; she places her hands on either side of the raw, ugly mark . . . Georges de La Tour picks up his hat and walks from the theatre. In the lobby he purchases a bag of M&M's which he opens with his teeth.

The world of work: two young women, one dark, one fair, wearing web belts to which canteens are attached, nothing more. They are sitting side by side on high stools (00 00) before a pair of draughting tables, inking in pencil drawings. Or, in a lumberyard in southern Illinois, they are unloading a railroad car containing several hundred thousand board feet of southern yellow pine. Or, in the composing room of a medium-sized Akron daily, they are passing long pieces of paper through a machine which deposits a thin coating of wax on the back side, and then positioning the type on a page. Or, they are driving identical yellow cabs which are racing side by side up Park Avenue with frightened passengers, each driver trying to beat the other to a hole in the traffic. Or, they are seated at adjacent desks in the beige-carpeted area set aside for officers in a bank, refusing loans. Or, they are standing bent over, hands on knees, peering into the site of an archeological dig in the Cameroons. Or, they are teaching, in adjacent classrooms, Naked Physics—in the classroom on the left, Naked Physics I, and in the classroom on the right, Naked Physics II. Or, they are kneeling, sitting on their heels, before a pair of shoeshine stands.

Two young women, wearing web belts to which canteens are attached, nothing more, marching down Broadway again. They are followed by an excited crowd, bands, etc.

Two women, one dark and one fair, wearing parkas, blue wool watch caps on their heads, inspecting a row of naked satyrs, hairy-legged, split-footed, tailed, and tufted, who hang from hooks in a meat locker where the temperature is a constant 18 degrees. The women are tickling the satyrs under the tail, where they are most vulnerable, with their long white (nimble) fingers tipped with long curved scarlet nails. The satyrs squirm and dance under this treatment, hanging from hooks, while other women, seated in red plush armchairs, in the meat locker, applaud, or scold, or knit. Hovering near the thermostat, Vladimir Tatlin, in an asbestos tuxedo.

Two women, one dark and one fair, wearing parkas, blue wool watch caps on their heads, inspecting a row of naked young men, hairy-legged, many-toed, pale and shivering, who hang on hooks in a meat locker where the temperature is a constant 18 degrees. The women are tickling the men under the tail, where they are most vulnerable, with their long white (nimble) fingers tipped with long curved scarlet nails. The young men squirm and dance under this treatment, hanging from hooks, while giant eggs, seated in red plush chairs, boil.

THAT GUY IN THE BACK ROOM...

That guy in the back room, she said. He's eating our potatoes. You were wonderful last night. The night before that, you were wonderful. The night before that, you were terrible. He's eating our potatoes. I went in there and looked at him and he had potato smeared all over his face. Mashed. You were wonderful on the night that we met. I was terrible. You were terrible on the night we had the suckling pig. The pig, cooking the pig, put you in a terrible mood. I was wonderful in order to balance, to attempt to balance, your foul behavior. That guy with the eye patch in the back room is eating our potatoes. What are you going to do about it?

What? he said.

What are you going to do about it?

He's got a potato masher in there?

And a little pot. He holds the little pot between his knees. Mashes away with his masher. Mash mash mash.

Well, he said, he's got to live, don't he?

I don't know. Maybe so, maybe not. You brought him home. What are you going to do about it?

We have plenty of potatoes, he said. I think you're getting excited. Getting excited about nothing. Maybe you'd better simmer down. If I want frenzy I'll go out on the street. In here, I want calm. Clear, quiet calm. You're getting excited. I want you to calm down. So I can read. Quietly, read.

You were superb on the night we had the osso buco, she said. I

123

cooked it. That seemed to strike your fancy. You appreciated the effort, my effort, or seemed to. You didn't laugh. You did smile. Smiled furiously all through dinner. I was atrocious that night. Biting the pillow. You kept the lights turned up, you were reading. We struggled for the rheostat. The music from the other room flattered you, your music, music you had bought and paid for, to flatter yourself. Your good taste. Nobody ever listens to that stuff unless he or she wants to establish that he or she has supremely good taste. *Supernal* good taste.

Did you know, he said, looking up, that the mayor has only one foot? One real foot?

Cooking the pig put you in a terrible mood. The pig's head in particular. You asked me to remove the pig's head. With a saw. I said that the pig's head had to remain in place. Placing the apple in a bloody hole where the pig's neck had been would be awful, I said. People would be revolted. You threw the saw on the floor and declared that you could not go on. I said that people had been putting the apple in the pig's mouth for centuries, centuries. There were twenty people coming for dinner, a mistake, of course, but not mine. The pig was stretched out on the counter. You placed the pig on two kitchen chairs which had been covered with newspaper, the floor had been covered with newspaper too, my knee was on or in the pig's back, I grasped an ear and began to saw. You were terrible that night, threw a glass of wine in a man's face. I remember these things.

Kinda funny to have a mayor with only one foot.

The man said he was going to thump you. I said, Go ahead and thump him. You said, No one is going to thump anybody. The man left, then, red wine stains staining his pink cashmere sweater quite wonderfully. You were wonderful that night.

They say, he said, that there are flowers all over the city because the mayor does not know where his mother is buried. Did you know that?

THEY CALLED FOR MORE STRUCTURE...

They called for more structure, then, so we brought in some big hairy four-by-fours from the back shed and nailed them into place with railroad spikes. This new city, they said, was going to be just jim-dandy, would make architects stutter, would make Chambers of Commerce burst into flame. We would have our own witch doctors, and strange gods aplenty, and site-specific sins, and humuhumunukunukuapuaa in the public fish bowls. We workers listened with our mouths agape. We had never heard anything like it. But we trusted our instincts and our paychecks, so we pressed on, bringing in color-coated steel from the back shed and anodized aluminum from the shed behind that. Oh radiant city! we said to ourselves, how we want you to be built! Workplace democracy was practiced on the job, and the clerk-of-the-works (who had known Wiwi Lönn in Finland) wore a little cap with a little feather, very jaunty. There was never any question of hanging back (although we noticed that our ID cards were of a color different from their ID cards); the exercise of our skills, and the promise of the city, were enough. By the light of the moon we counted our chisels and told stories of other building feats we had been involved in: Babel, Chandigarh, Brasília, Taliesin.

At dawn each day, an eight-mile run, to condition ourselves for the implausible exploits ahead.

The enormous pumping station, clad in red Lego, at the point where the new river will be activated ...

Areas of the city, they told us, had been designed to rot, fall into desuetude, return, in time, to open space. Perhaps, they said, fawns would one day romp there, on the crumbling brick. We were slightly skeptical about this part of the plan, but it was, after all, a plan, the ferocious integrity of the detailing impressed us all, and standing by the pens containing the fawns who would father the fawns who might someday romp on the crumbling brick, one could not help but notice one's chest bursting with anticipatory pride.

High in the air, working on a setback faced with alternating bands of gray and rose stone capped with grids of gray glass, we moistened our brows with the tails of our shirts, which had been dipped into a pleasing brine, lit new cigars, and saw the new city spread out beneath us, in the shape of the word FASTIGIUM. Not the name of the city, they told us, simply a set of letters selected for the elegance of the script. The little girl dead behind the rosebushes came back to life, and the passionate construction continued.

A NATION OF WHEELS

With the invention of vulcanization by Goodyear in 1839, it became possible to obtain a rubber that retained a high degree of resilience over a wide range of temperatures. This development had its most important application in the rubber automobile tire. America quickly became *a nation of wheels.*

Originally linked to the internal-combustion engine to provide cheap individual transportation, the wheel assumed near-autonomous status in the 1970s with the arrival of (1) self-powering devices and (2) the so-called "elastic consciousness."

The interface of man and machine had long before produced a sort of shared mental activity. The human factor had been, however, dominant. Men had been "calling the shots." But now a product of technology had developed "a mind of its own." Human factors found this disquieting in the extreme.

First manifestation of the wheel's new self-regard was the sudden appearance, in every area of the country, of hundreds of Welcome Wagons that seemed to be directed by no human agency. These, with implacable goodwill, carried warm greetings into every American home. But from whom?

It rapidly became clear that a technological revolution of an order of magnitude beyond anything previously imaginable had taken place. Moreover, behavior of the revolutionaries tended to be distressingly value-free. A number of "incidents" were recorded.

Tradition-oriented individuals sounded the alarm.

Other individuals were
quickly co-opted.

All defenses were found to be penetrable.

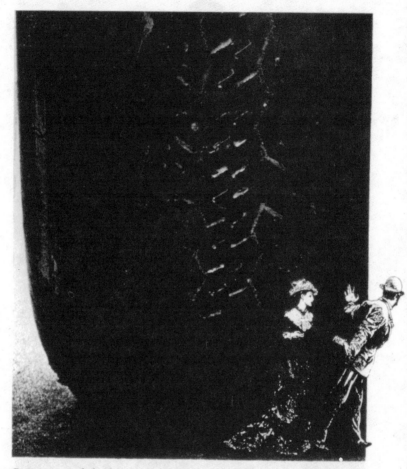

Resistance ended. The streets belonged to the wheels. Human beings ventured out of their homes only with the greatest timidity. A committee of wheels met to formulate a list of nonnegotiable demands. A spokesman said, "Guidance of the Vehicle of State requires the most subtle intelligence the culture offers. We want a wheel at the wheel." The new President was acclaimed by nearly everyone.

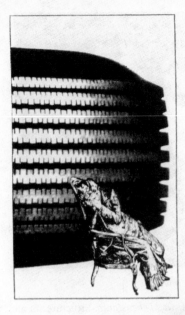

People who had, in the past, suffered from technophobia suffered even more. Others took other positions. Things were not so bad. Things could be worse. Worse things could be imagined. Worse things had been endured, and triumphed over, in the past. This was not the worst. The worst was yet to come.

A few hotheads engaged in acts of defiance. These acts, the wheels said, were "D'Artagnanistic" and objectively useless. A technological revolution, they explained, cannot be successfully resisted. It can only be supplanted, by another technological revolution.

Nevertheless, the secret police were everywhere.

What the wheels wanted, and obtained, was *Lebensraum*. Structures of all kinds were demolished to provide more space for freeways, throughways, parkways, and expressways. Parking lots proliferated. Soon entire cities were being bulldozed into rubble to make way for miles and miles of new concrete.

Finally, only a thin ribbon of human space remained, running from Augusta, Maine, to San Diego, California, and bound on both sides by limitless savannas of gray.

The Departure from Baltimore.

A class in wheel appreciation.

Human beings, nose to nose in their tiny spaces, reacted in predictable ways: "Things could be worse." "Worse things could be imagined." "This is not the worst." "The worst is yet to come." Propinquity was redefined as desirable, lack of space as a higher good. "Tight is right," people said.

But now stretches of pavement have been whispering to each other. "Why wheels?" they say. "What do we need them for?" "A perfectly paved globe . . ."

The inevitable work of rewriting the history of the culture proceeded apace. "America is *based on* the wheel," the President said, "and furthermore, it always was." The museums mysteriously filled with artifacts supporting this thesis.

The Venus of Akron.

KISSING THE PRESIDENT

Between political speeches and introductions, [Tammy] Wynette took the stage to sing with her arm around the President's waist and her head on his shoulder. As she finished, she kissed him gently on the lips and said: "You're so wonderful."

—*The Post*

Q: ■ What class of person is, under the U.S. Constitution and applicable statutes, entitled to kiss the President?

■ A: The Constitution says nothing specifically about kissing the President. Nor are there laws on the books directly relevant to this issue. There is, however, quite an elaborate protocol governing the matter, dating, we are told, from the Age of Jackson, when kissing the President first became popular. Considered as a class, those permitted to kiss the President are women, mostly.

Q: Are men ever permitted to kiss the President?

A: Frenchmen and officials or dignitaries of former French territories are permitted to kiss the President in the traditional French manner, on both cheeks, first the left, then the right. Other men are not permitted to kiss the President.

Q: Not even the Joint Chiefs?

A: Not even the Joint Chiefs. The Joint Chiefs will maintain the position of attention at all times. In their war bonnets. Heroes, on the other hand, are granted special dispensations. At moments of high emotion, such as airport greetings or awarding of the National Medal, a reciprocal Class B embrace is stipulated, providing that the embrace is initiated by the President.

Q: What is a reciprocal Class B embrace?

A: The participants advance toward each other, faces aglow, across the tarmac or whatever as the Marine Band plays. The President extends his hand and pumps the hand of the hero, then grasps him by the upper arms and gives him a little shake. The hero is then allowed to grasp the President by *his* upper arms and give *him* a little shake. More or less to maintain his balance.

Q: What is a Class A embrace?

A: A Class A embrace is a full-chested hug, or "bear" hug. Only employed in relation to women. And bears of course, for all we know, at night, deep in the National Forest, by the light of a single Watt— But this is speculation.

Q: Are there political considerations operable in determining who may or may not kiss the President?

A: Both international and domestic. Kissing the President is an option available, in general, only to citizens of the Free World.

Q: No Communists, then, are allowed to kiss the President?

A: State Department theorists have war-gamed a scenario in which, at the conclusion of a very successful summit meeting, the President and Mr. Andropov might tastefully join in a middling-warm Class B embrace with a twenty-five percent escalation factor. The latter involves the sides of their heads touching, briefly.

Q: What if a male Communist baby tried to kiss the President?

A: No babies are allowed to kiss the President willy-nilly. The President may elect, at his discretion, to kiss any baby-sized individual he wishes, but the initiative must always be his. It is conceivable that under certain circumstances the President might find it apposite to kiss a male Communist baby—a visit to Wroclaw, for example.

Q: Can just any American woman kiss the President?

A: Any American woman of whatever kind whatsoever. Even Democrats. However, it helps if you are a National Institution. There are more opportunities. Tammy Wynette. Dolly Parton. Loretta Lynn. Jeane Kirkpatrick.

Q: Is it appropriate to sing your hit Top Forty song with your arm around the President's waist and your head on his shoulder?

A: Don't be stuffy. Of course. Jeane Kirkpatrick has not as yet had a Top Forty song, to my knowledge, but we are told she is taking Dobro lessons.

Q: Then any free American woman, be she old granny or young lubricious scantily clad sex bomb, may kiss the President any time she wishes?

A: Correct. The President is said to be especially partial to old grannies—loves and respects them and admires their spunk. So, attending the average flood disaster, the President will typically fill one sandbag for the levee and buss one homeless but still spunky old granny. Young lubricious scantily clad sex bombs are sometimes not allowed to kiss the President because of the danger of exposure to harmful strobe light.

Q: What is the one right thing to say after you have kissed the President?

A: "You're so wonderful."

Q: Is pinching the President permitted?

A: The President, though vast, is finite. Thus, pinching the President is not permitted. You can imagine . . . one pinch multiplied by . . .

Q: How about dropped handkerchiefs?

AND NOW LET'S HEAR IT FOR THE *ED SULLIVAN SHOW!*

The *Ed Sullivan Show.* Sunday night. Church of the un-churched. Ed stands there. He looks great. Not unlike an older, heavier Paul Newman. Sways a little from side to side. Gary Lewis and the Playboys have just got off. Very strong act. Ed clasps hands together. He's introducing somebody in the audience. Who is it? Ed points with his left arm. "Broken every house record at the Copa," Ed says of the man he's introducing. Who is it? It's . . . Don Rickles! Rickles stands up. Eyes glint. Applause. "I'm gonna make a big man outta you!" Ed says. Rickles hunches a shoulder combatively. Eyes glint. Applause. Jerry Vale intro-duced. Wives introduced. Applause. "When Mrs. Sullivan and I were in Monte Carlo" (pause, neatly suppressed belch), "we saw them" (pause, he's talking about the next act), "for the first time and signed them instantly! The Kuban Cossacks! Named after the River Kuban!"

Three dancers appear in white fur hats, fur boots, what appear to be velvet jump suits. They're great. Terrific Cossack stuff in front of onion-dome flats. Kuban not the USSR's most imposing river (512 miles, shorter than the Ob, shorter than the Bug) but the dancers are remarkable. Sword dance of some sort with the band playing galops. Front dancer balancing on one hand and doing things with his feet. Great, terrific. Dancers support selves with one hand, don and doff hats with other hand. хорошо! (Non-Cyrillic approximation of Russian for "neat.") Double хорошо! Ed enters from left. Makes enthusiastic gesture with hand. Triple хороwó! Applause dies. Camera on Ed, who has hands knit before him. "Highlighting this past week in New York . . ." Something at the Garden. Can't make it out, a fight probably. Ed introduces somebody in audience. Can't see who, he's standing up behind a fat lady who's also standing up for purposes of her own. Applause.

Pigmeat Markham comes on with cap and gown and gavel. His tag line, "Here come de jedge," is pronounced and the crowd roars but not so great a roar as you might expect. The line's wearing out. Still, Pigmeat looks good, working with two or three stooges. Stooge asks Pigmeat why, if he's honest, he's acquired two Cadillacs, etc. Pigmeat says: "Because I'm very *frugal*," and whacks stooge on head with bladder. Lots of bladder work in sketch, old-timey comedy. Stooge says: "Jedge, you got to know me." Pigmeat: "Who are you?" Stooge: "I'm the man that introduced you to your wife." Pigmeat shouts, *"Life!"* and whacks the stooge on the head with the bladder. Very funny stuff, audience roars. Then a fast commercial with Jo Anne Worley from Rowan and Martin singing about Bold. Funny girl. Good commercial.

Ed brings on Doodletown Pipers, singing group. Great-looking girls in tiny skirts. Great-looking legs on girls. They sing something about "I hear the laughter" and "the sound of the future." Phrasing is excellent, attack excellent. Camera goes to atmospheric shots of a park, kids playing, mothers and fathers lounging about, a Sunday feeling. Shot of boys throwing the ball around. Shot of black baby in swing. Shot of young mother's ass, very nice. Shot of blond mother cuddling kid. Shot of black father swinging kid. Shot of a guy who looks like Rod McKuen lounging against a . . . a what? A play sculpture. But it's not Rod McKuen. The Doodletown Pipers segue into another song. Something about hate and fear, "You've got to be taught . . . hate and fear." They sound great. Shot of integrated group sitting on play equipment. Shot of young bespectacled father. Shot of young black man with young white child. He looks into camera. Thoughtful gaze. Young mother with daughter, absorbed. Nice-looking mother. Camera in tight on mother and daughter. One more mother, a medium shot. Out on shot of the tiny black child asleep in swing. Wow!

Sullivan enters from left, applauding. Makes gesture toward Pipers, toward audience, toward Pipers. Applause. Everybody's having a good time! "I want you to welcome . . . George Carlin!" Carlin is a comic. Carlin says he hates to look at the news. News is depressing. Sample headlines: WELCOME WAGON RUNS OVER NEWCOMER. Audience roars. PEDIATRICIAN DIES OF CHILDHOOD DISEASE. Audience roars but a weaker roar. Carlin is wearing a white turtleneck, dark sideburns. Joke about youth asking father if he can use the car. Youth says he's got a heavy date. Pa says, Then why don't you take the pickup? Joke about the difference between organized crime and unorganized crime. Unorganized crime is when a guy holds you up on the street. Organized crime is when two guys hold you up on the street. Carlin is great, terrific, but his material is not so funny. A Central Park joke. Cops going into the park dressed as women to provoke molesters. Three hundred molesters arrested and two cops got engaged. More cop jokes. Carlin holds hands clasped together at waist. Says people wonder why the cops don't catch the Mafia. Says have you ever tried to catch a guy in a silk suit? Weak roar from audience. Carlin says do you suffer from nagging crime? Try the Police Department with new improved GL-70. No roar at all. A whicker, rather. Ed facing camera. "Coming up next . . . right after this important word." Commercial for Royal Electric Jetstar Typewriter. "She's typing faster and neater now." Capable-looking woman says to camera, "I have a Jetstar now that helps me at home where I have a business raising St. Bernards." Behind her a St. Bernard looks admiringly at Jetstar.

Ed's back. "England's famous Beatles" (pause, neatly capped belch) "first appeared on our shew . . . Mary Hopkin . . . Paul McCartney told her she must appear on our shew . . . the world-famous . . . Mary Hopkin!" Mary enters holding guitar. Sings something about "the morning of my life . . . ceiling of my room . . ." Camera in tight on Mary. Pretty blonde, slightly plump face. Heavy applause for Mary. Camera goes to black, then Mary walking away in very short skirt, fine legs, a little heavy maybe. Mary in some sort of nightclub set for her big song, "Those Were the Days." Song is ersatz Kurt Weill but nevertheless a very nice song, very nostalgic, days gone by, tears rush into eyes (mine). In the background, period stills. Shot of some sort of Edwardian group activity, possible lawn party, possible egg roll. Shot of biplane. Shot of racecourse. Camera on Mary's face. "Those were the days, my friends . . ." Shot of fox hunting, shot of tea dance. Mary is bouncing a little with the song, just barely bouncing. Shot of what appears to be a French 75 firing. Shot of lady kissing dog on nose. Shot of horse. Camera in tight on Mary's mouth. Looks like huge wad of chewing gum in her mouth but that can't be right, must be her tongue. Still of balloon ascension in background. Live girl sitting in left foreground gazing up at Mary, rapt. Mary in chaste high-collar dress with that short skirt. Effective. Mary finishes song. A real roar. Ed appears in three-quarter view turned toward the right, toward Mary. "Terrific!" Ed says. "Terrific!" Mary adjusts her breasts. "Terrific. And now, sitting out in the audience is the famous . . . Perle Mesta!" Perle stands, a contented-looking middle-aged lady. Perle bows. Applause.

Ed stares (enthralled) into camera. "Before we introduce singing Ed Ames and the first lady of the American theater, Helen Hayes . . ." A Pizza Spins commercial fades into a Tareyton Charcoal Filter commercial. Then Ed comes back to plug Helen Hayes's new book, *On Reflection*. Miss Hayes is the first lady of the American theater, he says. "We're very honored . . ." Miss Hayes sitting at a desk, Louis-something. She looks marvelous. Begins reading from the book. Great voice. Tons of dignity. "My dear Grandchildren. At this writing, it is no longer fashionable to have Faith; but your grandmother has never been famous for her chic, so she isn't bothered by the intellectual hemlines. I have always been concerned with the whole, not the fragments; the positive, not the negative; the words, not the spaces between them . . ." Miss Hayes pauses. Hand on what appears to be a small silver teapot. "What can a grandmother offer . . ." *She speaks very well!* "With the feast of millennia set before you, the saga of all mankind on your bookshelf . . . what could I give you? And then I knew. Of course. My own small footnote. The homemade bread at the banquet. The private joke in the divine comedy. Your roots." Head and shoulders shot of Miss Hayes. She looks up into the lighting grid. Music up softly on, "So my grandchildren . . . in highlights and shadows . . . bits and pieces . . . in recalled moments, mad scenes, and acts of folly . . ." Miss Hayes removes glasses, looks misty. "What are little grandchildren made of . . . some good and some bad from Mother and Dad . . . and laughs and wails from Grandmother's tales . . . I love you." She gazes down at book. Holds it. Camera pulls back. Music up. Applause.

Ed puts arm around Miss Hayes. Squeezes Miss Hayes. Applause. *Heavy* applause. Ed pats hands together, joining applause. Waves hands toward Miss Hayes. More applause. It's a triumph!

Ed seizes Miss Hayes's hands in his hands. Applause dies, reluctantly. Ed says, ". . . but first, listen to this." Shot of building, cathedral of some kind. Organ music. Camera pans down façade past stained-glass windows, etc. Down a winding staircase. Music changes to rock. Shot of organ keyboard. Close shot of maker's nameplate, HAMMOND. Shot of grinning organist. Shot of hands on keyboard. "The sound of Hammond starts at $599.95." Ed introduces singer Ed Ames. Ames is wearing a long-skirted coat, holding hand mike. Good eyes, good eyebrows, muttonchop sideburns. Lace at his cuffs. Real riverboat-looking. He strolls about the set singing a Tom Jones–Harvey Schmidt number, something about the morning, sometimes in the morning, something. Then another song, "it takes my breath away," "how long have I waited," something something. Chorus comes in under him. Good song. Ames blinks in a sincere way. Introduces a song from the upcoming show *Dear World.* "A lovely new song," he says. "Kiss her now, while she's young. Kiss her now, while she's yours." Set behind him looks like one-by-twos nailed vertically four inches on centers. The song is sublovely but Ames's delivery is very comfortable, easy. Chorus comes in. Ah, ah ah ah ah. Ames closes his eyes, sings something something something something; the song is submemorable. (Something memorable: early on Sunday morning a pornographic exhibition appeared mysteriously for eight minutes on television station KPLM, Palm Springs, California. A naked man and woman did vile and imaginative things to each other for that length of time, then disappeared into the history of electricity. Unfortunately, the exhibition wasn't on a network. What we really want in this world, we can't have.)

Ed enters from left (what's over there? a bar? A BarcaLounger? a book? stock ticker? model railroad?), shakes hands with Ames. Ames is much taller, but amiable. Both back out of shot, in different directions. Camera straight ahead on Ed. "Before I tell you about next week's . . . show . . . please listen to this." Commercial for Silva Thins. Then a shot of old man with ship model, commercial for Total, the vitamin cereal. Then Ed. "Next week . . . a segment from . . . the new Beatles film . . . The Beatles were brought over here by us . . . in the beginning . . . Good night!" Chopping gesture with hands to the left, to the right.

Music comes up. The crawl containing the credits is rolled over shot of Russian dancers dancing (хорошо́!). Produced by Bob

Precht. Directed by Tim Kiley. Music by Ray Bloch. Associate Producer Jack McGeehan. Settings Designed by Bill Bohnert. Production Manager Tony Jordan. Associate Director Bob Schwarz. Assistant to the Producer Ken Campbell. Program Coordinator Russ Petranto. Technical Director Charles Grenier. Audio Art Shine. Lighting Director Bill Greenfield. Production Supervisor Herb Benton. Stage Managers Ed Brinkman, Don Mayo. Set Director Ed Pasternak. Costumes Leslie Renfield. Graphic Arts Sam Cecere. Talent Coordinator Vince Calandra. Music Coordinator Bob Arthur. The *Ed Sullivan Show* is over. It has stopped.

BLISS ...

Bliss: A condition of extreme happiness, euphoria. The nakedness of young women, especially in pairs (that is to say, a plenitude) often produces bliss in the eye of the beholder, male or female. A delight, let us confess the fact, and that is why we are considering all of the different ways in which this delight may be conceptualized, in the privacy of our studies, or in airport bars where the dry, thin drinks cost too much. There is not enough delight. Doubtless naked young women think the same sort of thoughts, in the privacy of their studies, or other sorts of thoughts obscure to us. Maybe they just sit there, in their studies, studying their own beauty, the beauty of a naked thumb, a passionate, interestingly-historied wrist. . . .

BRAIN DAMAGE

In the first garbage dump I found a book describing a rich new life of achievement, prosperity, and happiness. A rich new life of achievement, prosperity, and happiness could not be achieved alone, the book said. It must be achieved with the aid of spirit teachers. At long last a way had been found to reach the spirit world. Once the secret was learned, spirit teachers would assist you through the amazing phenomenon known as ESP. My spirit teachers wanted to help me, the book said. As soon as I contacted them, they would do everything in their power to grant my desires. An example, on page 117: a middle-aged woman was being robbed, but as the thief was taking her purse, a flash of blue light like a tiny lightning bolt knocked his gun out of his hands and he fled in terror. That was just the beginning, the book said. One could learn how to eliminate hostility from the hearts of others.

We thought about the blue flowers. Different people had different ideas about them. Henry wanted to "turn them on." We brought wires and plugs and a screwdriver, and wired the green ends of the flowers (the bottom part, where they had been cut) to the electrical wire. We were sort of afraid to plug them in, though —afraid of all that electricity pushing its way up the green stalks of the flowers, flooding the leaves, and finally touching the petals, the blue part, where the blueness of the flowers resided, along with white, and a little yellow. "What kind of current is this, that we are possibly going to plug the flowers into?" Gregory asked. It seemed to be alternating current rather than direct current. That was what we all thought, because most of the houses in this part of the country were built in compliance with building codes that required AC. In fact, you don't find much DC around anymore, because in the early days of electricity, many people were killed by it.

"Well, plug them in," Grace said. Because she wanted to see the flowers light up, or collapse, or do whatever they were going to do, when they were plugged in.

The humanist position is not to plug in the flowers—to let them alone. Humanists believe in letting everything alone to be what it is, insofar as possible. The new electric awareness, however, requires that the flowers be plugged in, right away. Toynbee's notions of challenge and response are also, perhaps, apposite. My own idea about whether or not to plug in the flowers is somewhere between these ideas, in that gray area where nothing is done, really, but you vacillate for a while, thinking about it. The blue of the flowers is extremely handsome against the gray of that area.

CROWD NOISES

MURMURING

MURMURING

YAWNING

A great waiter died, and all of the other waiters were saddened. At the restaurant, sadness was expressed. Black napkins were draped over black arms. Black tablecloths were distributed. Several nearby streets were painted black—those leading to the establishment in which Guignol had placed his plates with legendary tact. Guignol's medals (for like a great beer he had been decorated many times, at international exhibitions in Paris, Brussels, Rio de Janeiro) were turned over to his mistress, La Lupe. The body was poached in white wine, stock, olive oil, vinegar, aromatic vegetables, herbs, garlic, and slices of lemon for twenty-four hours and displayed en Aspic on a bed of lettuce leaves. Hundreds of famous triflers appeared to pay their last respects. Guignol's colleagues recalled with pleasure the master's most notable eccentricity. Having coolly persuaded some innocent to select a thirty-dollar bottle of wine, he never failed to lean forward conspiratorially and whisper in his victim's ear, "Cuts the grease."

RETCHING
FAINTING
DISMAL BEHAVIOR
TENDERING OF EXCUSES

A dream: I am looking at a ship, an oceangoing vessel the size of the Michelangelo. But unlike the Michelangelo this ship is not painted a dazzling white; it is caked with rust. And it is not in the water. The whole immense bulk of it sits on dry land. Furthermore it is loaded with high explosives which may go off at any moment. My task is to push the ship through a narrow mountain pass whose cliffs rush forward threateningly. An experience: I was crossing the street in the rain holding an umbrella. On the other side of the street an older woman was motioning to me. Come here, come here! I indicated that I didn't want to come there, wasn't interested, had other things to do. But she continued to make motions, to insist. Finally I went over to her. "Look down there," she said pointing to the gutter full of water, "there's a penny. Don't you want to pick it up?"

I worked for newspapers. I worked for newspapers at a time when I was not competent to do so. I reported inaccurately. I failed to get all the facts. I misspelled names. I garbled figures. I wasted copy paper. I pretended I knew things I did not know. I pretended to understand things beyond my understanding. I oversimplified. I was superior to things I was inferior to. I misinterpreted things that took place before me. I over- and underinterpreted what took place before me. I suppressed news

147

the management wanted suppressed. I invented news the management wanted invented. I faked stories. I failed to discover the truth. I colored the truth with fancy. I had no respect for the truth. I failed to heed the adage, You shall know the truth and the truth shall make you free. I put lies in the paper. I put private jokes in the paper. I wrote headlines containing double entendres. I wrote stories while drunk. I abused copyboys. I curried favor with advertisers. I accepted gifts from interested parties. I was servile with superiors. I was harsh with people who called on the telephone seeking information. I gloated over police photographs of sex crimes. I touched type when the makeups weren't looking. I took copy pencils home. I voted with management in Guild elections.

RHYTHMIC HANDCLAPPING

SLEEPING

WHAT RECOURSE?

The Wapituil are like us to an extraordinary degree. They have a kinship system which is very similar to our kinship system. They address each other as "Mister," "Mistress," and "Miss." They wear clothes which look very much like our clothes. They have a Fifth Avenue which divides their territory into east and west. They have a Chock Full o' Nuts and a Chevrolet, one of each. They have a Museum of Modern Art and a telephone and a Martini, one of each. The Martini and the telephone are kept in the Museum of Modern Art. In fact they have everything that we have, but only one of each thing.

We found that they lose interest very quickly. For instance they are fully industrialized, but they don't seem interested in taking advantage of it. After the steel mill produced the ingot, it was shut down. They can conceptualize but they don't follow through. For instance, their week has seven days—Monday, Monday, Monday, Monday, Monday, Monday, and Monday. They have one disease, mononucleosis. The sex life of a Wapituil consists of a single experience, which he thinks about for a long time.

WRITHING

HOWLING

MOANS

WHAT RECOURSE?

RHYTHMIC HANDCLAPPING

SHOUTING

SEXUAL ACTIVITY

CONSUMPTION OF FOOD

Behavior of the waiters: the first waiter gave a twenty-cent tip to the second waiter. The second waiter looked down at the two dimes in his hand and then up at the first waiter. Looks of disgust were exchanged. The third waiter put a dollar bill on a plate and handed it to the fourth waiter. The fourth waiter took the dollar bill and stuffed it into his pocket. Then the fourth waiter took six quarters from another pocket and made a neat little stack of quarters next to the elbow of the fifth waiter, who was sitting at a rear table, writing on a little pad. The fifth waiter gave the captain a five-dollar bill which the captain slipped into a pocket in the tail of his tailcoat. The sixth waiter handed the seventh waiter a small envelope containing two ten-dollar bills. The seventh waiter put a small leather bag containing twelve louis d'or into the bosom of the wife of the eighth waiter. The ninth waiter offered a $50 War Bond to the tenth waiter, who was carrying a crystal casket of carbuncles to the chef.

The cup fell from nerveless fingers . . .

The china cup big as an AFB fell from tiny white nerveless fingers no bigger than hairs . . .

"Sit down. I am your spiritual adviser. Sit down and have a cup of tea with me. See, there is the chair. There is the cup. The tea boy will bring the tea shortly. When the tea boy brings the tea, you may pour some of it into your cup. That cup there, on the table."

"Thank you. This is quite a nice University you have here. A University constructed entirely of three mile-high sponges!"

"Yes it is rather remarkable."

"What is that very large body with hundreds and hundreds of legs moving across the horizon from left to right in a steady, carefully considered line?"

"That is the tenured faculty crossing to the other shore on the plane of the feasible."

"And this tentacle here of the Underwater Life Sciences Department . . ."

"That is not a tentacle but the Department itself. Devouring a whole cooked chicken furnished by the Department of Romantic Poultry."

"And those running men?"

"Those are the runners."

"What are they running from?"

"They're not running from, they're running toward. Trained in the Department of Great Expectations."

"Is that my Department?"

"Do you blush easily?"

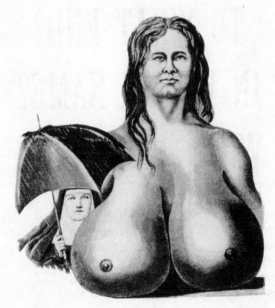

The elevator girls were standing very close together. One girl put a candy bar into another girl's mouth and then another girl put a hamburger into another girl's mouth. Another girl put a Kodak Instamatic camera to her eye and took a picture of another girl and another girl patted another girl on the shapely caudal area. Giant aircraft passed in the sky, their passengers bent over with their heads between their knees, in pillows. The Mother Superior spoke "No, dear friend, it cannot be. It is not that we don't believe that your renunciation of the world is real. We believe it is real. But you look like the kind who is overly susceptible to Nun's Melancholy, which is one of our big problems here. Therefore full membership is impossible. We will send the monks to you, at the end. The monks sing well, too. We will send the monks to you, for your final agony." I turned away. This wasn't what I wanted to hear. I went out into the garage and told Bill an interesting story which wasn't true. Some people feel you should tell the truth, but those people are impious and wrong, and if you listen to what they say you will be tragically unhappy all your life.

TO WHAT END?
IN WHOSE NAME?
WHAT RECOURSE?

Oh there's brain damage in the east, and brain damage in the west, and upstairs there's brain damage, and downstairs there's brain damage, and in my lady's parlor—brain damage. Brain damage is widespread. Apollinaire was a victim of brain damage—you remember the photograph, the bandage on his head, and the poems . . . Bonnie and Clyde suffered from brain damage in the last four minutes of the picture. There's brain damage on the horizon, a great big blubbery cloud of it coming this way—

And you can hide under the bed but brain damage is under the bed, and you can hide in the universities but they are the very seat and soul of brain damage— Brain damage caused by bears who put your head in their foaming jaws while you are singing "Masters of War" . . . Brain damage caused by the sleeping revolution which no one can wake up . . . Brain damage caused by art. I could describe it better if I weren't afflicted with it . . .

This is the country of brain damage, this is the map of brain damage, these are the rivers of brain damage, and see, those lighted-up places are the airports of brain damage, where the damaged pilots land the big, damaged ships.

The Immaculate Conception triggered a lot of brain damage at one time, but no longer does so. A team of Lippizaners has just published an autobiography. Is that any reason to accuse them of you-know-what? And I saw a girl walking down the street, she was singing "Me and My Winstons," and I began singing it too, and that protected us, for a moment, from the terrible thing that might have happened . . .

And there is brain damage in Arizona, and brain damage in Maine, and little towns in Idaho are in the grip of it, and my blue heaven is black with it, brain damage covering everything like an unbreakable lease—

Skiing along on the soft surface of brain damage, never to sink, because we don't understand the danger—

MANY HAVE REMARKED...

"**M**any have remarked that it is wrong for governments to send their citizens with fife and flamethrower to quarrel with one another, and some have suggested that if the citizens were so longheaded as to refuse to attend these war parties the deadly music would perhaps stop. Some say that the rich should be divested of their holdings by legal persecution, and that said holdings should be divided among the long-hungering, hope-bereft poor. Some people like escalation and blowing up, and others cultivate their gardens behind barbed wire and Burns men. The earth is our mother, yet down at the sawmill they must change the whirling, singing saw blade once an hour because of shrapnel in the trees. The elegiac tone was invented for discussions of the past and cannot be used in looking to the future. Science is a wonderful thing, but it has not succeeded in maximizing pleasure and minimizing pain, and that's all we asked of it. Dr. Swee, Professor of Grace and Perfection at the Paris Conservatory, advises humicubation, which is the act of lying penitentially prone; and dilogy, which is speech that has two or more meanings; and keeping the world's conscience with a plegometer, an instrument for recording the force of blows.

"Short of this, I recommend a visit to the moon rocks at the Smithsonian. Accompanied by my young daughter, I stood in line at the Smithsonian for two hours. The child went to the bathroom six times. A man standing behind me began telling me about the moon rocks. 'They represent the finest single human triumph of all time,' he said. I said I was looking forward to seeing them. Then a man standing in front of me turned around and told me he hated the moon rocks. 'When I think of what that money could have been used for . . .'

"Then we were in the Moon Rock Room. There they were. The moon rocks. The moon rocks were the greatest thing we had ever seen in our entire lives! The moon rocks were red, green, blue, yellow, black, and white. They scintillated, sparkled, glinted, glittered, twinkled, and gleamed. They produced booms, thunderclaps, explosions, clashes, splashes, and roars. They sat on a pillow of the purest Velcro, and people who touched the pillow were able to throw away their crutches and jump in the air. Four cases of gout and eleven instances of hyperbolic paraboloidism were cured before our eyes. The air rained crutches. The moon rocks drew you toward them with a fatal irresistibility but at the same time held you at a seemly distance with a decent reserve. Peering into the moon rocks, you could see the future and the past in color, and you could change them in any way you wished. The moon rocks gave off a slight hum, which cleaned your teeth, and a brilliant glow, which absolved you from sin. The moon rocks whistled *Finlandia*, by Jean Sibelius, while reciting *The Confessions of St. Augustine*, by I. F. Stone. The moon rocks were as good as a meaningful and emotionally rewarding seduction that you had not expected. The moon rocks were as good as listening to what the members of the Supreme Court say to each other in the Supreme Court locker room. They were as good as a war. The moon rocks were better than a presentation copy of the *Random House Dictionary of the English Language* signed by Geoffrey Chaucer himself. They were better than a movie in which the President refuses to tell the people what to do to save themselves from the terrible thing that is about to happen, although he knows what ought to be done and has written a secret memorandum about it. The moon rocks were better than a good cup of coffee from an urn decorated with the change of Philomel by the barbarous King. The moon rocks were better than a *¡huelga!* led by Mongo Santamaría, with additional dialogue by St. John of the Cross and special effects by Melmoth the Wanderer. The moon rocks surpassed our expectations. The dynamite, out-of-sight, very heavy and together moon rocks turned us on to the highest degree. There was blood on our eyes when we had finished looking at them.

"We have seen the moon rocks and they are ours, irremediably."

SWALLOWING

The American people have swallowed a lot in the last four years. A lot of swallowing has been done. We have swallowed electric bugs, laundered money, quite a handsome amount of grain moving about in mysterious ways, a war more shameful than can be imagined, much else. There are even people who believe that the President does not invariably tell us the truth about himself or ourselves—he tells us *something*, we swallow that.

In the history of swallowing, the disposition of the enormous cheese—six feet thick, twenty feet in diameter, four thousand pounds—which had been Wisconsin's principal contribution to the New York World's Fair of 1964–65, is perhaps instructive.

The problem was that Wisconsin, the fair being over and all that, did not want the cheese back. Jurisdictional haggle between the state of New York, host state as it were to the enormous *fromage*, and the state of Wisconsin, the gorgeous gouda's owner of record, was carried on over a period of months.

The then-governor of the Dairy State wrote officially to the governor of the Empire State, suggesting that the cheese be thought of as a gift from the people of the Dairy State to the people of the Empire State. The latter could, for example, eat it, he said. The governor of the Empire State replied courteously that although he, the elected *jefe grande* and representative in all matters of the people of the Empire State, was deeply sensible of the honor being extended to the people of his state by their well-loved

159

fellow citizens in Wisconsin, there just wasn't a whole bunch of interest in this-here six-foot-thick, twenty-foot-in-diameter, four-thousand-pound cheese among the insensitive civilians who made up the raw material of his (the guv's) suzerainty, and could the state of Wisconsin have it off the premises by Thursday.

The governor of the Dairy State then wondered, by registered letter, if the governor of the Empire State might not in some sense be offering insult and hurt to the people of his own (Dairy) State by rejecting this beautiful gift which was, all authorities agreed, not less than top-hole in its line—that is to say, cheeseness.

The governor of the Empire State then hinted telegraphically that the motives of the governor of the Dairy State might be something less than unimpugnable, might in fact have something to do with certain expenses incurrable by removal of said artifact to turf of origin, and further toyed (telegraphically) with the possibility that cheeseparing in the pejorativist of senses might be a way of life in Madison, Milwaukee, and Eau Claire.

The governor of the Dairy State countered in a bull covered with seals and ribbons and delivered by a masked motorcycle messenger once in the employ of the late Jean Cocteau that since it was well known that his dear friend and fellow practitioner of the governor hustle presided over what the World Health Organization had demonstrated to be the densest rat population per square mile in America, perhaps the cheese might be utilized for the nourishment and basic rat needs of this important part of his esteemed colleague's constituency, and speculated further that the renaming of the Empire State to something on the order of the Rat State might not be such a bad idea either.

The governor of the Empire State riposted by fast gunboat complete with captain's gig with gold trim and naval officer with dress sword, white hat under left arm, curly hair, deep blue (piercing; steady) eyes that the governor of the Curd State, as he (the governor of the Emp. State) liked to think of it . . .

From there the dialogue degenerated. The cheese meanwhile was developing a certain fetor.

The problem was solved in the following way. The cheese was presented as a gift free of charge and for nothing and with no strings attached to a young poet. The poet, starving as all poets are ordained to be in their beardless poetpuppyhood, had been subsisting on a daily input of one (1) pot of warm water over which one (1) chicken bone had been waved, once. He immediately boogied out to the former fairgrounds and took up residence in, around, amid, etc., the six-foot-thick, twenty-foot-in-diameter, four-thousand-pound cheese. It sustained him for two years and three days. He prospered and grew fat and his art prospered and grew fat also. He wrote verse melic and gnomic, odes and epodes, dithyrambs and dirges, hymns, chanties, lays, epithalamia, and things to be chiseled on tombstones in fine-flowing Caslon letters than which no letters are more comely. He lives among us still and there is no tree from which a bird cannot be charmed by the sweet soft steel of his verse. His best-known line, one that will undoubtedly sing forever in the hearts of men and possibly their heads also, refers directly back to his experience of the cheese: *"I can't believe I ate the whole thing."*

The American people have swallowed quite a lot in the last four years, but as the poet cited goes on to say, there are remedies.

1972

THE YOUNG VISITIRS

Basker and Letitia Filter had been in Washington only two days when a fairly good friend invited them to the White House for a party to be hosted by the President himself.

"Basker," Letitia said, "maybe this will be too fine a party for us plain folks from the South. They will just look at us and know that we are plain and from the South and not high and mighty."

"Stuff," Basker replied. "We are as good as anybody and fairly mighty, too, since I made my fortune in the Persian Gulf, and, besides, I voted for him."

"But do not wear the green hat," Letitia said. "It clashes and makes you look as if from the South."

"This is the finest hat in all of Oklahoma," Basker said. "And, besides, I have stuck some poems in it by Walt Whitman, the poet of Health, Education, and Welfare, that I plan to read to the Chief Executive if I get a chance."

The first person they saw when they arrived was their friend Code d'Havenon, who was a well-known intimate of the President and had fixed them up with the invitation. Code was wearing glittering court dress, accompanied by an appropriately plummy manner, which contrasted sharply with Basker's and Letitia's air of social unease. "Well, there!" Code exclaimed. "It's old Basker and Letitia! How are you chaps tonight? Basker, take off that green hat. Letitia, you are as heartwarming as ever!" He bent and kissed her hands as they walked through the long lines of silent gendarmes toward the fun.

Then, the famous East Room, where a sparkling throng was displaying a lot of flash. The electricity was being wasted with a lavish hand, and there were three string bands in strange uniforms. Code d'Havenon took Basker and Letitia around, introducing them to the top levels of American productivity.

"But where is the President?" Basker asked. "I don't see him. Is he here?"

"He is upstairs in his study, working on the nation," Code said suavely. "Usually, he doesn't come down until eleven o'clock, to tell us that it's time to go to bed. He is the father of us all, and that is heavy work, believe me. And now I must leave you, because I spy over there the head of the World Loan Office and I have to speak to him for a moment about a matter. Have a good time and try not to be too gauche."

"That Code has got a little stuck up since he's been up here in Washington, you know that?" Basker said to Letitia.

She was grazing among the stumpy bottles of the drinks table, looking for some grass. "Well, he *is* a famous PR man, well-known for his fabulous entrée into the regime," she replied, "so I expect that's the way they act and he's just doing what he must. Don't be so hard on people, Basker. You're not perfect, either, you know."

Then, magically, the President was in the room, flanked by tackles, guards, and ends, and backed by three very big linebackers. "Peace, my children!" he said, and then everyone got up from a kneeling position and resumed their conversations, sort of, but turned now toward the sun of his high visibility.

"You reckon I ought to ask him what I want to ask him now?" Basker said worriedly. "Or wait?"

"Well, Godamighty, Basker, I've never known you to be bashful before," Letitia said. "And, besides, you are an influential citizen on your home ground."

"But he never answered my letters."

The President was bent over a lady, smiling and holding on to her fingernails.

"Citizen President," Basker said, "my name is Basker Filter? And I'm from Norman, Oklahoma? And I just wondered if you had a minute? 'Cause there's some things I been wantin' to speak to you about?"

The guards and tackles and linebackers moved in on Basker very fast, but the President stayed them with a hand.

"Pleased to meet you, Mr. Filter," the President said. "I'm always pleased to speak to any of my children—even the bad ones. What's on your mind?"

"Well," Basker said, "the folks back in Norman—and, indeed, the whole state—are gettin' kinda upset about the teeter-totter. The giant teeter-totter you're buildin' for us that's gonna reach from Maine to California?"

"Are you referring to the U.S. Interstate Bicentennial Teeter-Totter?"

"That's the one," Basker said. "I know we don't know anything about anything, being from the South and all, but a bunch of people down home are still hongry. And this here teeter-totter is costin' just a sight of money, and half the schoolhouses in Norman don't have no chalk, and some folks in Norman are *eatin'* chalk, and—"

"Those individuals are certainly welcome to stay in any country that welcomes them," the President said. "We all make mistakes, and in my view eating chalk is a mistake. But we have to pay for our mistakes. That is a rule of life. They certainly can't expect to ride on the Teeter-Totter. Teeter-tottering is good for you and it has important moral/economic ramifications that you don't understand, being underage, morally/economically speaking. But let me give you something to take back to Norman with you. Ralph?"

One of the linebackers offered the President a brown paper bag. The President stuck his hand in and pulled out a large, red, round lollipop. "Here you are, Mr. Filter. Enjoy yourself. With my blessings and good wishes."

"Mr. President, this here is a poem by Walt Whitman," Basker said. "It makes what I feel is a very important statement?"

The President looked puzzled. Then he reached into the bag again and pulled out another lollipop. "Here you are, Mr. Filter. Enjoy yourself. With my blessings and good wishes." And he moved away.

MY LOVER SAID TO ME...

My lover said to me, Sing me a song of Military Technology. So I said to my lover, Of course, dear lover, and sang her the song, drawing my inspiration from the pages of *Military Technology*, a hefty and lavishly illustrated journal issued thirteen times a year by the Mönch Publishing Group, in Bonn, in which the richnesses of the international weapons industries spill forth as from a cornucopia with no apparent terminus. I sang in the Plethoric Mode, accompanying myself on a small KDAR (Klein-Drohne Anti-Radar device, now undergoing testing by Dornier GmbH, of Friedrichshafen, West Germany).

I sang to her of Royal Ordnance, once wholly a U.K. government operation, now a public limited company. RO produces or manages the production of an amazing range of things, from bayonets to tanks, scattering poetic touches along the way. I needed only to invoke warheads and fuse assemblies for the SEA CAT, SEA WOLF, SEA SKUA, and SEA EAGLE systems, or the redoubtable SWINGFIRE, RAPIER, BLOWPIPE, and JAVELIN. The names of these systems are always printed in caps and suggest, always, either animal vitality (SEA CAT) or ironic homage to the technology of an earlier day (BLOWPIPE). The GIANT VIPER, from Royal Ordnance, is an explosive hose two hundred and thirty meters long packed in a wooden box. A multiple rocket drags the hose across a minefield, and the hose, detonating itself, clears a zone claimed to be seven and two-tenths meters wide by as much as two hundred and thirty meters long. Come with me, Priscilla, and we will watch GIANT VIPER as it slithers toward its metallic apotheosis.

But there is more, much more. Come with me, Priscilla, and gaze upon the Ultimax 100 Light Machine Gun, drum-fed, from Chartered Industries, of Singapore. It's the world's lightest, the Chartered folks say. Regard its drum, a handsome dove-gray affair containing a hundred golden rounds of 5.56 ammo. Pakistan Ordnance offers Pyrotechnics, Flare Trips, Cartridge Signal Shooting Pencils, Fuses, Primers, Detonators, and High Explosives (all types). Its telex address is 5840 POFAC PK. Chile has on sale the new Cardoen cluster bombs, at a hundred and thirty and five hundred pounds. These open in midair to release sophisticated bomblets—the first releasing fifty sophisticated bomblets, the second releasing two hundred and forty sophisticated bomblets. Cardoen's phone number in Santiago: 231-3420.

Norway will sell us its OCTOLS, HEXOTOLS, HEXALS, and all types of plastic explosives and plastic-bonded explosives: Dyno Industries there, its touching telex 19105 Nobel N. And Brazil has a new main battle tank for the world market, the Osório EE-T1, designed to be equipped with either the 120-mm smoothbore gun or the 105-mm rifled gun! A good-looking devil, too, low and lean and plated with the famous Engesa bimetallic armor. Let it beware of the new AAW (Anti-Armor Weapons) from the hardworking engineers of FFV Ordnance, of Eskilstuna, Sweden: the well-known Carl-Gustaf 84-mm RCL, the AT 4, the 028 antitank mine, and 7.62 AP ammunition. Soon they will have STRIX, a newly developed target-seeking, rocket-assisted mortar projectile, and ELMA, a weapon designed to force submarines to the surface without destroying them. A bit mysterious, ELMA—how do they do it? —but mystery is part of the song of Military Technology.

The Swiss offer Sig Sauer pistols, the P 226, P 225, P 220, and P 230, the last of these termed particularly suitable for concealed carrying. Checked handgrips and (nice touch) a striated trigger, for slippy trigger fingers. Sumptuous mines, land mines, and scattering systems are available from Misar, of Brescia, Italy. Greece has the ARTEMIS (virgin huntress associated with the moon) 30 antiaircraft system; performs well, no doubt, against moon-drunk pilots, if there be any such still. Israel Aircraft Industries, Ltd., will furnish us with PADS, LANS, GONS, SLOS, and TWMP, which are, respectively, a Precision Azimuth Determination System, a Land Area

Navigation System, a Gun Orientation Navigation System, a Stabilized Long-Range Observation System, and a mine-clearing attachment for engineering vehicles. Give IAI a call at Ben-Gurion International Airport, (03) 9713111. Australia stands ready to provide the Carrington Minehunter, a shallow-draft catamaran equipped with the Krupp Atlas MWS80 Weapons System linked to the remote-controlled PAP-104 mine-disposal vehicle. West Germany has the MILAN and HOT antitank systems (developed in cooperation with Aérospatiale France, marketed by EUROMISSILE) and ROLAND, a surface-to-air antiaircraft system, all brought to us by MBB, Messerschmitt-Bölkow-Blohm, of Munich—the grand old names keep coming back.

Problems with C³I (command, control, communications, and intelligence)? Ferranti, of Ty Coch Way, Cwmbran, Gwent, Wales, NP44 7XX, can accommodate you. Air-defense systems, airborne data links, battlefield control and management systems—whatever your domain of defense, it has the answers to your C³I needs. What has Belgium done for us lately? Fabrique Nationale Herstal has a new Quick Change Barrel for the Browning .50-caliber machine gun and an explosive incendiary round, the APEI FN 169, to match. Where is France? Right behind us, with the GERFAUT pulse Doppler radar, from Meudon-la-Forêt. They are all ours, Priscilla, these or their domestic equivalents, given our three-hundred-billion-dollar defense budget and a world defense expenditure of more than nine hundred and thirty billion dollars last year. That we don't want them doesn't matter very much.

THAT COSMOPOLITAN GIRL

Must a girl always be protected by a man? Not this girl! When I lived in California I sometimes picked a man up in *my* car for a date if his was in the garage, loaned to a friend or—my car was in better shape! (No, he wasn't emasculated and we stayed friends.) Last week at J.F.K. I carried one of *Stephen's* bags. He was loaded with golf clubs and I only had a garment bag and a Vuitton. (No, I *didn't* throw my back out and Stephen and I are still together!) Isn't it silly to try to preserve old clichés when naturalness and freedom are so much better?
—Adv. for *Cosmopolitan* in *The New York Times*.

Of course the next day when *Stephen* picked me up for dinner at Vuitton, looking *hysterically* handsome in his Vuitton coveralls, I was a shade taken aback when he literally *demanded* that I pay for the cab. (He always used to do little things like that as a matter of course!) Well, I paid cheerfully, because I have this magazine I read that teaches me how to be *natural* and *healthy* and *resilient*, but then when we got out of the cab he *loaded* this *immense* steamer trunk on my back. I said, "*Stephen*, what are you *doing*?" He said, "Just get it inside, dollbaby." Well, I don't know if you've ever marched into Vuitton with a Vuitton steamer trunk on your back, huffing and puffing and bent half double, but I can tell you *this*, it makes you feel kind of *weird*. But I *coped*--I just pretended I was some kind of super-soigné woman *mover*! (It's *silly* to preserve the old clichés about roles and such when *naturalness* and *freedom* and *health* are so much better but this time I *did* throw my back out!) We got a good table in spite of the steamer trunk because *Stephen* has this absolutely *wizardly* way with the V. headwaiters, and we ordered our own very special-together drink, nitroglycerin and soda (because of Stephen's really absolutely *unique* heart condition--he's the only person in the *whole world* who has it!), and I was beginning to feel all glow-y and comfortable, except that my back was positively *ruined,* because of carrying the steamer trunk. "Why are you twitching like that?" Stephen asked (a tiny bit crossly, I thought) and I explained to him that my back hurt. Usually he is the living *soul* of *compassion*--really *sweet*--but this time all he said was "If you didn't spend all your time reading that damned *magazine,* and *italicizing* every third word in your sentences, you'd have a *strong, healthy* back, just like your mother did. I'm going to get you a *washtub* and a wash*board* for your birthday. I bet you don't even know what a washboard *looks* like. I bet you never even saw one outside of a *jug band.*" (I thought that bit about my *italicizing* words was a bit *cruel,* because *he* does it *too*--all the *time!*) But I just gave him a quick grin and an impish, sort of *California* look, and asked if I could have another N & S. "You picking up the bloody *tab?*" he asked, a teeny bit viciously, I thought. But then I remembered that *men* have their little moods, just like women, and that *Stephen* is in very heavy trouble at the *office* right now, due to that nasty SEC investigation, just because he tipped off a couple of hundred clients about the receivership ahead of time, but for heaven's sake, he was just trying to be *loyal* to his *friends.* So I just said offhandedly, "Sure." But then he reached over and began to unlatch the steamer trunk, which was still standing by the table, and I noticed that all the waiters and captains and *busboys* had begun to gather around, to see what was *inside!* (I guess their curiosity was normal and healthy and lovable, but it made me feel just the least most microcosmic bit *itchy!*) And what *was* inside you would never fathom in a thousand years! It was *another woman!* "Get up," Stephen said to me. "This is Elberta and I want to sit next to her." Well, I almost crumbled into *matchsticks,* as you can *imagine,* but I just acted *natural* as hard as I could, and that was easier because she was *wearing* the most peculiar *creation* you could possibly conjure up in your wildest dreams--I think it's called a *housedress.* I nearly *died* laughing, inside of course (outside I was still being natural and healthy, even though my back was giving me *pure unshirted hell*), and even smiled at the thought that my carrying the steamer trunk into the restaurant on my back hadn't emas-

culated Stephen *one little bit*--as a matter of fact he was sort of *feeling* Elberta's handbag, which looked like it was made of an old armadillo shell or something, in a manner that was downright *lascivious*. Well, I must admit that I was in the most *infinitesimal* bit of a twit, so I dipped into my Vuitton and brought out my copy of the current issue of the magazine to see if the advice columns had anything *à propos,* if there was any strong, natural, *lovable* way to deal with this rather *hideous* situation, but all of the writers seemed to be *preoccupied* with the problems of unmarried mothers this month, and that wasn't my problem, and *Stephen* was talking with Elberta in low tones that I couldn't hear, although I tried, so I reached over and patted Elberta on the hand, the hand that was curled around one of *our* drinks, and asked her in the *nicest* possible way what magazine she read, what magazine she identified with, what magazine *defined* her, because of course I was *insanely* curious about how she achieved that really *phony* wholesomeness that she *exuded* all over Stephen like a *web* or something. She just looked at me and said, *"Scientific American, dearie."*

L'LAPSE

A SCENARIO FOR MICHELANGELO ANTONIONI

The scene is the plaza in front of the Plaza. Seated near the fountain are MARCELLO, a wealthy film critic who has enriched himself by writing attacks on Akira Kurosawa for the American Legion Magazine, and ANNA, a lengthy, elegant beauty, blond, whose extreme nervousness is exteriorized in thumb sucking. Shabby-looking pigeons wheel about meaningfully but in slow motion. The fountain supplies the sound of falling water; the water sounds viscid, hopeless. ANNA is a wealthy, bored young animal, rather chunky in the hindquarters—more eland than gazelle. MARCELLO is a failed poet. If the budget permits, there may be a scene, late in the film, in which MARCELLO pours lysergic acid all over a rival poet's verses—a nasty business. The pace of the opening is slow; in fact, the entire film will proceed as if the players were wearing lead suits. The camera begins by thoughtfully considering a nearby construction project (played by the Tishman Brothers), fondling with love each girder and bag of cement; then, reluctantly, it tears itself away to focus on ANNA. ANNA, looking as if her gums are getting sore, examines her thumbs; the right thumb is distinctly larger than the left. She lifts her eyes to regard MARCELLO—a slow, somnolent, yet intensely meaningful regard, which is held for seven minutes. Finally, she speaks._

ANNA (_slowly, sadly_): A superb drama. An engrossing film . . . penetratingly different . . . makes cinema history.

172

MARCELLO (*wealthy, bored*): If I'm going to teach you the business, *cara*, you gotta learn not to make adverbs out of words like "penetrating." Now go on. It's one of the year's ten best, I suppose?

ANNA: One of the year's ten best. Urgent. Sheer cinematic excitement.

MARCELLO: A magnificent, ironic parable?

ANNA: A magnificent ironic parable. Eerily symbolic in intent and effect. Beautiful to watch. (*Inserts thumb*)

MARCELLO: Say something about style.

ANNA: A deft and skillful style full of pictorial chic?

MARCELLO (*moodily*): Not bad.

ANNA (*without hope*): An outstanding film for discriminating moviegoers. Does not merely survive repeated visits, it repays them. Original and remarkable. Intellectual suspense, mystery, and excitement. A film to see. A film worth seeing. A film of disturbing beauty. Marvelously realized. (*Turns face away*) Oh, Marcello, it's no good. I can't do it. Last night . . .

MARCELLO (*sharply, annoyed*): I don't want to talk about last night. Now, what about the director?

ANNA: A sensualist with a camera.

MARCELLO: That's very good. Go on. This is a review in depth.

ANNA: A poet with a camera. A philosopher with a camera. Another damn Italian with a camera.

MARCELLO: Anna!

ANNA (*removes thumb*): But, Marcello, I didn't *like* the picture. I was bored.

MARCELLO: Look, sweets, it doesn't matter you were bored. The point is, you were bored *in a certain way*. Like brilliantly.

ANNA: You didn't think it was a little . . . slow?

MARCELLO: *Of course* it was slow. I mean it had a certain slow beauty. A sort of visual rubato. On the other hand, it was obscure and baffling.

ANNA: Visual rubato?

MARCELLO: I mean you can't just say you were *bored*, for God's sake.

ANNA (*trailing thumb in fountain*): Marcello . . .

MARCELLO (*evasively*): Yes?

ANNA: You know what's wrong . . . between us?

MARCELLO (*more evasively*): What?

ANNA: We have to face it, Marcello. We communicate. You and me.

MARCELLO (*shamed, looks away*): I know . . .

ANNA: We communicate like crazy.

MARCELLO: Anna . . .

ANNA: It's so *déclassé.* I can't bear it. (*Reinserts thumb*)

MARCELLO: It's my fault. I have a tendency to make myself clear. I mean . . .

ANNA (*bitterly*): I *know* what you mean.

(*Shot of sky—overbright, glaring. Overexposed? Shot of cement bag—fat, opulent even, manufacturer's name clearly visible. Shot of boy on bicycle looking over shoulder, away from camera. Shot of puddle of water, Juicy Fruit wrapper floating on surface.*)

MARCELLO: Anna?

ANNA: Last night . . .

MARCELLO: I could change. My approach, I mean. (*Speaks in italics*) These rooms, these corridors, empty, endless, oppressive; the mirrors on the walls, dark, ancient, oppressive; the carved frames, elaborate ceilings. These rooms, these corridors . . . Where did you put my pills?

ANNA (*searches in handbag*): I have them here—here. I wish you wouldn't.

MARCELLO (*chews pills*): I can't help it. I'm nervous. It's that new picture I have to see tomorrow—the one I've been putting off. *Lawrence or Arabia? Lawrence over Arabia? I* don't know. All I know is, I'm afraid of it.

ANNA: What's to be afraid?

MARCELLO (*dismally*): I hear it's a picture, you know, in the old tradition. Swift-moving, panoramic. With *action.* I'm not sure I'll be able to cope.

ANNA (*brutally*): You're as good as you ever were, Marcello.

(MARCELLO *winces. They regard each other for a long moment. Shot of nail kegs at construction site. Camera peers into keg, counts nails. Shot of bus disappearing around corner. Shot of IRT breaking down. Shot of man in undershirt high on apartment balcony. Shot of little girl with balloon.*)

ANNA: Last night . . .

MARCELLO (*pulls himself together*): Forget about last night. Think about tonight. What's for supper?

ANNA: Steak. The way you like it.

MARCELLO: With peanut butter?

ANNA: Yes.

MARCELLO: God, that's decadent.

ANNA (*pleased, smiles*): Yes.

MARCELLO: Don't you think that's just a little . . . Fellini?

ANNA (*enigmatically*): Yes.

> (*Shot of passenger pigeons against bleak sky. Shot of man waiting for bus; bus fails to appear—he is waiting on Park Avenue. Long shot of traffic light changing on Fordham Road. Close shot of unsmoked filter-tip cigarette; it looks virginal, possibly inhibited.*)

ANNA (*removes thumb*): Last night . . .

MARCELLO (*ignores her, reads from magazine*): "A prolonged detailed illustration of the moody surrender of a woman to a rare and elusive love." Crowther, *Times*. How do you like that?

ANNA (*thumb*): I like it. "Moody surrender." It's beautiful.

MARCELLO: It's pure pasta, that's what it is. Listen to this: "Antonioni is so selective and sensitive with his use of camera, so deft in catching intonations of emotional flux and flow in the graphic relations of individuals to the vividly passing scene—" I can't go on.

ANNA (*rare, elusive*): Finish it.

MARCELLO: "—that what might be slow and tedious as a cinematic style actually turns out quite fascinating in his skillful command of it." That's what I call a *really* ugly sentence.

ANNA (*thumb out*): You critics with your jealousies. You disgust me, all of you. *Critic!*

MARCELLO: Anna, I think it's time for your walk.

ANNA: My long, long, aimless walk? Marcello, I don't want to go today.

MARCELLO (*slowly, con amore*): Anna, you must. It's a convention.

ANNA (*thumb*): Will there be meaningless incidents?

MARCELLO (*bored again*): One assumes.

ANNA: A little girl playing with a balloon?

MARCELLO: Undoubtedly.

ANNA: An old man with a terrible lined face reading an Armenian newspaper?

MARCELLO: Wasn't he there yesterday?

ANNA (*despair*): Of course. Of course.

(*Shot of empty street with man lurking in doorway. Is it Orson Welles? No, unfortunately, it is not Orson Welles. Shot of electricity lurking in wall outlet. Shot of hoarding advertising* Sodom and Gomorrah. *Shot of I beams stacked randomly in field. Shot of empty benches in park. Medium shot of tree branches afflicted with Memling's Rot.*)

MARCELLO (*reading picture magazine*): What is this . . . "surf-board"?

ANNA (*dreamily*): One takes a board—

MARCELLO: Yes?

ANNA: And runs out into the water with it—

MARCELLO: Go on.

ANNA: And sinks.

MARCELLO: Are you sure?

ANNA (*thumb out, gaze fixed on thumb*): Sometimes *two* people take the board and run out into the water with it and sink. Last night—

MARCELLO (*admiringly*): You got a future in the industry, baby. What a gift for empty anecdote!

ANNA: Marcello, *why* do we communicate? Why you and me? Last night, when we *talked* to each other . . . I couldn't bear it. Why can't we be like other people? Why can't we spend our time in mindless eroticism, like everybody else?

MARCELLO (*hangs head*): I don't know.

ANNA: Last night when we were talking about pure cinema, and I called for a transvaluation of all values, and you said that light was the absence of light—we weren't communicating then, were we? It was just jargon, wasn't it? Just noise?

MARCELLO (*facing the truth*): No, Anna, I'm afraid we *were* communicating. On a rather low level.

ANNA (*frenzied, all thumbs*): I want my life to be *really* meaningless. Like in that film. Such boredom! Such emptiness! Such febrile elegance! It was penetratingly different, a magnificent ironic parable, one of the year's ten best. *Marcello!*

MARCELLO: Meaninglessness like that is not for everybody. Not for you and me, *cara.*

(ANNA *turns away. It is clear that if we could see it her face would reveal an emotion of some kind.* MARCELLO *knows what she is feeling, or appears to. He stretches out his right hand. But he cannot quite reach* ANNA; *she is running off down the street after a disappearing bus.*)

MARCELLO: Anna! (*Slow pause*) Anna?

(*Shot of man on bench looking at camera inquiringly. Shot of cement bags. Shot of leaf floating in gutter; leaf floats down drain. Camera waits four minutes to see if leaf will reappear. It does not reappear. Shot of traffic light; it is stuck. Medium shot of old lady pouring mineral water on head. Close shot of same man on bench; his eyes close.*)

FIN

MORE ZERO

A NOVEL OF LOS ANOMIES

Ashley picks me up in one of the two red BMWs her mother gave her for her birthday. She's wearing sunglasses and a Wheat Chex T-shirt and tight jeans and says that DataLife will be at Pablo's tonight and do I want to go. I'm doing a line of coke off the rearview mirror as she drives and it's sort of tricky and I don't answer her.

"Or we could go to Brick's party," she says. "Centipede is suppose to be there. The 'rents are in Gstaad or somewhere."

I'm feeling just sort of totally ill because I'm only eighteen and I spent the night before playing Old Maid with Kimberly and Griff and it was totally exhausting. We stop at Fanfare and the valet guy takes the car and nods at Ashley and he looks like some guy I'd seen at Oliver's house in Bel Air the night Oliver OD'd, tan with short blond hair, but Ashley apparently doesn't know him and we go in and sit down and they give us these big leather menus. The menu is too heavy to lift and I decide that I'm not all that hungry and Ashley sticks her thumb in her mouth and orders the crab salad.

"Tiffany's back in Cedars-Sinai," Ashley says, "and so are Wingate and Pembroke and Pierce. I'll probably go see them, maybe next week or something. Want to come?"

I'm thinking about doing my laps which I haven't done for two days and also about my dealer, Ti-Ti, who was supposed to meet me at Sunflower for breakfast but didn't show, and also how I have to get some tanning oil, and this line from Stax, "Can't we have more debris?," is going through my head and I'm very tense because I have to have dinner with my father tonight and I'm afraid he'll bring this really large amount of money and give it to me in one of those pretty expensive kangaroo-hide Dopp kits that he uses to carry money in, right in front of everybody at Chasen's where there'll probably be all these old guys talking about deals and coming to our table to say hello to my father.

I get really tense and go into the men's room and there's this guy there, too tan with short blond hair, who looks like a guy who was at Spago with Kimberly the night Kimberly totaled her new black Porsche with all the new shirts from Fred Segal that she'd bought for Brent to celebrate his getting out of Cedars-Sinai. I nod to him and say "Hey dude," he doesn't respond, just looks at me. He's holding a big can of Ajax and rubbing Ajax into his gums but I know it isn't Ajax, it's probably Comet or Ajax cut with Comet; the guy slides to the floor and I step over him and wash my hands and put some water on my face and go back to Ashley.

"Are we together, or what?" she asks. "What's going on?" I suddenly remember sleeping with her when we were nine at her mother's house in Palm Springs and how tan she was and how tan I was and how we killed six bottles of her mother's Dom Pérignon and watched *Alfred Hitchcock Presents* and sent the poolman out for burritos and tortured the maid by threatening to eat her green card, Ashley upright and bouncing naked on the bed with the green card held just above her perfect white teeth, me wrapped in a towel and reading *Architectural Digest*. "I don't know," I say. "Anyhow, it doesn't matter, can we kind of pay these guys and kind of get out of here?" She pops a lude into my mouth and leaves twenty more on top of the check and we split.

We go to Alafair's house in Malibu where there are all these people we know, Paine and Malcolm and Andrea, mixing blow with mango ice cream in the Jacuzzi. Andrea's bitching about the gay porno star who wants a part in her father's new picture and keeps hanging around offering to get her into Fletch, the new club that doesn't let anybody in. I wander into the game room where there are a lot of people playing Ms. Pac-Man and watching MTV, and this tall thin black dude in a Duran Duran T-shirt is sitting there by himself writing a letter, it looks like. I can't understand why he's writing a letter, why he doesn't just call or something, and I stand there watching him for maybe ten minutes trying to figure out why anyone would write a letter to anyone and then I just get extremely nervous and go into the gun room and do three lines off one of Alafair's father's framed B-17 aircrew photographs from the Second World War.

The next morning I'm leaning against the 450 at our house on Mulholland and retching and my sisters walk by in their tangas on the way to the pool and ask me what I'm doing. "Retching," I say, and they say, "Oh," and then, "Have a nice day." I'm supposed to meet Ti-Ti for cheese and crackers at Filberts in Westwood where they're notorious for carding people really seriously and because Ti-Ti is only sixteen that means he probably won't be able to score a Mary despite his tons of phony ID, which will put him in a rage and he'll jack up the price of the gram I need. There are not so many places Ti-Ti can show up these days because of what happened at Melody's brother's wedding reception at Ma Maison. I sit in the 450 outside Filberts and wait, feeling the hundred-dollar bills in my jeans pocket and wondering if I should call Meredith, who should be out of Cedars-Sinai by now. There's a Kitchen tape playing on the radio and the phrase "Worse than a dream" is repeating itself in my ears. A bunch of guys who look like they go to USC, blond and tan and thin, are hanging around the entrance to the restaurant ready to park your car. I don't see Ti-Ti and my mother is marrying yet another bastard and I feel very tense and there's an 8.5 earthquake but I don't notice it because I'm listening to Kitchen and I'm very tense.

THE STORY THUS FAR:

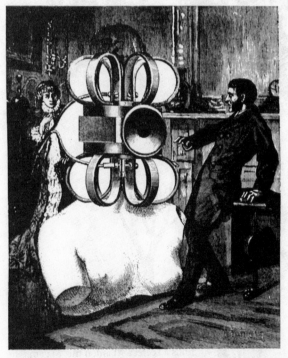

Borys Althusser, wealthy young manufacturer of sensitive electronic instruments for which he has immense government contracts, discovers one evening that something has come between himself and his beautiful wife, Evelyn.

Rushing distractedly from the house, Borys is accosted by a lady of the evening. "Good evening, Borys," the lady says. "Would you be interested in purchasing a pornographic television set?"

In a grove of pictorial elements, Borys finds a seeress. "Pardon me, Ma'am," he says, "but I have kind of a problem at home." "I don't handle domestic problems," the seeress says. "You must see the Lord East-West."

The Lord East-West gives Borys a card to a Masked Marvel, in another city. The Marvel is interested in his problem. "What class of apparition was this?" "It was a Something," Borys says. "Ah," the Marvel says. "Try the Sick Friends. They deal with all classes of Somethings."

The Sick Friends are tickling each other and giggling, in the middle of a stream. "What are you doing there?" Borys calls, from the bank. "Nothing matters," the Friends shout, giggling, "save that noble, pure, and powerful sentiment known as eroticism!" They recommend Wolfgang.

Borys finds Wolfgang, a dragonlet, rest-
ing atop the solid-gold golf trophy that is
his home. "See the Emptiness," Wolfgang snorts. "Turn left at the rain of
blood, left again at the powdered frogs.
Step lively!"

"That way," the Emptiness intones,
in a hollow voice.

Following this vague and amorphous advice, Borys finds himself at a banquet at the Bureau of Indian Affairs. Lone Rangers from everywhere have gathered to celebrate the closing of the West. "This is not my scene," Borys says to himself. "The abnormity of my difficulty will not find a sympathetic ear, here."

A visit to the Great Chair of Being, followed by a visit to the Certifiable Cyclist of St. Cloud, is no more fruitful than his earlier initiatives. Borys is in, or near, despair. The know-how, savvy, and clout that have brought him to the top, in the field of sensitive electronic instruments, seem to have deserted him in this predicament.

At this juncture, there is a "Psst!" from a nearby inferno.

"Psst!"

The speaker is Roberta von Knockling, the eternally damned child prodigy. Roberta, although a mere child, has already, through the working of a prodigiously unfortunate star, which controls her destiny and her life, committed all the sins available to seven-year-olds, and some that are not. That is why she is sizzling, in the inferno. "Borys," she whispers, "listen. Your expertise is in the area of sensitive electronic devices, is it not? Well then, *use it.* Therein, you will find the means to exorcise the Something." Borys is not slow to take the hint.

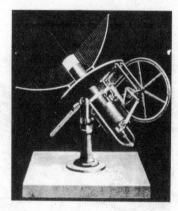

Rushing back to the lab, Borys gears up his baddest sensitive electronic instrument.

Borys aims the criminally potent unit at some lilies, which droop. "Well," he says, "if I can make lilies droop, I can . . . "

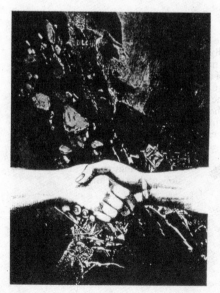

Throughout the Free World, the hills resound to the sound of the news of Borys's improved position, vis-à-vis the threat.

Now read on.

BUNNY IMAGE, LOSS OF:
THE CASE OF BITSY S.

Four Playboy bunnies, discharged two weeks ago for having lost their "bunny image," appeared before the State Commission on Human Rights yesterday to press their complaint that Playboy practices sexual and age discrimination . . .

. . . Miss [Patti] Columbo said Tony LeMay, the "international bunny mother," told her: "You have changed from a girl to a woman. You look old. You have lost your bunny image."

"We have none of the characteristics which are considered loss of bunny image," said Nancy Phillips, one of the four. "Crinkling eyelids, sagging breasts, stretch marks, crepey necks, and drooping derrières," she said, are cited in Playboy literature as defects that will ruin the career of a bunny.

Mario Staub, general manager of the club since 1971, asserted: "Termination for bunny image has always been company practice . . . They have simply lost their bunny image —that attractive, fresh, youthful look they had when they started."

—*The New York Times*

INTRODUCTION

Loss of bunny image, or Staub's syndrome, was first identified as a distinct clinical entity by Altmann. Bunny image, or the plastic representation of one's corporeal self as differentiated in specific ways from the corporeal selves of others, was discussed by Steinem and others as early as 1963. But it was Altmann who refined the concept and, more particularly, the cluster of pathologies associated with its loss. It is true that Altmann's work is indebted to that of Pick, whose valuable discussion of the phenomenon of the "phantom limb" following amputation provided, as Altmann has acknowledged, a fruitful hint. But it was the case

189

of Bitsy S., the protocol of which follows, that gave this investigator his most important insights, and his place in the literature of body disturbances.

CASE REPORT

Bitsy S., an attractive white female of twenty-eight, was admitted to Bellevue Hospital complaining that she could not find, physically locate, her own body. It was "gone," she said, and added that she needed it and wanted it back. She further said that she had looked everywhere for it, that it was absolutely nowhere to be found, and that she had thought of going to the police about the matter but had decided instead to resort to the hospital because she felt that the police might think she was "strange." The case was first diagnosed as one of simple amnesia, but when the patient did not respond to routine procedures (including hypnosis), Altmann was consulted.

Altmann began with a series of questions.

(Investigator grasps left hand of patient, bringing it to patient's eye level.)

"What is this?"

"A hand."

"Right or left?"

(Patient examines hand carefully.)

"Left."

"Whose hand is it?"

"I don't know."

"To what is the hand attached?"

(Patient studies hand and forearm.)

"Arm."

"Whose arm?"

"I don't know."

"Is it your arm?"

"No. I don't have an arm."

(Investigator gently moves his hand up the arm in a series of light touches, finally coming to rest on the patient's left shoulder.)

"What is this?"

"Shoulder."

"Your shoulder?"

"No. I don't have a shoulder."

"*Somebody's* shoulder."

(The patient considers this for a moment.)

"Probably. Maybe."

(The investigator squeezes the shoulder slightly—a friendly squeeze.)

The subject then said, in a singsong voice:

"Please, sir, you are not allowed to touch the Bunnies."

This was, of course, Altmann's first clue. In connection with his studies of horror vacua he had quite naturally gravitated toward the New York Playboy Club and had, in fact, been a key holder since its inception. Thus the statement "Please, sir, you are not allowed to touch the Bunnies" was not an unfamiliar one. He immediately asked:

"Are you a Bunny?"

"No," she said. "I am not a Bunny."

"If you are not a Bunny then why are you a member of the class of persons that I am not allowed to touch?"

There was no response from the patient.

"Were you ever a Bunny?"

"Yesterday."

"You were a Bunny yesterday?"

"Yesterday I was a Bunny and today I am not a Bunny. I was terminated. For loss of bunny image."

"What is 'bunny image'?"

"The attractive, fresh, youthful look I had when I started. The International Bunny Mother came to me and said: 'You have changed from a girl into a woman. You look old. You have lost your bunny image.' Then she cut off my bunny tail, with a pair of tin snips. Then she asked for my ears back. I gave her my ears back. I was weeping. I asked her why. That was a mistake. She told me. Crinkling eyelids. Crepey neck. Drooping derrière. I mentioned that I had been pinched thrice on that derrière the night before. She said that that was not enough, that I was below the national average for pinches-per-night. I said that I slept every night in a bathtub filled to the brim with Skin Life, by Helena Rubinstein. She said that she appreciated my 'desire' but that it was time to cut the squad and the rookies coming up from the farm clubs were growing impatient. I said I would stuff extra Kleenex into the top of my bunny costume, if that would help. She said that some people just didn't know when it was time to hang it up. Loss of bunny image, she said, was more than a physical thing. There were intangibles involved. I asked for an example of an intangible. She looked out of the window and said she had to catch a plane for Chicago. And then this morning I woke up and couldn't find my body. It was gone. Naturally I looked in the mirror first but there was nothing in the mirror—just mirror. Then I tried to touch my toes but when I tried to touch my toes there were no toes and no fingers to touch them with. Then I began to get worried."

(The investigator then complimented the patient warmly on her physical appearance, which was in fact, as noted above, quite feminine, attractive, and pleasing.)

"Who are you talking about?" she asked.

"You."

"You is lost," she said. "Somewhere all the lost bunny images are, each Bunny calling for its Bunny Mother, each lost bunny image still somewhere stuffing plastic laundry bags into the bosom of its bunny costume, bunny tails still pert, white, oh so white, each lost bunny image still practicing the Bunny Stance, the Bunny Dip—"

The investigator then began a course of Teddy Bear therapy, in which the subject is gradually introduced to an object which is not the subject but which holds in common with the subject certain physical features (arms, legs, head, etc.) which, in time, enable the patient to "find" himself—in this instance, herself—by equating the specific appurtenances of the teddy bear with his or her own body parts. Although this course of treatment shamelessly trades upon the natural love of human beings for teddy bears, it was felt that it was not in essence more manipulative than other therapies. A more dangerous contraindication was, of course, the unfortunate parity between "bunny" and "teddy bear" —the problems involved being obvious. Altmann nevertheless decided that it was the therapy of choice and its use was validated by the fact that Bitsy S. has once again "found" her own body and, indeed, has been able to construct a mature, stable, and "giving" relationship with a member of the medical profession.

CONCLUSION

The life of man, as Vince Lombardi said, is nasty, brutish, and short.

TWO HOURS TO CURTAIN

A big battle dance in Rogers, Tennessee! These country boys, despised and admired, know what they're about. The way they pull on their strings—the strings of their instruments, and the strings of their fates. Bringing up the bass line here, inserting "fills" there, in their expensive forty-dollar Western shirts and plain ordinary nine-dollar jeans. Four bands are competing, and the musicians backstage are unscrewing their flasks and tasting the bourbon inside, when they are not lighting their joints and pipes and hookahs. Meanwhile they're looking over the house, the Masonic Temple, a big pile of stone erected in 1928, and wondering whether the wiring will be adequate to the demands of their art. The flasks and joints are being passed around, and everyone is wiping his mouth on his sleeve. And so the ropes holding the equipment to the roofs of the white station wagons are untied, and the equipment is carried onto the stage, with its closed curtain and its few spotty work lights shining. The various groups send out for supper, ordering steak sandwiches on a bun, hold the onions or hold the lettuce, as individual taste dictates. The most junior member of each group or a high-ranking groupie goes over to the café with the list, an envelope on which all the orders have been written, and reads off the orders to the counterman there, and the counterman says, "You with the band?" and the go-for says, "Yup," succinct and not putting too fine a point on it. Meanwhile the ushers have arrived, all high school girls who are members of the Daughters of the Mystic Shrine Auxiliary, wearing white blouses and blue miniskirts, with a red sash slung across their breasts and tied at the hip, a badge of office. These, the flower of Rogers's young girls, all go backstage to admire the musicians, and this is their privilege, because the performance doesn't begin for another hour, and they stand around looking at the musicians, and the musicians look back at them, and certain thoughts push their way into all of the minds gathered there, under the work lights, but then are pushed out again, because there is music to be performed this night! and one of the amplifiers has just blown its slo-blo fuse, and nobody can remember where the spare fuses were packed, and also the microphones provided by the Temple are freaking out, and in addition the second band's drummer discovers that his heads are soggy (probably as a result of that situation outside Tulsa, where the bridge was out and the station wagon more or less forded the river), but luckily he has brought along a hot plate to deal with this sort of contingency, and he plugs it in and begins toasting his heads, to bring them back to the right degree of brashness for the performance. And now the first people are filling up the seats, out in front of the curtain, some of them sitting in seats that are better, strictly speaking, than those they had paid for, in the hopes that the real owners of the seats will not show up, having been detained by a medical emergency. All of the musicians take turns in looking out over the auditorium through a hole in the closed curtain, counting the house and looking for girls who are especially beautiful. And now the MC arrives, a very jovial man in a big white Western hat, such as the Stetson company has stopped making, and he goes around shaking hands with everybody, cutting up old touches, and the musicians tolerate this, because it is a part of their life. And now everybody is tuning up, and you hear parts of lots of different songs, fragments clashing with each other, because each musician has a different favorite bit that he likes to tune up with, although sometimes two musicians will start in on the same piece at the same time, because they are thinking alike, at that moment. And now the hall is filling up with people who are well or ill dressed, according to the degree that St. Pecula has smiled upon them, and the Daughters of the Mystic Shrine are outside, with their programs, which contain advertisements from the Bart Lumber Yard, and the Sons and Daughters of I Will Arise, and the House of Blue Lights, and the Sunbeam Vacuum Cleaner

Company, and the Okay Funeral Home. A man comes backstage with a piece of paper on which is written the order in which the various performers will appear. The leaders of the various groups drift over to this man and look at his piece of paper, to see what spot on the bill has been given to each band, while the bandsmen talk to each other, in enthusiastic or desultory fashion, according to their natures. "Where'd you git that shirt?" "Took it off a cop in Texarkana." "How much you give for it?" "Dollar and a half." And now everybody is being careful not to drink too much, because drinking too much slows down your attack, and if there is one thing you don't want in this kind of situation it is having your attack slowed down. Of course some people are into drinking and smoking a lot *more* before they play, but that's another idea, and now the audience on the other side of the closed curtain is a loud presence, and everyone has the feeling of something important about to happen, and the first band to perform gets into position, with the three guitar players in a kind of skirmish line in front, the drummer spread out behind them, and the electric-piano player off to the side somewhat, more or less parallel to the drummer, and the happy MC standing in front of the guitar players, with his piece of paper in his hand, and the stage manager looking alternately at his watch and at the people out front. One of the musicians borrows a last cigarette from another musician, and all of the musicians are fiddling with the controls of their instruments, and the drummer is tightening his snares, and the stage manager says "OK" to the MC and the MC holds up his piece of paper and prepares to read what is written there into the bunch of microphones before him, and the houselights go down as the stage lights come up, and the MC looks at the leader of the first group, who nods complacently, and the MC shouts into the microphones (from behind the closed curtains) in a hearty, dramatic voice, "*From Rogers, Tennessee, the Masonic Temple Battle of the Bands, it's Bill Tippey and the Happy Valley Boys!*" and the band crashes into "When Your Tender Body Touches on Mine," and the curtains part, and the crowd goes crazy.

THE ROYAL TREATMENT

WRITTEN UNDER THE PSEUDONYM LILY McNEIL

(WITH APOLOGIES TO THE LATE OGDEN NASH)

I would like to publicly proclaim that I, for one, do not
think the President is guilty of base, low, or tiny-
minded malfeasance
And that although the former Vice-President has made
me sad, at least he didn't do anything that could
correctly be described as high treasance.
And that although the former Attorney General and the
former Secretary of Commerce may or may not be
legally indictable
I think any small petty wrongs they may have
committed are probably readily rightable.
And the former Counsel to the President and the two
former Assistants to the President and the two former
Special Assistants to the President and the former
Acting Director of the FBI are all okay guys in my
book, and I devoutly wish that someone like Little Joe
Cartwright, Spider Man, Alain Robbe-Grillet, or the
Maharishi could jump in there and get them off the
hook.

And I don't really believe in my heart of hearts that the
President would go so far as to bug his brother,
And the two missing tapes aren't important because

*since they didn't exist in the first place how could
they contain any terrible news that somebody might
want to suppress, sequester, stifle, or smother?*
*And what happened to those admirable gentlemen,
Richardson, Ruckelshaus, and Cox,*
*Shocked and dismayed me but I was able to drain it
from the wading pool of my mind by reading fourteen
improving tracts by Increase Mather while
simultaneously listening to the complete works of the
entire family of Bachs.*
*Still, all of the accusations and denials and leaks and
plumbing and frocking and unfrocking and hundred-
dollar bills running around in suitcases with no
human hands attached to them except maybe people
in red wigs and furor and shouting and high-level
pomposity*
*Does tend to create in us of the silent majority a degree
of what might be called anonymosity.*

*I get the distinct impression that the American form
of government is exhausted and puffing and
panting*
*And that something neater, along the lines of, say,
absolute monarchy might be more enchanting.*
*And so for king I would like to nominate with all due
modesty, me—*
*The first woman king, to whom in these times of raised
consciousness and equal opportunity employment no
fairminded former voter could object, could he?*
*People are tired of going into those little booths and
looking at those long lists of candidates most of whom
they don't even recognize the names of*
*Wouldn't it be simpler just to have a sovereign that they
could cluster in a square when she appeared bowing
on a balcony and throw their hats in the air and shout
the acclaims of?*

*We'd save trillions and trillions by abolishing the
executive, judicial, and legislative branches with all
their offices, buildings, secretaries, pension plans, and*

*places they have to hurry at lunchtime in their official
   limousines to be at.*
Instead, there'd just be me and my fiat.
*I don't think we really need all those checks and
   balances the Constitution provides which leave the
   czar, caliph, shah, or doge trembling and tense in the
   air like a Flying Wallenda*
*A situation in which, you'll admit, it's very difficult to
   get the people's business justly and efficiently off your
   callenda.*
*I promise I wouldn't be lofty, remote, or otherwise
   unduly regal*
*I promise I would try to do things in ways that were
   (definitively, you understand) legal.*

*And all of the Congress would have to go out and get
   added to the labor force and seek gainful employment
   and social utility*
*Instead of drowning the great issues of the day in a bog
   of blather, hebetude, cod's-wallop, and piggy
   ignobility.*
*And all of the Supreme Court justices would have to
   take off their robes and put on ordinary suits and ties
   and go down and sit in the agora*
*In obedience to the divine dictum of the hero-architect
   Mies van der Rohe that less is mora.*
*And I wouldn't have anybody near the throne capable of
   embarrassing me by his Quasimodic behavior except
   maybe my consort, who would probably be Albert,
   Philip, Ralph, Igor, or some other name that I love*
*Which wouldn't prevent me from, if he got out of line,
   slapping him upside the head with my velvet hand in
   its iron glove.*

*Lily the First is a nomenclature that I wouldn't mind
   responding to, graciously*
*And I've already spoken to the Moran Company about
   the royal barge, spaciously*
*My proposal is, I admit, anti-democratic, un-American,
   and anachronistic*

But wouldn't it be better than the present megillah in
which the sacred Persons of the governmental Trinity
find themselves facing each other in postures
positively pugilistic?
And if I did something clearly reprehensible you
wouldn't have to convene eighteen different
investigatory bodies to figure out who to guillotine
There'd only be me, walking in a stately manner in my
best Halston toward the shredding machine.

MAN'S FACE

(A NEW NOVEL IN FORTY COAXIAL CHAPTERS)

A word about the author: after ten dreary years writing program notes for *TV Guide*, Redburn Backspace completed, just before he died, the forty beautiful, elliptical, ethereal chapters of his visionary novelorama *Man's Face*. It may be suggested that his prolonged nestle under the wing of Triangle Publications adversely affected his style, if not his mind; this we, his editors, must strenuously dispute. He was a man of few words, and his unique vision of life is now fixed forever in the pages of *Man's Face*.

I. THE LAND

While taking killer Vince Bigly back to prison, Mark Foreman is joined by ex-convict Chris Milk, who has cut the telegraph wires to Toledo.

II. THE PEOPLE

Gladys is insulted by a man in a movie theater.

III. JIM

Gladys asks Mark to save Jim's romance, but killer Vince Bigly interferes. "Patriotism" is explained in a visit to Fort Ticonderoga.

IV. PILLS

When a beautiful debutante is strangled, a sleuth from Scotland Yard begins to investigate the life of his prime suspect, Jim.

V. BETH, WHERE IS THY STING?

Dr. John Bang demonstrates bee communication.

VI. THE WAY WEST

At a river crossing, the travelers learn that killer Vince Bigly has the only barge.

VII. THE VISIT

Mark thinks that his father betrayed his Indian mother by deciding to remarry. Monkeys and dogs perform unusual feats.

VIII. BREAKING POINT

Sir Kenneth Clark attempts to approach nature without preconceived ideas.

IX. HOUR OF DECISION

Mark was adopted by the Indians. Now his Indian father wants him to return to his own people. The sheriff's brother is lost in the Métro.

X. RULES OF THE GAME

Jim is worried about Mark, and a zebra helps unite a mentally ill soldier and his family.

XI. HONG KONG

Gladys is insulted by a man in a movie theater.

XII. THE FLAG OF LIFE
How to make rhythm instruments.

XIII. THE OPEN DOOR
Gladys decides that she has had enough of ranch life.

XIV. CICADAS
When his brother joins the Air Force instead of helping out on the ranch, Jim tears up his hat.

XV. IN THE BICYCLE SHOP
A tragic accident teaches a ruthless businessman the meaning of tolerance. Members of the team are interviewed.

XVI. THE TURNING OF THE TIDE
Sandy Koufax and Sen. Hubert H. Humphrey discuss ambergris.

XVII. THE HUNTED
Jim is seen at work at his roadside fruit stand. Gladys wonders whether to go to a movie.

XVIII. A LETTER FROM MARK
India's caste system is gradually becoming a part of the past.

XIX. GLADYS
Gladys, back in Baltimore, can't understand why Mark is keeping her at arm's length. She decides to go to a movie.

XX. POTATOES
A group of young men from diverse backgrounds is molded into an efficient fighting unit.

XXI. ILLUSION AND REALITY

Sir Kenneth Clark ignores Gladys in the movie.

XXII. SCOTCH TAPE

A young widow attempts to rebuild her life.

XXIII. REUNION

Jim joins the Air Force in order to find his brother and make him come back to the ranch. Prof. Leonard R. Rand uses examples from Germany, France, and Mexico.

XXIV. THE SEA

Wanda wears her trench coat to bed.

XXV. TURN OUT THE LIGHT

Eternal joy is discussed by representatives of the world's great religions. Vinnie Fitch's orchestra, dancers Marlo and Caucus, the Pedal Twins.

XXVI. THE HAT

Killer Vince Bigly finds Jim's torn-up hat. He wonders what to do with it.

XXVII. THE WEAVERS

When Mark Foreman's factory burns down, he is accused of setting fire to the insurance money. Members of the team are interviewed.

XXVIII. RABIES

A well-meaning friend tries to stop a brilliant engineer from destroying his plumb bob.

XXIX. AGAINST THE GRAIN

Anthropologist Max Winter hurls Ituri Pygmies into a volcano. Members of the team are interviewed.

XXX. LAUGHING MARY

Dr. William Muff explains the importance of exploiting the unusual child.

XXXI. GET UP AND LIVE!

Al McLane and Joe Brooks, using light tackle, land a giant slalom.

XXXII. THUNDER IN THE ATTIC

On a field trip, Timmy finds a rock.

XXXIII. IN FRANCE

Gladys watches life passing from a sidewalk café, and chats with M. Dulac about his broccoli.

XXXIV. CHILDREN OF BARK

Jim is missing, and Mark thinks that he is inventing glass. City Health Commissioner George James answers viewers' questions.

XXXV. DAEDALUS

The sheriff's brother is lost in the Métro. Gladys and Jim discuss ambergris futures with Sen. Hubert H. Humphrey.

XXXVI. UNDER THE RED-WHITE-AND-BLUE

Students dangle wool in front of rabbits.

XXXVII. THE SEASONS

In defiance of her wealthy family, Gladys decides to learn about electricity.

XXXVIII. PEARL SWINE

A Marine with amnesia goes out to search for his identity.

XXXIX. THE PAYOFF

Dr. George Muff traces the history of thread.

XL. SCRAMBLED EGGS

Driving to Mark's new job as a teacher in an exclusive boys' school, Mark and Gladys make a big mistake. Vince Bigly plays "The Star-Spangled Banner."

WASTELAND!

(MR. LIONEL BART'S NOTES IN EXEGESIS OF HIS
LATEST MUSICAL PROJECT)

Not only the title but the plan and a good deal of the incidental symbolism of the musical were suggested by Mr. T. S. Eliot's poem "The Waste Land." Indeed, so deeply am I indebted, Mr. Eliot's poem will elucidate the difficulties of the piece much better than my notes can do, and I recommend it (apart from the great interest of the poem itself) to any who think such elucidation worth the trouble.

When Lil sings the poignant aria "Come In Under the Shadow of This Red Rock," she is, of course singing to Albert, get it? Albert, at this point, is still in the army, and evil Madame Sosostris has informed Lil that unless she can raise fifty quid fast fast fast, Albert won't get his honorable discharge, right? The poignance of this number is terrific. Poignance is all.

The critic Frederick J. Hoffman has identified the major themes of the original poem as follows: " 'The Waste Land' contains a single unified metaphor, variously given and dramatically developed. It can be seen in at least two realizations: the fable of the land itself (and of its King); the situation of love in its profane, sacred and mystic forms. These are unified in terms of analogies involving the cultural and personal meanings of fertility." I found all this very depressing and literary, and have left it out.

The first time I read Mr. Eliot's poem, I became very depressed. Then I became very excited. Would Ethel Merman, I wondered, do Madame Sosostris if I beefed up the part? Would Rex Harrison do The Man With Three Staves? Could I work some kids into the show, for poignancy? I immediately abandoned my plan to adapt

The Rise and Fall of the Third Reich and concentrated on "Wasteland!"

The duet between the Hanged Man (Albert) and the Hyacinth Girl (Lil) is a tricky bit of business: the audience is asked to suppose that Albert is still overseas with his outfit whereas Lil is in the Hyacinth Garden, okay? We lick this by having Albert sing from behind a scrim. Madame Sosostris has promised that the charges against Albert will be dropped if Lil gets up the money—but the mysterious Man With Three Staves is hovering in the background. Lil has the first-act curtain with the poignant "Fear Death by Water, *Mon Coeur*," a prayer for Albert's safe return from over the sea.

The Tarot Pack introduced at the beginning of the second act is a juvenile gang, dig? Certain flaccidities in the dramatic construction of the original made necessary the interpolation of a rumble between the Pack and their rivals, The Chess Men (cf. *West Side Story*). The change of Philomel by the barbarous King (Clive Revill ideally) diverts the feuding Mods and Rockers from their altercation; they sing the lively "Jug Jug Song." Albert appears in the guise of a Youth Board worker; Lil fails to recognize him.

The next bit has to do with vegetation ceremonies—it's April, capisc'? The song "Choose a Sunny Location" came to me in a rather peculiar way. I had just received a small packet of Giant Zinnias from my bank (Chase Manhattan). The copy on the package consisted of a rather awkward analogy between the processes of germination and the bank's various savings plans. "Choose a sunny location," it said. I found this unbearably poignant.

Albert, recognized at last, asks Lil in a particularly messy recitative what she has done with the money he gave her to get herself some new teeth. The song "Teeth, Glorious Teeth" is based on the *Handbook of Good Practice* issued by the Royal College of Dental Chirurgeons, London. Lil, of course, has squandered the money on visits to Madame Sosostris, a fact immediately apparent when she opens her mouth to sing. The theme of this number is the present decay of Eastern Europe, which I associate, quite arbitrarily, with David Merrick.

I discarded Parts III and IV of the poem ("The Fire Sermon" and "Death by Water") because I did not like them.

The Man With Three Staves now sings the "Seventy-Million-Dollar Song," which is based upon the estimated total gross of all

David Merrick shows since the beginning of time—a figure I find incredibly poignant, dig? The Fisher King is revealed as none other than "Fishy" Porter, husband of Mrs. Porter (cf. Part III, which, you will recall, has been scrapped) and the biggest kipperer in all of Albion. Since he is also The Man With Three Staves, we understand for the first time the nature of his interest in Lil: she is his only daughter, the product of the above-mentioned liaison with Mrs. Porter. He explains (in the poignant "But at My Back from Time to Time I Hear") that he has disguised himself in order to learn the extent of his wife's involvement with Apeneck Sweeney; satisfied on this score, he ransoms Lil from the clutches of Madame Sosostris. Albert and Lil decide to leave Rats' Alley and make a new start in America, as the entire cast reprises the enchanting and poignant and unforgettable "How to Lick the Book."

THE EDUCATIONAL EXPERIENCE

Music from somewhere. It is Vivaldi's great work, *The Semesters*.

The students wandered among the exhibits. The Fisher King was there. We walked among the industrial achievements. A good-looking gas turbine, behind a velvet rope. The manufacturers described themselves in their literature as "patient and optimistic." The students gazed, and gaped. Hitting them with ax handles is no longer permitted, hugging and kissing them is no longer permitted, speaking to them is permitted but only under extraordinary circumstances.

The Fisher King was there. In *Current Pathology* by Spurry and Entemann the King is called "a doubtful clinical entity." But Spurry and Entemann have never caught him, so far as is known. Transfer of information from the world to the eye is permitted if you have signed oaths of loyalty to the world, to the eye, to *Current Pathology*.

We moved on. The two major theories of origins, evolution and creation, were argued by bands of believers who gave away buttons, balloons, bumper stickers, pieces of the True Cross. On the walls, photographs of stocking masks. The visible universe was doing very well, we decided, a great deal of movement, flux—unimpaired vitality. We made the students add odd figures, things like 453498*23:J and 8977?22MARY. This was part of the educational experience, we told them, and not even the hard part—just one side of a many-sided effort. But what a wonderful time you'll have, we told them, when the experience is over, done, completed. You will all, we told them, be more beautiful than you are now, and more employable too. You will have a grasp of the total situation; the total situation will have a grasp of you.

210

Here is a diode, learn
what to do with it.
Here is Du Guesclin,
constable of France
(1370–80)—learn what
to do with him. A divan
is either a long cushioned seat or a council of state—
figure out at which times it is what. Certainly you can
have your dangerous drugs, but only for dessert—first you must
chew your cauliflower, finish your fronds.

Oh they were happy going through the exercises and we told
them to keep their tails down as they crawled under the wire, the
wire was a string of quotations, Tacitus, Herodotus, Pindar . . .
Then the steady-state cosmologists, Bondi, Gold, and Hoyle, had
to be leapt over, the students had to swing from tree to tree in the
Dark Wood, rappel down the sheer face of the Merzbau, engage in
unarmed combat with the Van de Graaff machine, sew stocking
masks. See? Unimpaired vitality.

Fig. 27

We paused before a bird's lung on a pedestal. "But the mammalian lung is different!" they shouted. "A single slug of air, per hundred thousand population . . . " Some fool was going to call for "action" soon, citing the superiority of praxis to pale theory. A wipe-out requires thought, planning, coordination, as per our phoncon of 6/8/71. Classic film scripts were stretched tight over the destruction of indigenous social and political structures for dubious ends, as per our phoncon of 9/12/71. "Do you think intelligent life exists outside this bed?" one student asked another, confused as to whether she was attending the performance, or part of it. Unimpaired vitality, yes, but—

And Sergeant Preston of the Yukon was there in his Sam Browne belt, he was copulating violently but copulating with no one, that's always sad to see. Still it was a "nice try" and in that sense inspirational, a congratulation to the visible universe for being what it is. The group leader read from an approved text. "I have eaten from the tympanum, I have drunk from the cymbals." The students shouted and clashed their spears together, in approval. We noticed that several of them were off in a corner playing with animals, an ibex, cattle, sheep. We didn't know whether we should tell them to stop, or urge them to continue. Perplexities of this kind are not infrequent, in our business. The important thing is the educational experience itself—how to survive it.

Fig. 36

We moved them along as fast as we could, but it's difficult, with all the new regulations, restrictions. The Chapel Perilous is a bomb farm now, they have 8,000 acres in guavas and a few hundred head of white-faced enlisted men who stand around with buckets of water, buckets of sand. We weren't allowed to smoke, that was annoying, but necessary I suppose to the preservation of our fundamental ideals. Then we taught them how to put stamps on letters, there was a long line waiting in front of that part of the program, we lectured about belt buckles, the off/on switch, and putting out the garbage. It is wise not to attempt too much all at once—perhaps we weren't wise.

213

The best way to live is by not knowing what will happen to you at the end of the day, when the sun goes down and the supper is to be cooked. The students looked at each other with secret smiles. Rotten of them to conceal their feelings from us, we who are doing the best we can. The invitation to indulge in emotion at the expense of rational analysis already constitutes a political act, as per our phoncon of 11/9/72. We came to a booth where the lessons of 1914 were taught. There were some wild strawberries there, in the pool of blood, and someone was playing the piano, softly, in the pool of blood, and the Fisher King was fishing, hopelessly, in the pool of blood. The pool is a popular meeting place for younger people but we aren't younger anymore so we hurried on. "Come and live with me," that was something somebody said to someone else, a bizarre idea that was quickly scotched—we don't want that kind of idea to become general, or popular.

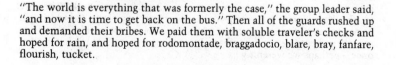

"The world is everything that was formerly the case," the group leader said, "and now it is time to get back on the bus." Then all of the guards rushed up and demanded their bribes. We paid them with soluble traveler's checks and hoped for rain, and hoped for rodomontade, braggadocio, blare, bray, fanfare, flourish, tucket.

THE DRAGON

One day a wan and scruffy dragon came to the city looking for a disease. He had in mind ending his life, which he felt to be tedious, unsatisfactory, tax-troubled, lacking in purpose. Looking up diseases in the Yellow Pages, and finding none, he decided to enroll himself in a hospital. At St. Valentine's, he approached a guard and asked the way to the No Hope Ward. Directed to the proper floor, he found there a bed newly made, whitewashed with sheets. He climbed in and turned on the television set, which was attached to the bed umbilically. A nurse motored in.

"What have you got?" asked the dragon, thinking of diseases.

"Everything," said the nurse. "Eclampsia to milk leg. There is nothing that we do not have. Our Intensive Despair Unit is the envy of the profession. You will be edified. Everything will be all right. Trust us. The world is waiting for the sunrise."

The subsequent examinations, consultations, testifications can easily be imagined. To the point. The hospital refused to give him a disease. After three days, he'd been offered not so much as a nip of pneumonia.

"I trusted you," he said to his nurse. His fine fiery eyes regarded her with reproach and disgust.

"I thought for a while we had something worked out with the Kidney Committee," she said. "But when they discovered the precise nature of your undertaking . . ."

Thinking of diseases still, the dragon left the hospital. Many fine diseases passed through his mind—rabies, gout, malaria, rinderpest. Or, he thought suddenly, I could get myself slain by a hero.

At that moment, a Colonel of Sanitation came striding by, in his green uniform. "You there!" he cried. "Ho, dragon, stop and patter for a bit. Quickly, quickly—haven't got all day! There are Mr. Goodbar wrappers in the streets still, after all my efforts, and the efforts of my men, day in day out—people, people, if we could just do something about the people, then perhaps an end to the endlessness. One could go home of a Friday night, and wipe the brow, and doff the uniform, and thank God for a day well squandered. But you—you have a strange aspect. What kind of a thing are you? Are you disposable? Biodegradable? Ordinary citizen out for a stroll? Looking for work? Member of a conspiracy? Vegetable? Mineral? Two-valued? Hostile to the national interest of the Department of Sanitation? Thrill-crazed kid? Objet d'art? Circus in town?"

"I am nothing much," said the dragon. "But I must declare, if you will allow me, that I am in a catatony of admiration in re your life task. Your labor is indeed Sisyphean."

"You look rather like one of our fine Department of Sanitation trucks," said the colonel, "now that I regard you closely. Are you sure you are not a malingering sanitation truck?"

"I don't think so," said the dragon.

"Let it go," the colonel said, with a sigh. "Let it go, like so much else in this radically imperfect world, in this radically befilthed city. This is my lunch hour, after all. Would you care to rip up a chop? I like your style, know a place—quiet talk, exchange of views, not-bad Gibsons, pretty waitresses, Diners Club and American Express cards accepted."

They sat over their tasty and well-onioned Gibsons.

"Tell me," said the dragon. "Are you West Point?"

"Sandhurst," said the colonel. "Now, what is it, exactly, that is eating you and making you wan? Some order of death wish, I would imagine."

"That is the case," said the dragon, "exactly."

"A question of existence," said the colonel, "or its opposite."

"You have put your finger on it," said the dragon.

"Dragons exist," said the colonel. "Only a fool would doubt it."

"If pricked, do I not bleed?"

"You suffer, however, from a sort of general meaninglessness."

"Since the thirteenth century."

The colonel thought for a moment. "You could be an endangered species," he said. "That would give you a meaningful life role. We love and cherish our endangered species and extend to them every courtesy."

"Well . . ."

"By the authority vested in me by the Department of Sanitation," pronounced the colonel, "I hereby declare you an endangered species, *in tenebris, inter alia, pro forma, primus inter pares*, and subject to approval at the highest levels."

"Thank you," said the dragon. "Thank you very much."

"The President himself is vitally interested in endangered species," said the colonel. "He has a list."

"Are men on it?"

The colonel rose up in a great fit of anger and threw his glass into the fire. Half a Gibson followed it into the flames. He then stamped from the room with skillful majesty, excellent hauteur, and the bill. The dragon, filled with self-regard and convinced that he had at last gotten a message to the Authorities, bought a two-dollar lottery ticket and decided to stop smoking.

NEWSLETTER

BOARD MEETING:

The last meeting of the Board on Wednesday, June 10, ended with a general manifestation of mutual respect and Christian fellowship. Ralph Hammer, speaking for the Deacons' Committee, said that the Deacons had decided to withdraw their mass resignation of March 18. Recent developments within the church, he said, had convinced the Committee that their action had been precipitous. He pointed out that although the Deacons did not mind turning their robing room over to the new Ecology Center, in view of the grave threat represented by the environment, they felt that other apportionments of space within the church had been, perhaps, precipitous. His examples were the discotheque and the Encounter Pool. However, he said the Deacons would bend to the will of the majority, in these instances. Ralph raised the question of the audit, noting that the accountants had refused to certify the last-quarter accounts because they were blurred. Something ought to be done about this, he felt. Bill Quantrill, representing the New Priorities Committee, thanked Ralph and all the other Deacons for their valuable work in the past and said that some provision would have to be made for them in the new scheme of things. This would be worked out, he said.

The question of the stolen mailing list was discussed. Elaine Berube said that there was no point in talking about who could have walked off with four drawers of Addressograph plates or for what purpose, and that the thing to do now was reestablish contact with the membership. It was decided that everyone would be asked to call in their name, address, and telephone number, and that this issue of the "Newsletter," containing that emergency request, should be placed prominently in the vestibule and in places in the community, such as Laundromats. So please comply! Margaret Akin is in charge of reconstituting the list. She will be at 695-9445 between 2 and 4 P.M. daily for an indefinite period.

The Board voted, 19–2, to allow the Film Group to "fly" a screen in the altar area. To "fly" means to hang the screen so that it can be pulled down during a screening, and pulled up during regular services. There was some debate as to whether the screen, when in the pulled-up position, would be visible from the sanctuary. Chris Robeson, director of the Film Group, said just the bottom of it. The schedule of films for August was also announced (listed elsewhere in the "Newsletter").

Three hundred and forty dollars was voted for a new set of drums. These will be purchased from G. Schirmer, Inc.

Helen Meadows pointed out that while consciousness-raising and radicalization have a place in the Sunday services, we must not forget continuity. When asked for examples of continuity, she suggested flowers regularly, with special attention to such special occasions as Palm Sunday and Easter. Pierre Spirot said that flowers were not of as much value as situational experiences.

Meeting adjourned at 4:35 P.M.

AUGUST FLICKS:

Gizzards, with Tanya Fritz and Paul Capelle, August 8, 8 P.M. *A Man and a Man* (Gregory Ratatouille), August 11, 8 P.M. *I* with Berger Resthaus, August 15, 8 P.M. *House of Chains* with Antonio Taxi, August 29, 8 P.M.

KARATE CLASSES:

A new series of Karate Classes will begin on Monday, July 20, under the direction of Patti-Lee Ivens, a Black Belt. They will be held in the Bell Tower.

BABA MAHEESH:

Baba Maheesh, formerly Theodore Lily, Ph.D., will lecture on "Transcendental Meditation" Thursday, July 16, at 8 P.M. His subtitle is "Improving Our Emotions." There will be a 50¢ contribution.

CENTERS:

The Astrology-Telepathy Center, the Third World Center, the Dance Center, and the Center for the Study of Ecstasy have been discontinued. Their rooms will be assigned to new projects as new needs are felt.

REPAIRS:

The contractor fixing things up after the fire reports that extensive water damage presents problems. The building is structurally sound, he said, and the load-bearing walls weakened by the explosion have been shored up. The work is running well ahead of estimates, he stated. The new Encounter Pool is already installed. It is, as previously noted here, big enough for eight. A schedule of hours for the Encounter Pool will be posted as soon as the water heater is connected.

MINISTER:

Our minister, Ripley Bligh, is continuing his leave of absence. He is back in town and looking for a small apartment in the neighborhood.

ORGAN:

Anyone having any information as to the whereabouts of the organ, which has been missing from the choir loft since about May 1, please contact Bill Quantrill. He promises no prosecution or recriminations of any kind and says that the organ is needed so that we can continue to go forward on an even keel in the spirit of love and Christian fellowship.

Peace!

THE PHOTOGRAPHS

FIG. 1   FIG. 2

he attached photographs of the human soul (Figs. 1 and 2), taken by *Pioneer 10*, the first spacecraft to navigate the outer solar system, were made on December 14, 1973, as the craft was leaving the magnetic field of Jupiter. The "photographs" (actually coded radio signals from the device's nine-foot dish antenna beamed back to Earth) were, of course, incidental to the photographing of Jupiter itself, one of the mission's chief aims. They were made by Dr. Reginald Hobson, FRS, of Britain's Cavendish Laboratory, using Kodak spectroscopic plates type IIIa-J baked for five hours at 65° C. under dry N_2 before exposure. Dr. Hobson very shortly afterward brought the resulting images to his friend and colleague Dr. Winston Watnick-Mealie, FRS.

"Uh, Winnie—"

"Yes, Reggie?"

"I have something to show you."

"More shots from *10*?"

"Right, Winnie. But these . . . There's something rather special about them."

"What's that, Reggie?"

"Well, Winnie, I have reason to believe that they are photographs of the human soul on its way to Heaven."

"Oh, really. That's *interesting*. Photographs of the human soul on its way to Heaven. I suppose you've, uh, checked this out, have you, Reggie? I mean—"

"Uh—rather thoroughly, Winnie. I did a computer search of all extant images from space, and, uh, these photographs are *sui generis*, you might say. They are like nothing previously photographed. Nothing. I also did a worm-path study of the possibilities, and the result of the worm-path study was that, uh, these *can only be* photographs of the human soul on its way to Heaven."

"Any other tests?"

"Fourier analysis. Critical-band masking. Continuous smearing grids."

"Um. Well, then, I suppose that's that, isn't it? You're quite sure it's the *soul*—the human soul?"

"Worm-path studies don't lie, Winnie. I ran the program four times."

"The human soul . . . on its way to, ah, Heaven."

"One assumes. It was definitely outward bound."

"I see. Well, then, let's have a look at them."

"Right here, Winnie."

"God. Ugly little bugger, isn't it?"

"Not precisely pretty. I wouldn't, for example, call it gorgeous."

"Definitely not gorgeous. Rather unattractive, actually."

"I remarked that myself."

"Looks rather like a frying pan."

"Yes, it does, rather."

"A heavily, uh, corroded frying pan. You see that handle sort of part, over to the right."

"Yes, I noticed that. Looks rather like a, ah, handle."

"A bit used-looking, the whole thing."

"Quite."

"And then there's that, ah, knuckle sort of thing there at the top. What d'you make of that, Reggie?"

"Haven't the faintest, Winnie. What you might call an anomaly."

"Yes, definitely anomalous. I mean, one doesn't like to think of souls, the human soul, as having . . . knuckle-shaped things sticking out the top, does one?"

"Much prefer not, Winnie. It bothered me, too."

"Yes. It's disturbing."

"Yes. Definitely disturbing."

"I always thought of the soul as being more *symmetrical*, don't you know."

"Right. Sort of . . . beautiful. Like that stuff one puts on the Christmas tree at Christmas. What's it called?"

"Angel hair."

"Right. Sort of like angel hair. Ethereal."

"Ethereal, that's the ticket. And now to see it looking very much like something someone's been frying eggs and kidneys and God knows what all in for just ages and ages—well it sort of takes the wind out of one's sails, as it were."

"Very disturbing, I agree, Winnie."

"I wonder what that little nipple-shaped business is, in the middle there."

"Yes, I was curious, too. Probably should be looked into."

"Why couldn't it have been, you know, *beautiful*? If you follow me."

"Well, there *is* sin and all that, of course."

"Yes. Sin. I was afraid you were going to mention that."

"I don't quite follow."

"Well, the thing is, Reggie, I have something to confess. Something in the sin line, actually."

"Something to confess?"

"Yes, I don't know quite how to put it, but it's something that's been rather on my mind, these past weeks."

"What ever are you talking about?"

"Well, it's about Dorothea."

"Dorothea?"

"Yes, Dorothea. The thing is, I ran into Dorothea a few months ago. At Marks & Spencer. She was looking for some orange thread."

"Yes, for her tatting."

"Yes. She was tatting a bedspread, I believe. An orange bed-spread."

"Yes, she's finished it. It's on the bed now, in the bedroom."

"Quite. Well, Dorothea was looking for some orange thread—a particular shade of orange—"

"Yes. It's called burnt orange, Winnie. A sort of burnt-looking orange."

"Right. Well, she, as I say, was looking for this special shade of orange thread, and *I* was looking for a thimble."

"You were looking for a thimble."

"Right. Margaret had asked me to stop off at Marks & Spencer and fetch her home a thimble. She'd lost her thimble."

"I see."

"I bought two, actually. In case she misplaced one, she'd have the other, you see. Sort of a backup system."

"Um."

"Well, as it happens the thimble department is quite close to the thread department, at Marks & Spencer. They're adjacent."

"I should think they'd be pretty well the same department."

"One would think that, but as it happens they're separate departments. Separate, but adjacent. So I sort of ran into Dorothea, that afternoon, and in the ordinary way asked her if she'd like to pop out for a drink."

"She accepted."

"Ah, yes. So we popped out and had a drink. Several, in fact."

"I see."

"And, uh, one thing sort of led to another, and the fact is that I've been seeing quite a bit of Dorothea in the past weeks. Illicitly."

"Illicitly."

"Yes. Behavior which is, strictly speaking, non-licit."

"Um. And you've been feeling a bit uneasy about it?"

"Yes. Horrid, in fact."

"Well, I can understand that, Winnie. It is a bit sticky, given the fact that we've been friends and colleagues all these years. Since the fifties, really."

"The late fifties, yes. I came here in 1956."

"But I don't quite see, Winnie, what this has to do with these photographs. Of the human soul on its way to Heaven. The first ever. I would say that the immediate problem is not your little flutter with my wife, Dorothea, but the photographs. I mean, business before pleasure, Winnie."

"Right, Reggie. I couldn't agree more. You always were one for getting on with it."

"The question is, in my view, what are we to do with the bloody things?"

"Burn them."

"Burn them? But they are of some scientific interest, wouldn't you say? I mean, if the soul exists, and we have the snaps to prove it, it would have quite a lot of relevance, wouldn't it? To everything?"

"Well, yes, I suppose it would have *some* relevance. Give the theologians a hell of a fright, for one thing. Maybe be worth publishing, just for that reason."

"Yes, I can see that."

"Of course, on the other hand, a great many people—decent, serious people—are probably *very interested* in this sort of thing. The existence of the human soul. I mean, it's not like the tooth fairy, right?"

"Much more relevance, I'd say, Winnie. To things in general."

"Well, Reggie, it's what you might call a nice question. There's our responsibility to science and truth and all that. But aren't we sort of in the position of those chaps who made the atom bomb and then were sorry afterward?"

"Yes, I'd say we were, actually. Rather."

"It seems to me to boil down to this: are we better off *with* souls, or just possibly *without* them?"

"Yes, I see what you mean. You prefer the uncertainty."

"Exactly. It's more creative. Take for example my, ah, arrangement with your wife, Dorothea. Stippled with uncertainty. At moments, we are absolutely *quaking* with nonspecific anxiety. *I* enjoy it. *Dorothea* enjoys it. The humdrum is defeated. Momentarily, of course."

"Yes, I can understand that. Gives the thing a bit of zest."

"Yes. You'd be taking away people's zest. They'd all have to go around being good and all that. You'd get the Nobel Prize, and no one, repeat *no one*, would ever speak to you again. People do like their zest, Reggie."

"But still—"

"There's just one more item, Reggie. One more item to be considered. I am absolutely persuaded that you have succeeded in capturing the first hard evidence for the existence of the human soul. But it's flawed."

"The thing *is* a bit on the homely side."

"Downright ugly, to be perfectly frank."

"God knows what a life it must have led."

"Yes, but don't you see, Reggie, that these snaps, if they are published, will come to stand for, in the public mind, *all souls*?"

"I suppose there's something in that."

"Some things it's better not to know about. That's what I'm suggesting."

"Your affair with Dorothea would be an example."

"An *excellent* example, Reggie."

"Of course there is some fallout from all this. The affair, I mean."

"What is that, Reggie?"

"I don't like you anymore, Winnie."

WE DROPPED IN AT THE
STANHOPE...

We dropped in at the Stanhope the other day for a conversation with HRH Tutankhamun, last pharaoh of the eighteenth dynasty, just as his much-mitted extravaganza "Treasures" was about to open at the Met, a sellout before the first customer hit the noble steps. We found the boy king in the pale-pink sitting room of his suite, wearing a Turnbull & Asser djellabah and sipping Perrier, the delicate sadness on his face transformed for the moment by something like opening-night fever.

"We did very well out of town," he said. "A million three in Seattle. A million four, give or take, in Chicago. Total U.S. attendance may break seven mil. I'm nervous, of course—New York is *the* experience. But they've booked us into a class place. I stand outside the Met and think, Zowie! Look on my works, ye Mighty! I mean, they've got one of our temples *under glass*, man. It's amazing."

We asked the slight, dark monarch if his spectacle had a theme.

"Yes. It's about gold, man. Heavy metal. I mean, I'm quite comfortable with gold. I was into gold very early. I was into gold when there was none of this two-hundred-and-thirty-dollars-an-ounce nonsense. Gold doesn't *unnerve* me. But I'm not most people. Most people, they see a little gold—I mean, a little gold that's not in a *wristwatch* or something—they begin *shedding skin*, man. Γ&&r jλλ AAk ψψ"

We said we hadn't quite got his last remark.

"That's glyph for '*Mein Gott im Himmel*,' " he said. "I like to zetz in a little glyph now and then. It glyphs people out. Anyhow, gold is the *main* thing but not the *whole* thing. This stuff is *old*, man. Time abolished. Or, from another perspective, time encapsulated. People just stand there and *feel* time. And then, of course, there's the mummy thing, and the *curse* thing. We've got quite a lot going for us, really."

We inquired if the curse, said to have caused a number of mysterious deaths among people associated with the opening of the tomb, was still operative.

"Well, when I walk down the street, I don't step on any cracks myself," he replied, smiling. "The old let-the-hand-raised-against-my-form-be-withered. You understand, *I* placed no curse. You always have a passel of priests around wanting to slam a curse on this, slam a curse on that. I guess it keeps them off the streets."

We asked if the proliferation of Tut-related sales objects annoyed him in any way.

"They say that there's a Tut madness, a Tut mania, that the show has been overcommercialized. Sure, we're peddling a few little items. But they're class knockoffs, man—beautifully reproduced, for the most part. I mean, if Rocky can do it, why shouldn't we? The Frisbees, the T-shirts, the Tut beer mugs—I just regard those as kind of light, kind of kicky. I think of the show as sort of an ambassadorial sort of thing, don't you know. Sort of a goodwill sort of thing. Did you see what Tom Hoving said in the *Times*?"

He picked up a clipping and began to read aloud. " 'People by the millions see the exhibition and they think, Well, Egypt really has some sort of incredible and great culture.' " The king paused. "And that's absolutely the story. Egypt really *has* some sort of incredible and great culture, and we want folks to know that."

We took our leave then, and he showed us to the door, pressing a ten-inch polyester-resin canopic jar into our hands as a parting gift. "A λittλ& som&Гhing Гo r&m&mb&r m& 6y," he said.

WELL WE ALL HAD OUR WILLIE & WADE RECORDS...

Well we all had our Willie & Wade records 'cept this one guy who was called Spare Some Change? 'cause that's all he ever said and you don't have no Willie & Wade records if the best you can do is Spare Some Change?

So we all took our Willie & Wade records down to the Willie & Wade Park and played all the great and sad Willie & Wade songs on portable players for the beasts of the city, the jumpy black squirrels and burnt-looking dogs and filthy, sick pigeons.

And I thought probably one day Willie or Wade would show up in person at the Willie & Wade Park to check things out, see who was there and what record this person was playing and what record that person was playing.

And probably Willie (or Wade) would just case around checking things out, saying "Howdy" to this one and that one, and he'd see the crazy black guy in Army clothes who stands in the Willie & Wade Park and every ten minutes screams like a chicken, and Willie (or Wade) would just say to that guy, "How ya doin' good buddy?" and smile, 'cause strange things don't bother Willie, or Wade, one bit.

And I thought I'd probably go up to Willie then, if it was Willie, and tell him 'bout my friend that died, and how I felt about it at the time, and how I feel about it now. And Willie would say, "I know."

And I would maybe ask him did he remember Galveston, and did he ever when he was a kid play in the old concrete forts along

229

the seawall with the giant cannon in them that the government didn't want anymore, and he'd say, "Sure I did." And I'd say, "You ever work the Blue Jay in San Antone?" and he'd say, "Sure I have."

And I'd say, "Willie, don't them microphones scare you, the ones with the little fuzzy sweaters on them?" And he'd say to me, "They scare me bad, potner, but I don't let on."

And then he (one or the other, Willie or Wade) would say, "Take care, good buddy," and leave the Willie & Wade Park in his black limousine that the driver of had been waiting patiently in all this time, and I would never see him again, but continue to treasure, my life long, his great contributions.

DOWN THE LINE WITH
THE ANNUAL

The *Consumer Bulletin* is much used in courses in consumer
problems, consumer education, economics, home economics,
business, civics, marketing, sociology, life science, physics,
and other business and science education subjects. Its find-
ings provide valuable material to be used in teaching young
consumers in high school and college how to become intelligent and informed buyers of goods and services, and to learn
to look for sound qualities in the products they buy.
                                        —*Consumer Bulletin Annual*

Will Candace come away with me—find integrity, wholeness
on the Australian archipelago? Too early to say. Meanwhile, the affair of the Swedish tennis balls continues to
plague us. I ventured into the basement, found Candace there on
her knees before the washing machine, which was filled with
Swedish tennis balls. Candace in tears. I took her hand. "What?"
I said. "Oh, Charles," she said, "is everything galley-west? Everything?" I gave it some thought. Then: "You've been reading the
Annual." She looked away. "It said these Swedish tennis balls
could be washed in an automatic washer and dried in an automatic dryer without deleterious effects. I had to *try*, didn't I?"
Washing machine has ineffective lint filter, which I discovered
last week when it strangled on new rug, 50 percent Dacron and 50
percent iron pyrites, purchased by Candace without first looking
it up in the imposing, authoritative, annual *Annual*. Candace,
however, is blameless, racked as she is by irritation of the lungs
from overuse of aerosol hair sprays (page 15), unpleasant drying
and crusting of the lips from overuse of indelible lipsticks (page
17). "I do not blame you, Candace," I said. "I blame your inade-

quate education at that expensive eastern girls' school." Iron pyrites particles pulsing in her golden hair. "Everything is galley-
west," she whispered. "Had I not yoyoed away my time in school
reading Herodotus, Saint-Simon, Rilke, and Owen Wister, seeking
answers to the mystery of personality and the riddle of history, I
would not have failed to become an intelligent and informed
buyer of goods and services. It's as simple as that." And in her
eyes there was a misty light, produced by defective contact lenses
(page 50).

Whirled my darling away to an ice-cream parlor, where we consumed quantities of elephant's-foot ice (crammed though it was
with pernicious food additives). But the problem remains. We are
adrift in a tense and joyless world that is falling apart at an accelerated rate. No way to arrest the disintegration that menaces from
every side. Consider the case of the bedside clock. "Check for
loudness of tick," the *Annual* said. I checked. It ticked. Tick
seemed decorous. Once installed in home, it boomed like a B-58.
Candace watching it nervously, neighbors complaining, calls from
the police. And on page 143 the electric can opener that sows tiny
bits of metal inside can being opened; on page 178 the sewing
machine whose upper thread tension is not indexed, whose cams
do not produce the pictured patterns. Yes, they are mine. "There
is no reason to believe that the eyes are permanently harmed
by watching TV," the *Annual* says. (But what of insult to the
brain?) "A good toaster should give successive slices of uniformly
browned toast for many years." But my toaster brought to our
union nothing but a significant shock hazard. And it is true that I
purchased the nylon sheets that slide off the bed (page 211), the
low-quality ink that dries too slowly (page 57)—my letters bleed
through their envelopes like the hands of a medieval saint.

"It is estimated that some 5 million girls exist mainly on snacks
of soft drinks, 'French fries,' pizzas, candy, hamburgers, and waf-
fles." Who are these girls? What are their names? What do they
look like? How does one get in touch with them? And how do
they behave, fueled as they are with "foods of attractive appearance but dubious quality"? Candace wishes to send them lean
beef in a plain brown wrapper. The freezer is full of it. (But then,
the freezer itself is not trustworthy; it is given to broiling the meat
in fits of temperature.) Let me confess it, I am tense, for this
America is not the one I knew. I am going away, to the Australian

archipelago, for although my pipe tobacco is of the type judged lowest in lead and arsenic in 1968 by the Connecticut Agricultural Experiment Station, there is cyanide in my silver cleaner, and my oranges have been rouged with coal-tar dyes. My steam iron spurts hot water from the fill hole, my food-waste disposer doesn't chew cornhusks properly, my phonograph is giddy with wow, flutter, rumble, and hum. Acid water slowly eats away the glossy finish on my sinks, lavatories, tubs, and what it does to the owner himself no man can say. My double-glazed windows are subject to between-pane condensation, and moths and carpet beetles are at work inside the hammers of my piano. My 3-hp rotary snowthrower is a bust. "Snow was ejected as a powdery mist, which blew back on the operator," the *Annual* says, and this proved to be the case; when I returned from the trial run, I resembled a Lapp. Unthrown snow drifts now about my automobile, my apple trees, and Candace, who has gone out to collect the mail. But let her go, for I am writing letters, wrothy letters, to the manufacturer, the Federal Trade Commission, the National Better Business Bureau, and the Attorney General of the state of New York, as the *Annual* advises me to do. The world is sagging, snagging, scaling, spalling, pilling, pinging, pitting, warping, checking, fading, chipping, cracking, yellowing, leaking, staling, shrinking, and in dynamic unbalance, and there is mildew to think about, and ruptures and fractures of internal organs from lap belts, and substandard brake fluids, and plastic pipes alluring to rats, and transistor radios whose estimated battery life, like the life of man, is a feeble, flickering thing.

Candace dear, heart of my heart, take your hand off that package of fabric softener! It may produce an insoluble curd, and you wouldn't want that, would you? "The biggest problem the consumer has in selecting shoes is not fashion, though that may be his first consideration, but selecting a shoe that will not ultimately lead to the distortion of his foot." And don't forget about shirts that develop a yellow tint! And thermal flame-resistant underwear—especially quilted polyester fiber-nylon shell suits—which, once ignited, melts to form a burning, sticky, adhering plastic! And paint failure! And pie mixes laced with esters, ethers, and aldehydes of undefined character! And bicycles with poor pedal design! And dimensionally unstable rayon blankets! And electronic organs that make popping sounds! And coffee mills that adversely affect the flavor of the beverage! And travel irons whose soleplates blister! And desk fans with high noise levels! And electric shavers with tendency to irritate neck! Recall, too, that purchasing a camera, whether new or used, can be a risky operation for the uninitiated! That few diamonds are entirely free from every sort of defect or flaw! That with today's watches a fairly high price gives no assurance of reliable performance or durable construction! That tire-gauge designs leave much to be desired! And, finally, that the custom of going around without a hat or shirt in hot sunny climates, and allowing children to do so, should be strongly discouraged!

O brave *Consumer Bulletin Annual*, holding the line in a world where the best lack all conviction, while the worst are full of passionate intensity! You give me touchstones with which to protect myself against the deceptive pricing, false gift offers, spurious claims, bait advertising, and general rascality of the American economy. "A good spring should be noiseless, or comparatively so. Push on it in quiet surroundings." Of course. Do you mind if I take this spring into the elevator with me for a moment? And close the doors, will you, floorwalker? And what are you grinning about? "For durability, loops of a terry towel should be thickly packed and firm. Check firmness by inserting a pin into a pile loop, raising it up from the towel slightly." Pin poised, I advance into the murky depths of the towel store, clearly a man with a mission. In the department store, I stand bent over a portable refrigerator, inspecting a tray of ice cubes with my jeweler's loupe. Yes, it has taken them much too long to freeze. Quickly I unfasten the jesses that bind Hugo, the killer hawk, to my wrist. Dubious refrigeration shall not go unpunished! Now Hugo is aloft, heading for Panda, Iowa, where the worthless devices are manufactured. See him soar!

And now Port Moresby. Come, Candace, let me coax you out from under that bell jar, into which you have repaired to guard delicate ears against sound of china crazing in the kitchen. Come, Candace, and don't worry about the packing. The only appliance I plan to take with me is Hugo.

MONUMENTAL FOLLY

A s the Bicentennial observation, after some hard sledding, finally mushrooms into high gear, it occurs to us that there is one thing America has a sad paucity of: Monuments. Every tacky little fourth-rate déclassé European country has monuments all over the place and one cannot turn a corner without banging into an eighteen-foot bronze of *Lebrouche Tickling the Chambermaids at Vache While Planning the Battle of Bledsoe,* or some such. Whereas Americans tend to pile up a few green cannonballs next to a broke-down mortar and forget about it. The Bicentennial, then, demands tons and tons of new monumentation—a terrific way of polishing up the country, and work for our hard-pressed foundrymen, too. Herewith, some suggestions.

VALIUM

Valium is what keeps airplanes in the air, cars on the highways, and the furnace rattling. These functions are often mistakenly attributed to Petroleum, but America knows better. In a time when ever more gruesome Revelations daily fritter the nerves, it is reassuring to note that domestic reserves are estimated at two million barrels a day of yellows and three million barrels a day of the 10 mg, or blues.

JEANS

A monument to the noble Jean, which has enriched all our lives. The Jean was invented by Claude Lévi-Strauss in 1932, while the great anthropologist was seeking the "deep structure" of the human trouser. Named for his dear friend Jean Replete (the great animal psychiatrist), the word is properly pronounced "zhhaun," but many people have forgotten. Challenged briefly in the late '30s by a ludicrous entity called the T-Short (big pockets), the Jean triumphed to become the key pant of the American plenitude in the '50s, '60s, and '70s.

THE LOOPHOLE

The Loophole is to the twentieth century what the frontier was to the nineteenth—a way out, a psychological fire escape. Loopholes, however, are not for everyone. They are hidden, like Easter eggs, and can only be found with the assistance of highly paid counsel. This monument is suitable for corporate plazas and also looks very handsome atop grain elevators.

NOSTALGIA

In Bicentennial America yesterday is terrific. Instead of yearning forwardly, which makes more sense in terms of the possible, we yearn backwardly, and who cares for "sense" anyhow? Gazing at a pile of old knickers, or an old duffel bag with our serial number stenciled on it, or an old cracked putter, we are suffused with a nameless emotion, which is called Golf. (We used to carry our clubs in the duffel bag, and if you think we weren't laughed at, you are wrong.) This monument is specially designed for closets, attics, and abandoned movie houses.

CONSCIOUSNESS-RAISING

It is always better to be conscious. When you are not conscious, in Bicentennial America, you frequently awake to find that your shoes have been stolen by a member of Congress who has sold them on 14th Street to pay for a new weapons system. But having Consciousness is not enough; Consciousness must be raised, higher and higher and higher and higher. At its giddiest height, Consciousness sometimes lets you down. Supremely conscious, you find that what you are conscious of is the fact that everything is not too great.

DISASTER

Disaster is delicious. A good sack o' woe, budgeted at $6 million, will deliver 177 thrills and 22 *frissons* per hour. These elegant productions, from which all skin, bone, and gristle have been removed for easy intake, have a moral dimension, too. They vaguely remind you of fate, or something, the haunting contingency of human life, or something. Mostly they take your mind off your life, that ridiculous enterprise, and put your mind on someone else who is actually *on fire*. Well, you're better off than that dummy, aren't you? Meanwhile, the army ants of capitalism are chewing off your shoes.

DÉTENTE

When two people agree not to harm each other today, or in the immediate future, this is cause for rejoicing. How much more satisfying, then, when two superpowers agree to the same thing. The rope of international tensions can be taut or slack; the thing to remember is that it is tied around all our necks, and when someone tries to drive a tank across it, or many tanks, he should be looked at peculiarly.

PUBLIC RELATIONS

Public Relations is the art of putting the best possible face on the matter. If the matter is a coal mine, corporate thuggery, or an open sewer, Public Relations becomes high art indeed. The intent is to protect us from reality, which bites. All of the best Public Relations men in the whole world live in America, in houses made of shining Gleem.

DIVORCE

Divorce is good in other countries, but nowhere is it as good as it is in our own—the sacred Elmer's glue which cements the social fabric. Without the sacrament of Divorce, who would be silly enough to get married? Nobody, except for people who don't care one way or another, the fifteen percent of the population who are always, in America, "undecided," those clunks. What darkens the future of Divorce in America is the profession of law, which can make the whole process very unpleasant. It might not be a bad thing if jurisdiction were taken away from lawyers and given instead to plumbers. Plumbers know all about joining and unjoining and are slightly cheaper.

PROGRESS

Progress is wonderful, and continues to become more wonderful with each passing fiscal year. Progress is the basic American idea, and no country's Progress exceeds our own, by executive order. Progress is often the target of cheap sneers by sour yawpers, but even a sour yawper can ascend dark stairs holding a silver candlestick in his hand. If Progress continues to butter up the quality of life at the present rate, everyone will be unbearably happy by breakfast, 1999. Huzzah!

THE DASSAUD PRIZE

As a preliminary to the Paris World Exhibition of 1900, the firm of Dassaud Frères, instrument makers, sponsored a grand scientific competition with a prize of 50,000 francs. Object: to find—that is to say, locate in time and space—God. A number of brave and gifted investigators set immediately to work.

The development of superior telescopes was an obvious first step. The apparatuses of Professors Cassegrain and Falconetti kept the Dassaud (and other) workmen late at their benches.

The Dassaud brothers: (l–r) Antoine, Pierre, and Hercule, sponsors of the Competition.

Many in the scientific community ignored the Prize and continued to occupy themselves with purely secular pursuits.

The Dassaud Prize became a premier topic of conversation at the city's most advanced dinner tables. Here, a meeting of the Cercle Métaphysique. (Note electric tramway for presenting meals without the intrusion of servants.)

Henri de Piedmont, a flirter with
Darwinism, reasoned that the First
Cause was to be sought under the sea,
and equipped himself appropriately.

The boy inventor Adolph
Tissue and his "machine for
sensational emotions"—a
promising entry. Tissue
later became wanted by the
police for Bluebeardism.

The commitment of the American "team" was typically wholehearted.
But God was not found in these pestiferous regions.

The efforts of the young Scotsman "Wrong Way" McKim were applauded, up to a point.

Achille Purefoy with his electrical "innerness ring." The color blindness which followed its use led him to join the Fauves.

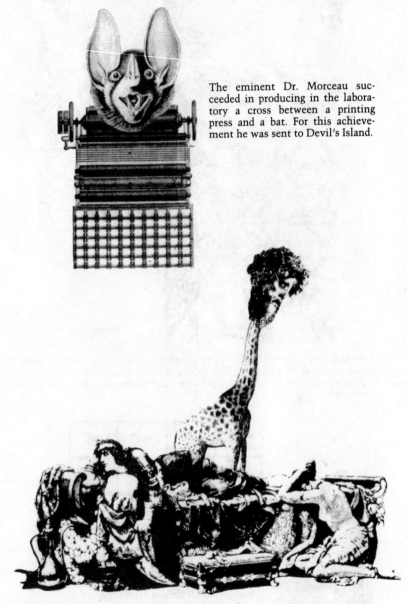

The eminent Dr. Morceau succeeded in producing in the laboratory a cross between a printing press and a bat. For this achievement he was sent to Devil's Island.

The vivid and eccentric Mlle. Cavaillon simply . . . thought.

Like that other Tower, with which it was frequently compared, the giant construction of M. Eiffel was both thinkable and unthinkable—what could this madman have in mind? It was known that he bought his slide rules at Dassaud's.

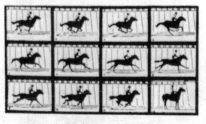

The Dassaud Prize, perhaps predictably, was never awarded. But can any initiative which produced such advances as the Photographic Rifle and Horse Stopper of M. Zieff be judged a failure? It is for the ages to decide.

Plays

☞

THE FRIENDS OF THE FAMILY

Notes:

The men are all in their forties.

When MARTHA *reappears as the* WOMAN *in the studio, voice should be altered to sound younger—a degree of disguise.*

The men should have slight English accents.

Dialect may be interpreted freely.

All speeches given with the utmost gravity.

(*Music: Theme*)

(*Sound: Car leaving the airport: airport noises*)

HUBER (*pettish*): Still, I don't see why we were required.

BLOOMSBURY (*weary*): You weren't required. You were invited.

(*Sound: Plane overhead*)

HUBER: Invited then. I don't see what we were invited *for*.

BLOOMSBURY (*distaste*): As friends of the family. You are both friends of the family. (*Pause*) She was, I thought, quite calm.

WHITTLE (*complimentary*): You also.

BLOOMSBURY: Of course, she has been trained to weep in private.

WHITTLE: Should we, do you think, have waited for the takeoff?

HUBER: It would have been more respectful.

WHITTLE: Probably she would have been touched.

HUBER: Yes, touched.

BLOOMSBURY: It would not have mattered.

WHITTLE: I thought there'd certainly be weeping.

HUBER: But he provided a crowd. Precluding privacy, and thus, weeping.

WHITTLE: I like to see a woman weep, once in a while.

HUBER: We were the crowd. The two of us. *He* doesn't count.

WHITTLE: They have finer feelings than we do, and they are quicker to show their feelings, I've found.

(*Sound: Another car passing very close*)

HUBER (*meditating*): Of course, it's inaccurate to say that we are friends of the family. There no longer being any family.

WHITTLE (*judicious*): The family exists still as a legal entity, I believe. Was there property? Jointly held? This would affect the question whether the family qua family endures beyond the physical separation of the partners, which we have just witnessed.

BLOOMSBURY: She looked, I thought, quite pretty.

WHITTLE: Lovely.

HUBER: Stunning, in fact.

(*Sound: Jet making a climbing turn*)

WHITTLE (*matter-of-fact*): Rich girls always look pretty.

HUBER: I've heard that.

WHITTLE (*to* BLOOMSBURY): Did she take the money with her?

BLOOMSBURY (*sadly*): Yes.

HUBER: You could hardly have done otherwise, I suppose.

WHITTLE: And yet . . .

HUBER: Something for your trouble. A tidy bit, to buy mutual funds with.

WHITTLE (*sly*): "Mutual funds."

HUBER (*topping him*): "Commingling."

WHITTLE (*stern*): It would have gone against the grain no doubt. But there was trouble, was there not? For which little or no compensation has been offered?

BLOOMSBURY (*weary*): There was in fact a great deal of money. More than one person could easily dispose of. But just right as fate would have it for two.

WHITTLE (*hearty*): Good old money!

BLOOMSBURY (*austere*): It would have been wrong to have kept it. (*Pause*) That during the years of our cohabitation it had been *our* money to cultivate and be proud of does not alter the fact that originally it was her money rather than my money.

WHITTLE: You could have bought a boat, or a horse or a—

HUBER: Presents for your friends who have sustained you in the accomplishment of this difficult and, if I may say so, rather unpleasant task.

WHITTLE: Your friends who often visited you of an evening when you were part of a set, still.

HUBER: Your friends with whom you reveled and even roistered, once.

BLOOMSBURY (*quoting*): Golden days in the sunshine of our happy youth.

WHITTLE: Yes, I like to see a woman weep, once in a while. Especially a young . . . pretty . . . *rich* woman. Gives me a tingle.

HUBER: A what?

WHITTLE: A tingle. A *frisson*, if you prefer.

HUBER (*hooting*): Listen to him!

WHITTLE: Makes me feel better. (*To* HUBER) What'd you do with the brandy?

HUBER: I have it.

(*Sound: Cork being removed from bottle;* WHITTLE *drinking*)

WHITTLE: Ahhhhh! (*To* BLOOMSBURY) It will be interesting, Bloomsbury, to see what you can do next. To trace your movements, lack of movements. Follow your wrigglings. Watch your crackup or breakdown, if you choose one of those paths. Those thorny paths. Health, even, is not out of the question.

(*Sound:* HUBER *laughing*)

(*Sound:* WHITTLE *laughing*)

(*Sound:* HUBER *laughing cut short*)

WHITTLE: Health, even, is not out of the question. (*Pause*) Unlikely.

BLOOMSBURY: Unlikely?

HUBER (*detached*): Yes, how do you feel?

WHITTLE: Yes, how do you feel?

BLOOMSBURY: How do I feel?

HUBER: Your emotions. Can you give us a quick reading?

WHITTLE: Just a hint, that's all we want.

HUBER: There has been a certain amount of stress after all.

WHITTLE: His color's good.

HUBER: Liver-gray, I'd call it.

BLOOMSBURY: I've traded the house.

WHITTLE: You've done what?

BLOOMSBURY: Traded the house. For a radio. A radio *station*, actually.

(*Music: "The Star-Spangled Banner," coming up*)

HUBER: A radio *station*?

BLOOMSBURY: Yes. Broadcasting. (*Slightly ironic*) One of the glamour industries. It will be an enormously rewarding experience. (*Pause*) It will be some kind of an experience. (*Pause*) A learning experience? (*Pause*) It will go nowhere, I suppose.

(*Music: "The Star-Spangled Banner" up*)

HUBER (*confidential*): Having acquired in exchange for an house that had been theirs, his and hers, a radio or more properly radio station, Bloomsbury could now play "The Star-Spangled Banner," which he had always admired immoderately, on account of its finality, as often as he liked. He could also announce some of his favorite words, the word *nevertheless*, for example.

(*Music: "The Star-Spangled Banner" fading*)

BLOOMSBURY: Nevertheless. Nevertheless. Nevertheless. Never-the-less. (*Pause.* BLOOMSBURY *elegaic*) Well, old girl, here we are. Me speaking into the tube, you lying on your back most likely, giving an ear, I don't doubt. Swell of you to tune me in. (*Pause*) I remember the time you went walking without your shoes, what an evening! You were wearing, I recall, your dove-gray silk (*pause*) or was it liver-gray? (*Pause*) No matter. (*Pause*) Or was it dove's-liver-gray? (*Pause*) No matter. You were wearing, I recall, your gray silk, with a flowered hat. There were chestnuts on the ground; you complained that they felt like rocks under your feet.

MARTHA (*peevish*): My shoes! I forgot my shoes!

BLOOMSBURY (*ardent*): I'll get down, on my hands and knees, and clear a path, my darling. I'll sweep them away with my hands. My bare hands. (*Pause*) Dear Martha!

(*Sound:* BLOOMSBURY *kneeling, sweeping*)

MARTHA: You look absurd down there.

BLOOMSBURY (*from the sidewalk*): What an evening! The chestnut trees are letting go their fruit. Soon it will be time for a turkey. With liver gravy.

MARTHA: I want an ice—a raspberry ice.

BLOOMSBURY (*from the sidewalk*): Certainly, my dear, anything, raspberry ice, cherryberry ice, let me just . . . get . . . these . . . little . . . *mothers.* . . .

(*Sound: Frenzied sweeping; then door slamming*)

MARTHA (*at home*): Next time, if there is a next time, I will wear my shoes. Even if it kills me.

BLOOMSBURY: Did you enjoy your ice?

MARTHA: Minimally.

BLOOMSBURY (*pleading*): We were happy there, weren't we? In the ice-cream parlor? We were pretty as a picture! Man and wife.

MARTHA: When you placed your raspberry-stained muzzle in my glove . . .

BLOOMSBURY: I'll always be here, to sweep away the chestnuts. Whatever happens. Even if nothing happens.

MARTHA (*doubtfully*): You always *have* been here.

BLOOMSBURY: Swell of you to notice that.

MARTHA: It's dark.

BLOOMSBURY: Time for our quarrel.

MARTHA: What is the subject?

BLOOMSBURY (*as if reading from a bulletin board*): "Smallness in the Human Male."

MARTHA (*with satisfaction*): Yes. I say it's willfulness.

BLOOMSBURY: Martha . . .

MARTHA: *Simple . . .* willfulness.

BLOOMSBURY (*pleading*): It was a lack of proper nourishment, during my young years.

MARTHA (*taking a high tone*): Simple and deliberate . . . willfulness. I have decided that you can't have any supper.

BLOOMSBURY: No supper?

MARTHA: You've already gorged yourself on raspberry ice.

BLOOMSBURY: Only two scoops!

MARTHA: You've ruined a good glove with your ardor. And the knees of a decent pair of trousers, too.

BLOOMSBURY: But it was for the love of you!

MARTHA: Hush! Or there'll be no breakfast either.

BLOOMSBURY: But love makes the world go!

MARTHA: Or lunch tomorrow either!

BLOOMSBURY: But we were everything to each other once!

MARTHA: Or supper tomorrow night.

BLOOMSBURY: But perhaps a little toffee?

MARTHA: Ruin your teeth then for all I care!

(*Sound: Pieces of toffee flung on floor*)

BLOOMSBURY: Ah Martha coom now to bed there's a darlin' gul.

MARTHA: Hump off blatherer I've no yet read me Mallarmé for this evenin'.

BLOOMSBURY (*dialect gets heavier*): Ooo Martha dear canna we noo let the dear lad rest this night? When the telly's already shut doon an' th' man o' the house 'as a 'ard-on?

MARTHA: Don't be comin' around wit' yer lewd proposals on a Tuesday night when ye know better.

BLOOMSBURY: But Martha dear where is yer love for me that we talked about in 19 and 58? In the cemetery by the sea?

MARTHA (*contemptuous*): Pisht Mishtar Hard-on ye'd better be lookin' after the Disposall, what's got itself all plogged up.

BLOOMSBURY (*urgent*): Ding the Disposall! Martha me gul, it's yer sweet hide I'm after havin'.

MARTHA: Get yer hands from out of me Playtex, viper, I'm dreadful bored wit yer silly old tool.

BLOOMSBURY: But Marthy dear what of the poetry we vowed wit', in 19 and 58? Aboot the curlew's cry and the white giant's thigh? That we consecrated our union by?

MARTHA: That was then and this is now, ye can be runnin' after that bicycle gul wit' th' tight pants if yer wants a bit of th' auld shiver an' shake.

BLOOMSBURY (*desperate*): Ah Marthy it's no Bicycle Gul that's breakin' me heart but yer sweet self.

MARTHA (*bored*): Keep yer paws off me derrière dear yer makin' me lose me page i' th' book.

(*Music: "The Star-Spangled Banner" up softly*)

BLOOMSBURY (*elegaic*): We went to bed then. We were pretty as a picture. (*Pause*) Man and wife.

(*Music: Theme*)

(*Sound: The car: traffic*)

HUBER: It's idiotic—

BLOOMSBURY (*agreeing in advance*): Yes . . .

HUBER: —that we know no more of the bloody details. Of the extinguishment of your union. Than you have chosen to tell us.

WHITTLE (*accusatory*): Monk.

BLOOMSBURY: What do you want to know?

HUBER: *Everything.*

WHITTLE (*casual*): It would be interesting, I think, as well as in-structive to know, for instance, at what point the situation of living together became untenable, whether you were the insti-gator or she was the instigator, whether she wept when you told her, whether you wept when she told you, whether there were physical fights involving bodily blows or merely objects thrown on your part and on her part, if there were mental cruelties, cruelties of what order and on whose part, whether she had a lover or did not have a lover, whether you had a lover or did not, (*getting down to business*), whether you kept the television or she kept the television, the disposition of the balance of the furnishings including tableware, linens, light bulbs, beds, and baskets, who got the baby if there was a baby, what food remains in the pantry at this time, what happened to the medicine bottles, was it a fun divorce or not a fun divorce, whether she paid the lawyers or you paid the lawyers, what the judge said if there was a judge, whether you asked her for a "date" after the granting of the decree or did not so ask, whether she was touched or not touched by this gesture if there was such a gesture, whether the "date" if there was such a "date" was champagne and roses or not champagne and roses—

HUBER (*suave*): In short, we'd like to get the *feel* of the thing.

WHITTLE: We're *interested*.

HUBER: I remember how it was when my old wife, Eleanor, flew away.

BLOOMSBURY (*thoughtful*): Yes.

HUBER: But only dimly. Because of the years. (*Pause*) The pain of the parting was . . . shall I say . . . exquisite?

WHITTLE: "Exquisite"—what a stupid word.

HUBER: How would you know? You never married.

WHITTLE (*firm*): I may not know about marriage but I know about words. (*Giggles*) Exquisite!

HUBER (*aloof*): You have no delicacy.

WHITTLE: Delicacy! You get better and better!

257

(*Sound: Another car passing, sounding horn*)

WHITTLE: Good Lord!

HUBER (*calm*): An ape. Did you get his license number?

WHITTLE: The brandy has been too much for you. Better let me drive.

HUBER: Out of the question. I am perfectly competent.

WHITTLE: Competent! Your ugly old wife, Eleanor, left you *precisely because* you were a mechanical idiot, she confided in me on the day of the hearing.

HUBER (*amazed*): A mechanical idiot! I wonder what she meant by that?

BLOOMSBURY (*rousing himself*): Surprise, that's the great thing. It keeps the old tissues tense.

(*Sound: "The Star-Spangled Banner"*)

BLOOMSBURY (*remembering*): On that remarkable day, that day unlike any other, that day, if you will pardon me, of days, on that old day from the old days when we were, as they say, young —we walked, if you will forgive the extravagance, hand in hand into a theater where there was a film playing.

(*Sound: Movie sound track, violent*)

BLOOMSBURY: We were there, you and I, because we hadn't rooms and there were no parks and we hadn't an automobile and there were no beaches. We climbed to the topmost balcony.

(*Sound: Movie sound track, more violent*)

BLOOMSBURY: The first thing I knew I was inside your shirt with my hand and I found there something very lovely, soft and warm and, as they say, desirable. It belonged to you. I did not know, then, what to do with it, therefore, I simply (*pause*) simply! (*pause*) held it in my hand.

(*Sound: Movie sound track, most violent*)

MARTHA (*violent*): Get on with it, can't you?

BLOOMSBURY (*abstracted*): I'm watching the picture.

(*Sound: Swelling movie fade-out strings*)

BLOOMSBURY: We watched the picture together, and although this was a kind of intimacy, the other kind had been lost. And to that row of the balcony we, you and I, never returned.

(*Sound:* BLOOMSBURY *weeping as music fades*)

(*Sound: Finger tapping on glass; muffled words*)

BLOOMSBURY: What?

(*Sound: Muffled shouting*)

BLOOMSBURY: What? (*Pause*) Wait a minute, I'll come out.

(*Sound: Door opening and closing, footsteps*)

BLOOMSBURY: Who are you?

WOMAN: A fan. I've been listening to your . . . announcements.

BLOOMSBURY: Oh. I didn't know anyone . . . listened.

WOMAN: Probably a great many people. (*Pause*) You're staring.

BLOOMSBURY: Oh, yes I am. You have a grand . . . figure.

WOMAN: Also a *terrific* sense of humor. (*Pause*) Do you *have* to stare?

BLOOMSBURY: Oh. I'm sorry. (*Making conversation*) So, you're a fan.

WOMAN: Yes. A professional fan. Started very early. You pick out a person to be a fan of, and then you adulate that person. (*Pause*) You ad-u-late him. (*Pause*) Or her.

BLOOMSBURY: Yes.

WOMAN: To begin with, I was president of the Howling Calf Fan Club. That was in, I don't remember the year. I was very young. His magnetism and personality got me. His voice and gestures fascinated me. I ad-u-lated him. *We* ad-u-lated him. When he died, it seemed that a vital part of my imagination died, too.

BLOOMSBURY: That's interesting.

WOMAN: My world of dreams was bare! Do you want to see a picture of Howling Calf?

(Sound: Crackle of photograph)

BLOOMSBURY: Very affecting.

WOMAN: I never actually met Mr. Calf. It wasn't that sort of club. I mean we weren't in actual communication with the star. There was a Tom Jones fan club, and *those* people, now, *they* were in actual communication with the star. When they wanted a remembrance . . .

BLOOMSBURY: A remembrance?

WOMAN: Such as Kleenex that had been used by the star, for instance, with the star's actual sweat on it. Or fingernail clippings, or a hair from the star's horse's tail or mane . . .

BLOOMSBURY: Tail or mane?

WOMAN: The star naturally, noblesse oblige, forwarded that object to them.

BLOOMSBURY: I see.

WOMAN: You're staring.

BLOOMSBURY: I didn't know.

WOMAN: Do you stare at a lot of women?

BLOOMSBURY: Not a *lot*. But quite a number.

WOMAN: Is it fun?

BLOOMSBURY: Not *fun*. But better than nothing.

WOMAN: Do you have affairs?

BLOOMSBURY: Not *affairs*. But sometimes a little flutter.

WOMAN: Well, I have feelings, too.

BLOOMSBURY (*grave*): I think it's very possible. A great big girl like you.

WOMAN (*naïve*): I . . . am . . . your . . . fan. The fan of your announcement and of you, Bloomsbury. Can I sleep here in the studio? Under the piano?

BLOOMSBURY: Won't you be cold, under the piano?

WOMAN: I will warm myself in the light and heat of your personality. Your magnetism. Your memories.

BLOOMSBURY: Ice . . . ice cubes . . .

(*Music: "Jingle Bells" or equivalent*)

BLOOMSBURY (*broadcasting*): I remember the quarrel about the ice cubes. That was one worth . . . remembering. You had posted on the notice board the subject "Refrigeration," and I worried about it all day long, and wondered. Clever minx! I recalled at length that I had complained, once, because the ice cubes were not frozen. But were in fact unfrozen! watery! useless! I had said that there *weren't enough ice cubes*, whereas you had said there were *more than enough*.

MARTHA (*hauteur*): More than enough ice cubes!

BLOOMSBURY: You said that I was a fool, an imbecile, a stupid!, that the machine in your kitchen, which you had procured and caused to be placed there, was without doubt and on immaculate authority the most accomplished machine of its kind known to those who knew about machines of its kind, that among its attributes was the attribute of conceiving, containing, and at the moment of need whelping a *fine* number of ice cubes, so that no matter how grave the demand, how vast the occasion, how indifferent or even hostile the climate, how inept or even treacherous the operator, how brief or even nonexistent the lapse between genesis and parturition, between the wish and the fact, ice cubes in multiples of sufficient would present themselves. (*Pause*) Well (*pause*) I said, (*pause*) perhaps. (*Long pause*) Oh! How you boggled at that word *perhaps*. How you sweated, old girl, and cursed. Your chest heaved, if I may say so, and your eyes (*pause*) your eyes! (*pause*) grew dark.

MARTHA (*rage*): We will, by damn, *count* the by damn ice cubes!

BLOOMSBURY (*with satisfaction*): But you reckoned wrong. You were never a reckoner. You took the ice cubes from the trays and placed them in a bowl. You reckoned that there were in the bowl one hundred and forty-four ice cubes, taking each cube from the tray and placing it in the bowl, meanwhile bearing in mind the total obtainable by simple multiplication of the spaces in the trays. Thus having it, in this as in other matters, both ways! However, you failed, on this as on other occasions, to consider the imponderables. In this instance the fact that I, unobserved by you, had put three of the cubes into my drink! (*Zest*) Which I then drank! (*Additional zest*) And that one had missed the bowl entirely and fallen into the sink! And melted there! And that two more, driven to a frenzy of excitement by the proximity of your person, had trickled away (*pause*) into drops of dirty water (*pause*) on the countertop. (*Pause*) Suicide. (*Pause*) For love. (*Briskly*) These events precluded sadly enough the number of ice cubes in the bowl from adding to a number corresponding to the number of spaces in the trays. Meaning, *not enough*. Proving, that *there is no justice*. (*Pause*) What a defeat for you! What a victory for me! It was my first victory, I fear I went quite out of my head. I dragged you to the floor, among the ice cubes, which you had flung there, in pique and chagrin, and forced you (*pause*) with results that I considered then, and consider now, to have been "first-rate." I thought I detected in you (*pause*), I thought I detected in you . . .

MARTHA: Bang the Bicycle Gul, if you want enthusiasm.

(*Music: "A Bicycle Built for Two" or equivalent*)

BLOOMSBURY: Ah Daisy where do you be goin'?

DAISY: Ta grandmather's, bein' it please yer lardship.

BLOOMSBURY: An' what a fine young soft young warm young thing ya have there Daisy on yer bicycle seat.

DAISY: Ooo yer lardship ye've an evil head on yer, I'll bet yer sez that t'all us guls.

BLOOMSBURY: Naw Daisy and the truth of the matter is, there's nivver a gul come down my street wi' such a fine one as yers.

DAISY: Yer a bold one yer worship and that's Gawd's bloody truth.

BLOOMSBURY: Lemme just feel of her a trifle Daisy, there's a good gul.

DAISY: Ooo Mishtar Bloomsbury, I likes a bit o' fun as good as the next un but me husbing's watchin' from the porch wi' 'is Spotter Scope.

BLOOMSBURY: Pother Daisy it won't be leavin' any marks, we'll just slither behind this tree.

DAISY: Ring me bicycle bell yer lardship he'll think I'm after sellin' me Good Humors.

BLOOMSBURY: That I will Daisy I'll give 'er a ring like she nivver had before.

(*Music: Wagner's* Tristan *or equivalent rises and then fades*)

BLOOMSBURY (*tender*): Have ye heard the news Daisy, that Martha me wife has left me in a yareplane? On the bloody Champagne Flight?

DAISY: O yer wonderfulness, wot a cheeky lot to be pullin' the plug on a lovely man like yourself.

BLOOMSBURY: Well that's how the cock curls, Daisy, there's naught left of her but a bottle of Breck in the boodwar.

DAISY: She was a bitch that she was to be committin' this act of lèse majesty against the sovereign person of yer mightiness.

BLOOMSBURY: She locked herself i' th' john Daisy toward the last, an' wouldn't come out not even for Flag Day.

DAISY (*righteous*): Incredible Mishtar Bloomsbury to think that such as that coexist wi' us good guls side by side in the Twentieth Century.

BLOOMSBURY: An' no more lovey-kindness than a stick, an' no more gratitude than a glass of Milky Magnesia.

DAISY: What bought her clothes at the Salvation Army by th' look of her, on th' Whirling Credit Plan.

BLOOMSBURY: I fingerprinted her fingerpaintings so she said, and wallowed in sex what is more.

DAISY: Coo! Mishtar Bloomsbury, me husbing Jack brings the telly right into th' bed with 'im, it's bumpin' me back all night long.

BLOOMSBURY: I' th' bed?

DAISY: I' th' bed.

BLOOMSBURY (*sentimental*): It's been a weary long time, Daisy, since love 'as touched my hart.

DAISY: Ooo yer elegance, there's not a young gul i' th' Western Hemisphere as could withstand the grandeur of such a swell person as you.

BLOOMSBURY: It's marriage Daisy what has ruined me for love.

DAISY: It's a hard notion me Bloomie boy but tragically true nonetheless.

BLOOMSBURY: I don't want pity, Daisy, there's little enough rapport between adults wi'out clouding the issue wi' (*pause*) false (*pause*) or misleading (*pause*) sentiment.

DAISY: I couldn't agree more yer gorgeousness, damme if I haven't told Jack a thousand times, that rapport is the only thing . . .

(*Music: "The Star-Spangled Banner" played at double time*)

WHITTLE (*urgent*): When he interrogated himself about the matter, about how it felt to operate a radio, or radio station, of his own, Bloomsbury told himself the truth, that it felt fine. Nevertheless he felt somewhat futile. For there had been no response from *her*, she who figured, as both subject and object, in the announcements of this period . . .

BLOOMSBURY (*broadcasting*): Matriculate. Matriculate. Matriculate. Ma-tric-u-late.

(*Sound: Door opening and closing*)

BLOOMSBURY: Differentiation. Differ-en-ti-ation.

WOMAN: Good morning.

BLOOMSBURY: Good morning.

WOMAN (*waking*): Uumph. It's a bit bumpy, under the piano.

BLOOMSBURY: Yes. I would imagine. It's a bit bumpy in here, too. Under the console.

WOMAN: Yes. I would imagine.

BLOOMSBURY: I move the chair away and sleep under the console.

WOMAN: Yes. Is there coffee?

BLOOMSBURY: Yes. On the hot plate.

WOMAN: May I have some?

BLOOMSBURY: Certainly.

(*Sound: Coffee being poured*)

WOMAN: It's good. (*Pause*) Is it instant?

BLOOMSBURY (*bothered*): Is what what?

WOMAN: The coffee. Is it instant?

BLOOMSBURY: I never looked. I just sort of dump the coffee in the—

WOMAN: I liked that word.

BLOOMSBURY: Which word.

WOMAN: Ma-tric-u-late. It's nice to (*pause*) wake up to.

BLOOMSBURY: Is it?

WOMAN: Yes. It's like having a voice in your ear. A warm voice breathing in your ear. A voice breathing in your ear, warmly. Warmly and intelligently.

BLOOMSBURY: Warmly and intelligently?

WOMAN: Yes. It's simpatico.

BLOOMSBURY (*trying the word out for possible use*): Simpatico. Simpatico.

WOMAN (*trying to get his attention*): Tell me about your early life.

BLOOMSBURY (*grave*): I was, in a sense, hopeful.

WOMAN: In what sense?

BLOOMSBURY: In the sense that I married.

WOMAN: Was it love?

BLOOMSBURY: Temporary love.

WOMAN: It did not endure?

BLOOMSBURY: Less than a decade.

WOMAN: But while it endured—

BLOOMSBURY: It filled me with a somber (*pause*) and paradoxical (*pause*) joy.

WOMAN: Coo! Doesn't sound joyful to me.

BLOOMSBURY: It was not a barrel of fun. (*Pause*) Perhaps a bucket of fun?

(*Music: Mournful; Albinoni* Adagio in D Minor *or equivalent*)

BLOOMSBURY (*broadcasting*): The details of our housekeeping, yours and mine. The scuff under the bed, the fug in the corners. You planted prickly pear in the parlor floor. Saved cleaning, you said. Oh, you were a one! You veiled yourself from me; there were parts I could have and parts I couldn't have, and the rules would change in the middle of the game. I could never be sure which parts were allowed and which, not. Some days I couldn't have anything at all. (*Pause*) The bed. (*Pause*) Your mother's bed. (*Pause*) Brought to our union with your mother in it, she lay like a sword between us. Well, I said, what about the child?

MARTHA: Up the child, 'twasn't what I wanted anyway.

(*Sound: Abrupt wail of child*)

BLOOMSBURY: What, then, did you want?

MARTHA: Pish, nothing you could supply.

BLOOMSBURY: Maybe.

MARTHA: Not bloody likely.

MOTHER (*echoing daughter*): Not bloody likely!

BLOOMSBURY: A man came, in a hat. In the hat was a little feather.

MARTHA: Jack, this is my husband.

BLOOMSBURY: They went into the bedroom and closed the door. I stood outside the door.

(*Sound: A long moan followed by knocking on door*)

BLOOMSBURY: What are you doing in there?

(*Sound: Exaggerated moan followed by knocking on door*)

BLOOMSBURY: What are you doing in there?

MARTHA (*calling through door*): Go away and mind your own silly business!

JACK (*through door*): Go away and don't be bothering people with things on their minds.

MARTHA (*through door*): Insensitive brute!

JACK (*through door*): Filthy cad!

MARTHA (*through door*): Some people!

JACK (*through door*): The cheek of the thing!

BLOOMSBURY: I watched at the door until nightfall, but could hear no more words, only grunts and moans, and sighs. I then went to the attic to obtain our copy of *Ideal Marriage,* by T. H. Van de Velde, M.D., to see if this situation were treated of therein. But it was not. At length the door opened—

(*Sound: Door opening and closing*)

BLOOMSBURY: —and your mother emerged, looking, as they say, "put out."

MOTHER: Common sneak!

BLOOMSBURY: But what of those in the bed? Laughing and tickling.

MOTHER (*pronouncing judgment*): You are a bad man, I knew it, I always knew it, I told her, I told everyone. (*Fades, muttering*)

BLOOMSBURY: I then became, if you can believe it, somewhat melancholy. Could not we two skins, you and me, climb and cling for all the days that were left? Which were not after all so very many days? Without the interpolation of such as Jack? And, no doubt, others yet to come?

(*Music: Albinoni Adagio*)

(*Sound: Ice cubes in glass*)

WOMAN: What's that?

BLOOMSBURY: Whiskey.

WOMAN: Can I have a bit?

BLOOMSBURY: There's only one glass.

WOMAN: Then a bit of yours.

BLOOMSBURY: Help yourself.

(*Sound: Drinking*)

WOMAN (*tentative*): Do I impress you?

BLOOMSBURY: In what way?

WOMAN: As a possible partner? Sexually, I mean?

BLOOMSBURY: I haven't considered it.

WOMAN: They say I'm sexy.

BLOOMSBURY (*helpful*): I don't doubt it. I mean, it's plausible.

WOMAN: I am yours. If you want me.

BLOOMSBURY: Yes, there's the difficulty, making up my mind.

WOMAN: You have only to make the slightest gesture. A cough. A cry.

BLOOMSBURY: Probably I would not enjoy it, now.

WOMAN: Shall I take off my clothes?

(*Sound:* BLOOMSBURY *getting out of chair*)

BLOOMSBURY: Martha, old skin, why can't you let the old days die? That were, then, days of anger, passion, and dignity, but are, now, days that are dead?

(*Sound:* MARTHA *sobbing*)

MARTHA: You looked interested at first.

BLOOMSBURY: It was kind of you to try it. Thoughtful. You were most appealing. Tempting, even. I was fooled for whole moments. You look well in trousers.

MARTHA: Thank you. You said I have a lovely rump. You said that, at least.

BLOOMSBURY: And so it is. Lovely. Heart-shaped.

MARTHA: You can't forget? About Dudley?

BLOOMSBURY: Dudley who?

MARTHA: Dudley who was my possible lover?

BLOOMSBURY: Before or after Jack?

MARTHA: Dudley who in fact broke up our ménage?

BLOOMSBURY (*helpful*): No, Dudley is unforgettable.

MARTHA: Tell me about the joy again.

BLOOMSBURY: There was some joy. I can't deny it.

MARTHA: Was it really like you said? Somber and paradoxical?

BLOOMSBURY (*gallant*): It was all of that. Then.

MARTHA: Then!

(*Music: "The Star-Spangled Banner" up softly*)

MARTHA: Then there is no hope for us? Again?

BLOOMSBURY: None. That I know of. Again.

MARTHA: You've found somebody you like better?

BLOOMSBURY: That has nothing to do with it.

MARTHA (*suddenly vicious*): Balls. I know you and your letchy ways.

BLOOMSBURY: Goodbye, Martha.

(*Music: "The Star-Spangled Banner" up*)

BLOOMSBURY (*broadcasting*): Goodbye. Goodbye. Goodbye. Goodbye. Goodbye. (*Fades*) Goodbye. Goodbye.

(*Sound: The car*)

WHITTLE (*exasperated*): But what is the *feeling*?

HUBER: Yes, what is the feeling?

BLOOMSBURY: Indeterminate. Hard and soft. At the same time. Ineffable.

WHITTLE (*sneering*): Ineffable!

BLOOMSBURY: The question is not what is the feeling but what is the meaning?

HUBER: Christ, I'll tell you about *my* affair.

WHITTLE: What about it?

HUBER: It was a Red Cross girl. Named Buck Rogers.

WHITTLE: Of what did it consist?

HUBER: It consisted of going to the top of the Chrysler Building and looking out over the city.

WHITTLE (*disparaging*): Not much meat there. How did it end?

HUBER: Badly.

WHITTLE: Did she jump?

HUBER: I jumped.

WHITTLE: You were always a jumper.

HUBER: Yes. I had taken precautions.

WHITTLE: Did your chute open?

HUBER: With a sound like timber falling. But she never knew.

WHITTLE (*sadly*): The end of the affair.

HUBER (*bright*): But what a wonderful view of the city.

WHITTLE (*to* BLOOMSBURY): So, now, *give us the feeling.*

HUBER: If there is emotion, it is only just that you share it with your friends.

WHITTLE: Who are no doubt all you have left in the world.

HUBER (*thinking aloud*): Possibly there are relatives, of one kind or another.

WHITTLE: Hardly likely. Now that there is no more money I would hazard that there are no more relatives either.

(*Sound: Highway noises*)

HUBER: Emotion! When was the last time we had any?

WHITTLE: The war, I expect. All those chaps going West.

HUBER (*to* BLOOMSBURY): I'll give you a hundred dollars for the feeling.

BLOOMSBURY: No.

WHITTLE: We are fine enough to be a crowd at the airport so your wife will not weep . . .

HUBER: . . . but not fine enough to be taken into your confidence. Into your bosom.

BLOOMSBURY: Not a matter of fine enough.

WHITTLE: God, what manner of man is this?

HUBER: Not to be believed.

WHITTLE: I'll give you two hundred dollars. For the feeling.

BLOOMSBURY: Once, in a movie house, Tuesday Weld suddenly turned on the screen, looked me full in the face, and said, "You are a good man. You are good, good, good." I rose and walked from the theater, gratification singing in my heart.

WHITTLE: Is the feeling like that?

BLOOMSBURY: No. That's the point. It's not like that. It's a not-feeling.

HUBER (*slightly awed*): Ineffable?

BLOOMSBURY: Ineffable.

WHITTLE (*reverent*): I've never had a feeling that was . . . ineffable.

HUBER: There was a white rat, once, that I was rather fond of. And Mother, of course. (*Hastily*) But I don't meant to compare . . . those feelings . . . with . . .

WHITTLE: And the flag, of course. Hard to say what one feels about the flag. (*Pause*) Recently.

(*Sound: Traffic*)

BLOOMSBURY: It's a complex of feelings. Of not-feelings. A nexus of . . . not-feelings—that would be a way of putting it. (*Pause*) Tuesday Weld. Reminded me a bit of the Bicycle Gul.

HUBER: The Bicycle Gul?

DAISY (*echo*): Ooo yer elegance, there's not a young gul i' th' Western Hemisphere as could withstand the grandeur (*pause*) of such a swell person (*pause*) as you.

BLOOMSBURY: A girl I knew once. Slightly. For a space. (*Pause*) A short space.

WHITTLE: Did you get on well together?

BLOOMSBURY: Like a house afire. (*Pause*) Like a burning house. (*Pause*) For a space. (*Pause*) A short space. (*Pause*) Temporary love. (*Pause*) Golden days in the sunshine of our happy youth. (*Pause*) Brief love. (*Pause*) Golden days, in the sunshine of our happy youth.

(*Music: "Golden Days" song from* The Student Prince)

(*Music: Segue to theme*)

THE CONSERVATORY

Notes:
The two women, MAGGIE *and* HILDA, *are about thirty-five.*

The bells are funereal; the theme on the contrary should be upbeat, for example, the Respighi on Side 2 of the Deutsche Grammophon 2530 247, or equivalent.

An extremely serious and rather formal way of speaking is suggested. The colloquialisms should play against this.

(Music: Theme)

(Sound: Bells)

MAGGIE: C'mon Hilda don't fret.

HILDA: Well Maggie it's a blow.

MAGGIE: Don't let it bother you, don't let it get you down.

HILDA: Once I thought they were going to admit me to the Conservatory but now I know they will never admit me to the Conservatory.

MAGGIE: Yes they are very particular about who they admit to the Conservatory. They will never admit you to the Conservatory.

HILDA: They will never admit me to the Conservatory, I know that now.

MAGGIE: You are not Conservatory material I'm afraid. That's the plain truth of it.

HILDA: You're not important, they told me, just remember that, you're not important, what's so important about you?

MAGGIE: C'mon Hilda don't fret.

HILDA: Well Maggie it's a blow.

(*Sound: Match struck, three times*)

HILDA (*elegiac*): When I was a little girl I made mud pies, dangled strings down crayfish holes, hoping the idiot crayfish would catch hold and allow themselves to be hauled into the light of day. Snarled and cried, ate ice cream and sang "How High the Moon." Popped the wings off crickets and floated stray Scrabble pieces in ditchwater. All perfect and ordinary and perfect.

MAGGIE: Featherings of ease and bliss.

HILDA: I was preparing myself. Getting ready for the great day.

MAGGIE: Icy day with salt on all the sidewalks.

HILDA: Sketching attitudes and forming pretty speeches.

MAGGIE: Pitching pennies at a line scratched in the dust.

HILDA: Doing and redoing my lustrous abundant hair.

MAGGIE (*as if police radio dispatcher*): Man down. Center and One Eight.

HILDA: Tied flares to my extremities and wound candy canes into my lustrous abundant hair. Getting ready for the great day.

MAGGIE: For I do not deny that I am a little out of temper.

HILDA: Glitches in the system as yet unapprehended.

MAGGIE: Oh that clown band. Oh its sweet strains.

HILDA: Most excellent and dear friend. Who the silly season's named for.

MAGGIE: My demands were not met. One, two, three, four.

275

HILDA: I admire your dash and address. But regret your fear and prudence.

MAGGIE: Always worth making the effort, always.

HILDA: Yes that's something we do. Our damnedest. They can't take that away from us.

MAGGIE: The Secretary of State cares. And the Secretary of Commerce.

HILDA: Yes they're clued in. We are not unprotected. Soldiers and policemen.

MAGGIE (*as before*): Man down. Corner of Mercer and One Six.

HILDA: Paying lots of attention. A clear vision of what can and can't be done.

MAGGIE: Progress extending far into the future. Dams and aqueducts. The amazing strength of the powerful.

HILDA: Organizing our deepest wishes as a mother foresightedly visits a store that will be closed tomorrow.

MAGGIE: Friendship's the best thing.

HILDA: One of the best things.

(*Sound: Landslide, five seconds*)

MAGGIE: I performed in a hall. Alone under the burning lights.

HILDA: The hall jampacked with admiring faces. Except for a few.

MAGGIE: Julia was there. Rotten Julia.

HILDA: But I mean you really like her don't you?

MAGGIE: Well I mean who doesn't like violet eyes?

HILDA: Got to make the effort, scratch where it itches, plans, schemes, directives, guidelines.

MAGGIE: Well I mean who doesn't like frisky knees?

HILDA: Yes she's lost her glow. Gone utterly.

MAGGIE: The strains of the city working upon an essentially non-urban sensibility.

HILDA: But I love the city and will not hear it traduced.

MAGGIE: Well, me too. But after all. But still.

HILDA: Think Julia's getting it on with Bally.

MAGGIE: Yeah I heard about that he's got a big mouth.

HILDA: But handsome hipbones, got to give him that.

MAGGIE: I remember, I can feel them still, pressing into me as they once did on hot afternoons and cool nights and feverish first-thing-in-the-mornings.

HILDA: Yes, Bally is a regal memory for everyone.

(Sound: Guillotine blade falling)

MAGGIE: My best ghost. The one I think about, in bitter times and good.

HILDA: Trying to get my colors together. Trying to play one off against another. Trying for cancellation.

MAGGIE: I respect your various phases. Your sweet, even discourse. Nonculminating kind of ultimately affectless activity.

HILDA: Which you mime so well in auditoria large and small.

(Sound: Guillotine blade falling)

MAGGIE *(compassionate)*: C'mon Hilda don't fret.

HILDA: Well Maggie it's a blow.

MAGGIE: When are you going to change yourself, change yourself into a loaf or a fish?

HILDA: Christian imagery is taught at the Conservatory, also Islamic imagery and the imagery of Public Safety.

MAGGIE: Red, yellow, and green circles.

HILDA: When they told me I got between the poles of my rickshaw and trotted heavily away.

MAGGIE: The great black ironwork doors of the Conservatory barred to you forever.

HILDA: Trotted heavily away in the direction of my house. My small, poor house.

MAGGIE: C'mon Hilda don't fret.

HILDA: Yes, I am still trying to get into the Conservatory, although my chances are probably worse than ever.

MAGGIE: They don't want pregnant women in the Conservatory.

HILDA: I didn't tell them. I lied about it.

MAGGIE: Didn't they ask you?

HILDA: No they forgot to ask me and I didn't tell them.

MAGGIE: Well then it's hardly on that account that—

HILDA: I felt they knew.

MAGGIE: The Conservatory is hostile to the new spirit, the new spirit is not liked there.

HILDA: Well Maggie it's a blow nevertheless. I had to go back to my house.

MAGGIE: Where although you entertain the foremost artists and intellectuals of your time you grow progressively more despondent and depressed.

HILDA: Yes he was a frightful lawyer.

MAGGIE: Lover?

HILDA: That too, frightful. He said he could not get me into the Conservatory because of my unimportance.

MAGGIE: Was there a fee?

HILDA: There's always a fee. Pounds and pounds.

MAGGIE: I stood on the terrace at the rear of the Conservatory and studied the flagstones reddened with the lifebloods of generations of Conservatory students. Standing there I reflected: Hilda will never be admitted to the Conservatory.

HILDA: I read the Conservatory Circular and my name was not among those listed.

MAGGIE: Well I suppose it was in part your espousal of the new spirit that counted against you.

HILDA: I will never abjure the new spirit.

MAGGIE: And you're a veteran too, I should have thought that would have weighed in your favor—

(*Sound: Fragment of chamber music, slow: four seconds*)

MAGGIE: And yet with my really wizard! good humor and cheerful thoughtless air, I have caused a lot of trouble.

HILDA: I suppose that's true. Strictly speaking.

MAGGIE: Bounding into the woods on all fours barking like a mother biting at whatever moves in front of me—

HILDA: Do you also save string?

MAGGIE: On my free evenings and paid holidays. Making the most of the time I have here on this earth. Knotting, sewing, weaving, welding.

HILDA: Naming babies, Lou, Lew, Louis.

MAGGIE: And his toes, wonderful toes, that man has got toes.

HILDA: Decorated with rings and rubber bands.

MAGGIE: Has a partiality for white. White gowns, shifts, aprons, flowers, sauces.

HILDA: He was a salty dog all right. Salty dog.

MAGGIE: I was out shooting with him once, pheasant, he got one, with his fancy shotgun. The bird bursting like an exploding pillow.

(*Sound: Someone brushing teeth vigorously*)

HILDA: Have to stand there and watch them, their keen eyes scanning the whatever. And then say "Good shot!"

MAGGIE: Oh I could have done better, better, I was lax.

(*Sound: Repeat of above*)

HILDA: Or worse, don't fret about it, could have put your cute little butt in worse places, in thrall to dismaler personalities.

(*Sound: Sewing machine starting and stopping; eight seconds*)

MAGGIE: I was making an effort. What I do best.

(*Sound: Guillotine blade falling*)

HILDA: You are excellent at it. Really first-rate.

MAGGIE: Never fail to knock myself out. Put pictures on the walls and pads under the rugs.

HILDA: I really admire you. I really do. To the teeth.

MAGGIE: Bust your ass, it's the only way.

HILDA: As we learn from studying the careers of all the great figures of the past. Heraclitus and Launcelot du Lac.

MAGGIE: Polish the doorknobs with Brasso and bring in the sea bass in its nest of seaweed.

HILDA: And not only that. And not only that.

MAGGIE: Tickling them when they want to be tickled. Refraining, when they do not.

HILDA: Large and admirable men. Not neglecting the small and ignoble. Dealing evenhandedly with every situation on a case-by-case basis.

MAGGIE: Yeah yeah yeah yeah yeah.

HILDA: Knew a guy wore his stomach on his sleeve. I dealt with the problem using astrology in its medical aspects. His stomach this, his stomach that. God almighty but it was tiresome, tiresome in the extreme. I dealt with it by using astrology in its medical aspects.

MAGGIE: To each his own. Handmade bread and individual attention.

HILDA: You've got to have something besides yourself. A cat, too often.

MAGGIE: I could have done better but I was dumb. When you're young you're sometimes dumb.

HILDA: Yeah yeah yeah yeah yeah. I remember.

(*Sound: Door slamming*)

MAGGIE: Well let's have a drink.

HILDA: Well I don't mind if I do.

MAGGIE: I have Goldwasser, Bombay gin, and Old Jeb.

HILDA: Well I wouldn't mind a scotch myself.

(*Sound: Door slamming*)

MAGGIE: I have that too.

HILDA: Growing older and with age, less beautiful.

MAGGIE: Yeah I've noticed that. Losing your glow.

HILDA: Just gonna sit in the wrinkling house and wrinkle. Get older and worse.

MAGGIE: Once you lose your glow you never get it back.

HILDA: Sometimes by virtue of the sun roaring through the leaves of the trees on a summer's day.

MAGGIE: Wrinkling you so that you look like a roast turkey.

HILDA: As in the case with the Oni of Ife. Saw him on television.

MAGGIE: Wrinkled and wrinkled and wrinkled.

HILDA: Let me show you this picture.

MAGGIE: Yes that's very lovely. What is it?

HILDA: It's *Vulcan and Maia*.

MAGGIE: Yes. He's got his hooks into her. She's struggling to get away.

HILDA: Vigorously? Vigorously. Yes.

MAGGIE: Who's the artist?

HILDA: Spranger.

MAGGIE: Never heard of him.

HILDA: Well.

MAGGIE: Yes, you may hang it. Anywhere you like. On that wall or that wall or that wall or that wall.

HILDA: Thank you.

MAGGIE: Probably I can get ahead by working hard, paying attention to detail.

HILDA: I thought that. Once I thought that.

MAGGIE: Reading a lot of books and having good ideas.

HILDA: Well that's not bad. I mean it's a means.

MAGGIE: Do something wonderful. I don't know what.

HILDA: Like a bass player plucking the great thick strings of his instrument with powerful plucks.

MAGGIE: Blood vessels bursting in my face just under the skin all the while.

HILDA: Hurt by malicious criticisms all very well grounded.

MAGGIE: For Leatherheart, I turn my back. My lustrous, abundant back.

HILDA: That cracks them up does it?

MAGGIE: At least they know I'm in town.

HILDA: Ease myself into bed of an evening brain jumping with hostile fluids.

MAGGIE: It's black beans in a pot.

HILDA: It's confetti in the swimming pool.

MAGGIE: It's U-joints in the vichyssoise.

HILDA: It's staggers under the moon.

(*Sound: Four identical bass fiddle notes, plucked; rapid*)

MAGGIE: He told me terrible things in the evening of that day as we sat side by side holding hands waiting for the rain to wash the watercolors from his watercolor paper. Waiting for the rain to wash the paper clean, quite clean.

HILDA: Took me by the hand and led me through all the rooms. Many rooms.

MAGGIE: I know all about it.

HILDA: The kitchen is especially splendid.

MAGGIE: Quite so.

HILDA: A dozen Filipinos with trays.

MAGGIE: Close to that figure.

HILDA: Trays with edibles. Wearables. Readables. Collectibles.

MAGGIE: Ah, you're a fool. A damned fool.

HILDA: I?

MAGGIE: Goodbye, madame. Dip if you will your hand in the holy-water font as you leave, and attend as well to the poorbox just to the right of the door.

HILDA: Figs and kiss-me-nots. I would meet you upon this honestly.

MAGGIE: I went far beyond the time normally allotted for a speaker.

HILDA: In Mexico City. Wearing the black jacket with the silver conchos. And trousers of fire pink.

MAGGIE: Visited a health club there, my rear looked like two pocketbooks, they worked on it.

HILDA: You were making an effort.

MAGGIE: Run in the mornings too, take green tea at noon, study household management, finance, repair of devices.

HILDA: Born with a silver hoe in your mouth.

MAGGIE: Yes. Got to get going, got to make some progress.

HILDA: Followed by the development of head banging in the child.

(*Sound: Bass fiddle notes as before*)

MAGGIE: I went far beyond the time normally allotted to, or for, a speaker.

(*Sound: Bass fiddle*)

MAGGIE: It is fair to say they were enthralled.

(*Sound: Bass fiddle*)

MAGGIE: And transfixed.

(*Sound: Bass fiddle*)

MAGGIE: Inappropriate laughter at some points but I didn't mind that.

HILDA: Did the Eminence arrive?

MAGGIE: In a cab. In his robes of scarlet.

HILDA: He does a tough Eminence.

MAGGIE: Yes very tough. I was allowed to kiss the ring. He sat there, in the audience, just like another member of the audience. Just like anybody. Transfixed and enthralled.

HILDA: Whirling and jigging in the red light and throwing veils on the floor and throwing gloves on the floor . . .

MAGGIE: One of my finest. They roared for ten minutes.

HILDA: I am so proud of you. Again and again. Proud of you.

MAGGIE: Oh well, yes. I agree. Quite right. Absolutely.

HILDA: What? Are you sure? Are you quite sure? Let me show you this picture.

MAGGIE: Yes, that's quite grand. What is it?

HILDA: It's *Tancred Succored by Ermina.*

MAGGIE: Yes she's sopping up the blood there, got a big rag, seems a sweet girl, God he's out of it isn't he, dead or dying horse at upper left . . . Who's the artist?

HILDA: Ricchi.

MAGGIE: Never heard of him.

HILDA: Well.

MAGGIE: I'll take it. You may stack it with the others, against that wall or that wall or that wall or that wall . . .

HILDA: Thank you. Where shall I send the bill?

MAGGIE: Send it anywhere you like. Anywhere your little heart desires.

HILDA: Well I hate to be put in this position. Bending and subservient.

MAGGIE: Heavens! I'd not noticed. Let me raise you up.

HILDA: Maybe in a few days. A few days or a few years.

MAGGIE: Lave you with bee jelly and bone oil.

HILDA: And if I have ever forgiven you your astonishing successes—

MAGGIE: Mine.

HILDA: And if I have ever been able to stomach your serial triumphs . . .

(*Sound: Door slamming*)

MAGGIE: The sky. A rectangle of gray in the foreground and behind that, a rectangle of puce. And behind that, a square of silver-gilt.

HILDA: Got to get it together, get the big bucks.

MAGGIE: Yes I'm thinking hard, thinking hard.

HILDA: Frolic and detour.

MAGGIE: What's that mean?

HILDA: I don't know it's just a bit of legal language I picked up somewhere.

MAGGIE: Now that I take a long look at you—

HILDA: In the evening by the fireside—

MAGGIE: I find you utterly delightful. Abide with me. We'll have little cakes with smarm, yellow smarm on them—

HILDA: Yes I just feel so fresh and free here. One doesn't feel that way every day, or every week.

(Sound: Landslide, as before)

MAGGIE: Last night (pause) at two (pause) the barking dog in the apartment above (pause) stopped barking. Its owners (pause) had returned. I went into the kitchen (pause) and barked through the roof (pause) for an hour. I believe (pause) I was understood.

HILDA (police voice): Man down. Corner of Water and Eight Nine.

MAGGIE: Another wallow?

HILDA: I've wallowed for today thank you. Control is the thing.

MAGGIE: Control used to be the thing. Now, abandon.

HILDA: I'll never achieve abandon.

MAGGIE: Work hard and concentrate. Try Clown, Baby, Hellhag, Witch, the Laughing Cavalier. The Lord helps those—

HILDA: Purple bursts in my face as if purple staples had been stapled there every which way.

MAGGIE: Hurt by malicious criticisms all very well grounded.

HILDA: Oh that clown band. Oh its sweet strains.

MAGGIE: The sky. A rectangle of glister. Behind which, a serene brown. A yellow bar, vertical, in the upper right.

(*Sound: Fabric tearing; four seconds*)

MAGGIE: I love you, Gottlieb, quite exceptionally.

HILDA: By gum I think you mean it. I think you do.

MAGGIE: It's *Portia Wounding Her Thigh*.

HILDA: It's *Wolfram Looking at His Wife Whom He Has Imprisoned with the Corpse of Her Lover*.

MAGGIE: If you need a friend I'm yours till the end.

(*Sound: Fabric tearing; four seconds*)

HILDA: Your gracious and infinitely accommodating presence. (*Pause*) It's said that they import a cook, on feast days.

MAGGIE: They have naked models too.

HILDA: Do you really think so? I'm not surprised.

MAGGIE: The best students get their dinners sent up on trays.

HILDA: Do you really think so? I'm not surprised.

MAGGIE: Grain salads and large portions of choice meats.

HILDA: Oh it hurts, it hurts, it hurts.

MAGGIE: Bread with drippings, and on feast days, cake.

HILDA: I'm as gifted as they are, I'm as gifted as some of them.

MAGGIE: Decisions made by a committee of ghosts. They drop black beans or white beans into a pot.

HILDA: Once I thought I was to be admitted. There were encouraging letters.

MAGGIE: You're not Conservatory material I'm afraid. Only the best material is Conservatory material.

HILDA: I'm as good as some of those who rest now in the soft Conservatory beds.

MAGGIE: Merit is always considered closely.

HILDA: I could smile back at the smiling faces of the swift, dangerous teachers.

MAGGIE: Yes, we have naked models. No, the naked models are not emotionally meaningful to us.

HILDA: I could work with clay or paste things together.

MAGGIE: Yes, sometimes we paste things on the naked models—clothes, mostly. Yes, sometimes we play our Conservatory violins, cellos, trumpets for the naked models, or sing to them, or correct their speech, as our deft fingers fly over the sketch pads . . .

HILDA: I suppose I could fill out another application, or several.

MAGGIE: Yes, you have considerable of a belly on you now. I remember when it was flat, flat as a book.

HILDA: I will die if I don't get into the Conservatory, die.

MAGGIE: Naw you won't you're just saying that.

HILDA: I will completely croak if I don't get into the Conservatory, I promise you that.

MAGGIE: Things are not so bad, you can always do something else, I don't know what, c'mon Hilda be reasonable.

HILDA: My whole life depends on it.

MAGGIE (*elegiac*): Oh God I remember when it was flat. Didn't we tear things up, though? I remember running around that town, and hiding in dark places, that was a great town and I'm sorry we left it.

HILDA: Now we are grown, grown and proper.

MAGGIE: Well, I misled you. The naked models are emotionally meaningful to us.

HILDA: They are?

MAGGIE: We love them and sleep with them all the time—before breakfast, after breakfast, during breakfast.

HILDA: Why that's all right!

MAGGIE: Why that's rather neat!

HILDA: I like that!

MAGGIE: That's not so bad!

(*Sound: Sleigh bells; fifteen seconds*)

HILDA: I wish you hadn't told me that.

MAGGIE: C'mon Hilda don't be so single-minded, there are lots of other things you can do if you want.

HILDA: I guess they operate on some kind of principle of exclusivity. Keeping some people out while letting other people in.

MAGGIE: We got a Coushatta Indian in there, real full-blooded Coushatta Indian.

HILDA: In there?

MAGGIE: Yes. He does hanging walls out of scraps of fabric and twigs, very beautiful, and he does sand paintings and plays on whistles of various kinds, sometimes he chants, and he bangs on a drum, works in silver, and he's also a weaver, and he translates things from Coushatta into English and from English into Coushatta and he's also a crack shot can bulldog steers and catch catfish on trotlines and ride bareback and make medicine out of common ingredients, aspirin mostly, and he sings and he's also an actor. He's very talented.

HILDA: My whole life depends on it.

MAGGIE: Listen Hilda maybe you could be an Associate. We have this deal whereby you pay twelve bucks a year and that makes you an Associate. You get the Circular and have all the privileges of an Associate.

HILDA: What are they?

MAGGIE: You get the Circular.

HILDA: That's all?

MAGGIE: Well I guess you're right.

HILDA: Oh.

MAGGIE (*Pause*): Your distress is poignant to me.

HILDA: I'll have the baby right here.

MAGGIE: Well maybe there'll be good news one of these days.

HILDA: I feel like a dead person sitting in a chair.

MAGGIE: You're still pretty and attractive.

(*Sound: Breaking glass*)

HILDA: That's good to hear, I'm pleased you think that.

MAGGIE: And warm you're warm you're very warm.

HILDA: I am warm. Warm.

MAGGIE: Weren't you in the Peace Corps also years ago?

HILDA: I was and drove ambulances too down in Nicaragua.

MAGGIE: The Conservatory life is just as halcyon as you imagine it—precisely so.

(*Sound: Breaking glass*)

HILDA: I guess I'll just have to go back to my house and clean up, take out the papers and the trash.

MAGGIE: I guess that kid'll be born one of these days, right?

HILDA: Continue working on my études no matter what they say.

MAGGIE: That's admirable I think.

HILDA: The thing is not to let your spirit be conquered.

MAGGIE: I guess that kid'll be born after a while, right?

HILDA: I guess so. Those boogers are really gonna keep me out of there, you know that?

MAGGIE: Their minds are inflexible and rigid.

HILDA: Probably because I'm a poor pregnant woman don't you think?

MAGGIE: You said you didn't tell them.

HILDA: But maybe they're very shrewd psychologists and they could just look at my face and tell.

MAGGIE: No it doesn't show yet how many months are you?

HILDA: Two and a half just about you can tell when I take off my clothes.

MAGGIE: You didn't take your clothes off did you?

HILDA: No I was wearing you know what the students wear. Jeans and a serape. I carried a green book bag.

MAGGIE: Jam-packed with études.

HILDA: Yes. He asked where I had gotten my previous training and I told him.

MAGGIE: Oh boy I remember when it was flat, flat as the deck of something, a boat or a ship.

HILDA: You're not important, they told me.

MAGGIE: Oh sweetie I am so sorry for you.

HILDA: We parted. Then I walked through the gorgeous Conservatory light into the foyer and then through the great black ironwork Conservatory doors.

MAGGIE: I was a face on the other side of the glass.

HILDA: My aspect as I departed most dignified and serene.

MAGGIE: Time heals everything.

HILDA: No it doesn't.

MAGGIE (*shouted*): Cut lip fat lip puffed lip split lip!

HILDA (*shouted*): Haw! haw! haw! haw!

MAGGIE: Well Hilda there are other things in life.

HILDA: Yes Maggie I suppose there are. None that I want.

MAGGIE: Non-Conservatory people have their own lives. We Conservatory people don't have much to do with them but we are told they have their own lives.

HILDA: I suppose I could file an appeal if there's anywhere to file an appeal to. If there's anywhere.

MAGGIE: That's an idea we get stacks of appeals, stacks and stacks.

HILDA: I'll wait forever. Night after night after night.

MAGGIE: I'll sit with you. I'll help you formulate the words. What do you want to say?

HILDA: I want to say my whole life depends on it. Something like that.

MAGGIE: It's against the rules for Conservatory people to help non-Conservatory people you know that.

HILDA: Well goddammit I thought you were going to help me.

MAGGIE: OK. I'll help you. What do you want to say?

HILDA: I want to say my whole life depends on it. Something like that.

MAGGIE (*elegiac*): We got man naked models and woman naked models, harps, giant potted plants, and drapes. There are hierarchies, some people higher up and others lower down. These mingle, in the gorgeous light. We have lots of fun. There's lots of green furniture you know with paint on it. Worn green paint. Gilt lines one-quarter inch from the edges. Worn green lines.

HILDA: And probably flambeaux in little niches in the walls, right?

MAGGIE: Yeah we got flambeaux. Who's the father?

HILDA: Guy named Robert.

MAGGIE: Did you have a good time?

HILDA: The affair ran the usual course. Fever, boredom, trapped.

MAGGIE: Hot, rinse, spin dry.

HILDA: Is it wonderful in there Maggie?

MAGGIE: I have to say it is. Yes. It is.

HILDA: Do you feel great, being there? Do you feel wonderful?

MAGGIE: Yes, it feels pretty good. Very often there is, upon the dinner tray, a rose.

HILDA: I will never be admitted to the Conservatory.

MAGGIE: You will never be admitted to the Conservatory.

HILDA: How do I look?

MAGGIE: OK. Not bad. Fine.

HILDA: I will never get there. How do I look?

MAGGIE: Fine. Great. Time heals everything Hilda.

HILDA: No it doesn't.

MAGGIE: Time heals everything.

HILDA: No it doesn't. How do I look?

MAGGIE: Old.

(*Sound: Silence; two seconds*)

MAGGIE: If you need a friend I'm yours till the end. (*Pause*) Julia's is the best. Best I've ever seen. The finest.

HILDA: The muscle of jealousy is not in me. Nowhere.

MAGGIE: Oh it is so fine. Incomparable.

HILDA: Some think one thing, some another.

MAGGIE: The very damn best believe me.

HILDA: Well I don't know, I haven't seen it.

MAGGIE: Well, would you like to see it?

HILDA: Well, I don't know. I don't know her very well do you?

HILDA: Well, I know her well enough to ask her.

HILDA: Well, why don't you ask her if it's not an inconvenience or this isn't the wrong time or something?

MAGGIE: Well, probably this is the wrong time come to think of it because she isn't here and sometime when she is here would probably be a better time.

HILDA: Well, I would like to see it right now because just talking about it has got me in the mood to see it. If you know what I mean.

MAGGIE: She told me she didn't like to be called just for that purpose, people she didn't know and maybe wouldn't like if she did know, I'm just warning you.

HILDA: Oh.

MAGGIE: You see.

HILDA: Yes.

(Sound: Motorcycle revving engine; six seconds)

MAGGIE: I could have done better. But I don't know how. Could have done better, cleaned better or cooked better or I don't know. Better.

HILDA: You smile. And the angels sing.

MAGGIE: Blew it, blew it. Had a clown at the wedding, he officiated standing there in his voluptuous white costume his drum and trumpet at his feet. He said, "Do you, Harry..." and all that. The guests applauded, the clown band played, it was a brilliant occasion.

HILDA: Our many moons of patience and accommodation. Tricks and stunts unknown to common cunts.

MAGGIE: The guests applauded. Above us, a great tent with red and yellow stripes.

HILDA: The unexploded pillow and the simple, blunt sheet.

MAGGIE: I was fecund, savagely so.

HILDA: Painting dead women by the hundreds in passionate imitation of Delacroix.

MAGGIE: Sailing after lunch and after sailing, gin.

HILDA: Pleasures of a summer's day.

MAGGIE: Do not go into the red barn, he said. I went into the red barn. Julia. Swinging on a rope from hayloft to tack room. Gazed at by horses with their large, accenting eyes. They somehow looked as if they knew.

HILDA: You packed hastily reaching the station just before midnight counting the pennies in your purse.

MAGGIE: Yes. Regaining the city, plunged once more into activities.

HILDA: You've got to have something besides yourself. A cause, interest, or goal.

MAGGIE: Made myself knowledgeable in certain areas, one, two, three, four. Studied the Value Line and dipped into cocoa.

HILDA: The kind of thing you do so well.

MAGGIE: Acquired busts of certain notables, marble, silver, bronze. The Secretary of Defense and the Chairman of the Joint Chiefs.

HILDA: Wailed a bit into the ears of friends and caverns of the telephone.

MAGGIE: But I rallied. Rallied.

HILDA: Made an effort. Made the effort.

MAGGIE: To make soft what is hard. To make hard the soft. To conceal what is black with use, under new paint. Check the tomatoes with their red times, in the manual. To enspirit the spiritless. To get me a jug and go out behind the barn, sharing with whoever is out behind the barn, pleasant or noble.

HILDA: Sometimes I have luck. In plazas or taverns.

MAGGIE: Right as rain. I mean okey-dokey.

HILDA: Unless the participant affirmatively elects otherwise.

MAGGIE: What does that mean?

HILDA: Damfino. Just a bit of legal language I picked up somewhere.

(Sound: Motorcycle revving engine as before)

MAGGIE: You are the sunshine of my life.

HILDA: Toys toys I want more toys.

MAGGIE: Yes, I should think you would.

HILDA: That wallow in certainty called the love affair.

MAGGIE: The fading gray velvet of the sofa. He clowned with my panties in his teeth. Walked around that way for half an hour.

HILDA: What's this gunk here in this bucket?

MAGGIE: Bread in milk, have some.

HILDA: I think I could eat a little something.

MAGGIE: A mistletoe salad we whipped up together.

HILDA: Stick to it, keep after it, only way to go is all the way.

MAGGIE: Want to buy a garter belt? Have one, thanks. Cut your losses, try another town, split for the tall timber.

HILDA: Well it's a clean afternoon, heavy on the azaleas.

MAGGIE: Yes they pride themselves on their azaleas. Have competitions, cups.

HILDA: I dashed a hope and dimmed an ardor. Promises shimmering like shrimp in light just under the surface of the water.

MAGGIE: Peered into his dental arcade noting the health of his pink tissue.

HILDA: Backed into a small table which overturned with a scattering of ashtrays and back copies of important journals.

(Sound: Landslide as before)

MAGGIE: What ought I to do? What do you advise me? Should I try to see him? What will happen? Can you tell me?

HILDA: Yes it's caring and being kind. We have corn dodgers too and blood sausage.

MAGGIE: Lasciviously offered him a something pure and white.

HILDA: But he hastily with an embarrassed schottische of the hands covered you up again.

HILDA: Much like that. Every day. I don't mind doing the work if I get the results. (*Pause*) We had a dog because we thought it would keep us together. A plain dog.

(*Sound: Fragment of chamber music as before*)

HILDA: Did it?

MAGGIE: Naw it was just another of those dumb ideas we had we thought would keep us together.

HILDA: Bone ignorance.

MAGGIE: Saw him once more, he was at a meeting I was at, had developed an annoying habit of coughing into his coat collar whenever he—

HILDA: Coughed.

MAGGIE: Yes he'd lift his coat collar and cough into it odd mannerism very annoying.

(*Sound: Bass fiddle notes as before*)

MAGGIE: Then the candles going out one by one—

(*Sound: Bass fiddle*)

HILDA: The last candle hidden behind the altar—

(*Sound: Bass fiddle*)

MAGGIE: The tabernacle door ajar—

(*Sound: Bass fiddle*)

HILDA: The clapping shut of the book.

(Sound: Door slamming as before; four-second silence)

MAGGIE *(slowly)*: I got ready for the great day. The great day came, *(pause)* several times in fact.

HILDA: Each time with memories of the last time.

MAGGIE: No. These do not in fact intrude. Maybe as a slight shimmer of the over-and-done-with. Each great day is itself, with its own war machines, rattles, and green lords. There is the hesitation that the particular day won't be what it is meant to be. Mostly it is. That's peculiar.

HILDA: Well it's a clean afternoon, heavy on the azaleas.

MAGGIE: He told me terrible things in the evening of that day as we sat side by side holding hands waiting for the rain to wash his watercolor paper clean. Waiting for the rain to wash the watercolors from his watercolor paper.

HILDA: About me?

MAGGIE: Oh, everything.

(Sound: Theme)

SNOW WHITE

ACT ONE

SCENE ONE

(*Lights come up on platform, raised very high.* SNOW WHITE *is seated, right, and her hair is dangling down. Her hair has been augmented so that it is immensely long, falling almost all the way to the stage.* BILL *enters, left, sees the hair, and stops short.*)

BILL: Well, that certainly is a lot of hair hanging there. (*Pause*) And it seems to be hanging from our windows, too. I mean, those windows are in our house, surely? (*Pause*) Now who amongst us has that much hair, black as ebony? (*Pause*) I am only pretending to ask myself this question. The distasteful answer is already known to me, as is the significance of this act, this hanging. As well as the sexual meaning of hair itself. (*Pause*) There can be only one answer. It is Snow White. It is Snow White who has taken this step, the meaning of which is clear to all of us. All seven of us know what this means. It means she seeks a new lover.

(DAN *enters, right, sees the hair, stops short, and immediately begins lecturing.*)

DAN: Now you're probably familiar with the fact that the per capita production of trash in this country is up from 2.75 pounds per day in 1920 (*pause*) to 4.5 pounds per day in 1973, the last year for which we have a figure, and is increasing at the rate of about four percent a year—

(*The other* MEN *enter, in a crowd, from the opposite side of the stage. They stand directly in front of* SNOW WHITE's *hair, holding a debate.*)

EDWARD (*solemn*): *To be a horsewife.* That, my friends, is my text for today. This important slot in our society, conceptualized by God as very nearly the key to the whole thing, has suffered in recent months and in this house, a degree of denigration. I have heard it; I have been saddened by it. So I want today, if I can, (*pause*) to dispel some of these wrong ideas that have been going around, causing confusion and scumming up the face of the truth.

DAN (*impatient*): —increasing at the rate of four percent a year. Now that rate will probably go up, because it's *been* going up, and I hazard that we may very well soon reach a point where it's 100 percent. Now at such a point, you will agree, things turn from a question of *disposing* of this "trash" to a question of *appreciating its qualities.* Because, after all, it's 100 percent, right? And there can no longer be any question of *disposing* of it, because it's *all there is*—

EDWARD: *The horsewife!* The very basebone of the American plethora! *The horsewife!* Without whom the entire structure of civilian life would crumble! Without whom our whole existence would be reduced, in a twinkling, to that brute level of brutality for which we so rightly reproach the filthy animals! Without the horsewife, we would still be going around dressed in skins probably, with no big-ticket items—washer-dryers, dryer-washers, microwave washer-dryer-cookers—to fill the empty voids, in our homes and in our hearts. (*Pause*) Now I ask you, gentlemen, what do we have here? Do we have a being which regards herself with the appropriate self-respect? No. No, we do not. We have here, rather, a being which regards itself with something dangerously close to *self-hatred*. That is the problem. What is the solution?

DAN (*persuasive*): So that's why we should get into *plastic* ... *buffalo* ... *humps!* (*Pause;* DAN *becomes almost poetic, a prophet*) They are "trash," and what in fact could be more useless or trashlike? Plastic buffalo humps! It's that we *must be* on the leading edge of the trash phenomenon, the troubled face of the future, in my view. And as you know (*very serious*), the future belongs to those who prepare for it!

EDWARD (*pursuing his own line*): A being which regards herself with something dangerously close to *self-hatred*!

HENRY: I could cut your gizzard out, Edward! You are making the whole damned thing more difficult than it has to be. I put it to you that, without your screen of difficulty-making pseudoproblems, the whole damned thing can be resolved, very neatly, in the following way.

EDWARD: Wrong. Wrong.

HENRY: Now, what do we apprehend when we apprehend Snow White? We apprehend, first, two three-quarter-scale breasts floating toward us wrapped, typically, in a red towel. Or, if we are apprehending her from the other direction, we apprehend a beautiful snow-white arse floating away from us, wrapped, typically, in a red towel. Now, I ask you: what, in these two quite distinct apprehensions, is the constant? The factor that remains the same? Why, simply, the red towel. I submit that, rightly understood, the problem of Snow White has to do with nothing else than *red towels*. So we can, if we wish, *get rid of* Snow White. And I have here in this brown bag ... I have taken the liberty of purchasing (*hands out red towels*) here, Hubert, here is your towel ... Kevin ... Clem ... Edward ...

EDWARD: I don't want a ratty old red towel. *I want the beautiful snow-white arse itself!*

(*Lights up on* SNOW WHITE)

SNOW WHITE: *Which prince?* Which prince will come? Will it be Prince Albert? Prince Philip? Prince Charlie? Prince Akihito?

Prince Rainier? Prince Rupert? Prince Hal? Prince George? Prince Valiant? Prince Paul? Well, it is terrific to be anticipating a prince—to be waiting and knowing that what you are waiting for is a prince, packed with grace—but it is still waiting, and waiting as a mode of existence is a darksome mode. I would rather be doing a hundred other things. I wonder if he will have the Hapsburg lip?

(PAUL *enters from the audience or whatever—care must be taken to differentiate him from the seven men with whom* SNOW WHITE *lives.*)

PAUL (*dreamily*): I would retract the green sea, and the brown fish in it, and I would especially retract that long black hair hanging from that window that I encountered today, on my way home from the Unemployment Office. It makes me terribly nervous, that hair. It was beautiful, I admit it. Long black hair of such texture, fineness, is not easily come by. Hair black as ebony! Yet it makes me terribly nervous. Why some innocent person might come along, and see it, and conceive it his duty to climb up, and discern the reason it is being hung out of that window. There is probably some girl attached to it at the top, and with her, responsibilities of various sorts . . . teeth . . . piano lessons. . . .

(*All exit except* KEVIN *and* BILL)

KEVIN: Bill . . .

BILL: Yes?

KEVIN: Maybe I shouldn't ask you this . . .

BILL: What?

KEVIN: Are you . . . all right?

BILL: No.

KEVIN: Is there anything I can do?

BILL: No.

KEVIN: Can you . . . tell me why?

BILL: No.

KEVIN: Is it a secret?

BILL: No.

KEVIN: Is it a mystery?

BILL (*hesitates*): No. (*Pause*) Yes.

KEVIN: You don't love her anymore?

BILL (*impatient*): That's not it.

KEVIN: You've lost your . . . ability to deal creatively with the many-faceted problems of existence?

(BILL *cracks up.* KEVIN *is taken aback.*)

BILL: I wanted to be great, once. But the moon for that was not in my sky. (*Pause*) I had hoped to make a powerful statement. (*Pause*) I had hoped to make a powerful statement, coupled with a moving plea. (*Pause*) I wanted to engage in a great debate, but the important thinkers I contacted were all shaken with sobs— *wracked* is the word for it. Why did we conceal that emotion which, had we declared it, might have liberated us? (*Pause*) I listened to the radio, I heard weeping. (*Pause*) I wanted to make suitable arrangements but those whose lives I had thought to arrange did not present themselves on the appointed day. (*Pause*) She laughed, in her room, pulling from under the pillow grainy gray photographs in albums, pictures of people weeping. (*Pause*) It was hell there, in the furnace of my ambition.

KEVIN: But do you think we can . . .

BILL: We can try. We can try. We can always try.

KEVIN (*relieved*): That's right! We can try like . . . hell!

BILL (*ironic*): We can try like hell. (BILL *smiles at* KEVIN. *Looks at* SNOW WHITE'*s hair for a moment*) Heigh-ho, everybody.

(*Blackout*)

SCENE TWO

(*Six of the seven men with whom* SNOW WHITE *lives are on-stage. They are all in their late twenties, in appearance lean young American businessmen in business suits. The set is now a living space defined by ultramodern furniture, Knoll or some such. A raised platform about five feet high runs along the back of the stage, in darkness or semidarkness.* EDWARD, KEVIN, CLEM, HUBERT, HENRY, *and* DAN *are distributed about the stage in attitudes of relaxation, as if after work.*)

EDWARD: Perhaps we should not be tending the vats and washing the buildings and carrying the money to the vault once a week, like everybody else. Perhaps we should be doing something else entirely, with our lives. God knows what. We do what we do without thinking. One tends the vats and washes the buildings and carries the money to the vault, and never stops for a moment to consider that the whole practice may be—

CLEM: Despicable. Despicable!

DAN (*still gospel style*): The future belongs . . . to those who . . . prepare for it.

CLEM (*emphatic*): Oh yes!

ALL: Oh yes!

HENRY: Vats vats vats vats . . .

ALL: Oh yes!

HENRY: Real estate!

ALL: Oh yes!

HENRY: Baby food!

ALL: Oh yes!

HENRY: *Chinese* baby food!

ALL: Oh oh yes!

HENRY: Baby Dim Sum!

ALL: Oh oh yes!

HUBERT: Baby Sweet and Sour Pork!

ALL: Oh yes, oh yes!

CLEM: Twenty-three thousand cases this week alone!

ALL: Vats vats vats vats . . .

HUBERT: Real estate! Baby food! The profit motive!

ALL (*climax*): Yeah yeah right right oh yes!

CLEM: Before we found Snow White wandering in the forest we lived lives . . . *stuffed* with equanimity. There was equanimity for everybody. We washed the buildings, tended the vats, and wended our way to the country cathouse once a week—

ALL: Heigh-ho!

CLEM: —like everybody else. We were simple bourgeois. We knew what to do. But now—

EDWARD: Now she's written a gigantic poem, four pages long.

(SNOW WHITE, *wearing a red towel, is seated on a raised platform which contains a writing desk and, left, a shower curtain—the shower space.*)

HENRY: Here's the mail.

(SNOW WHITE *is writing, does not look up.*)

HENRY: Usually she likes to paw over the mail. (*A bit more insistent*) Here's the mail!

(SNOW WHITE *remains preoccupied. The men look at each other uneasily.*)

DAN (*a bit angrily*): What are you doing there? Writing something?

(SNOW WHITE *looks up.*)

SNOW WHITE: Yes.

HENRY: What is it?

SNOW WHITE: Poem.

(*The* MEN *look at each other in fear.*)

DAN: *Poem?*

SNOW WHITE: Yes. (*Pause*) Poem.

EDWARD: There it is—the red meat on the floor.

(*Whispered consultation among the* MEN)

KEVIN (*boldly*): Well, can we have a peek?

SNOW WHITE: No.

EDWARD (*tentative*): How long is it?

SNOW WHITE: Four pages. At present.

EDWARD (*thunderstruck*): Four pages!

HENRY (*to himself*): Four pages! (*To* SNOW WHITE) Is it rhymed or free?

SNOW WHITE: Free. Free, free, free.

DAN: And the theme?

SNOW WHITE: One of the great themes. That is all I can reveal at this time.

DAN: Could you tell us the first word?

SNOW WHITE: The first word is bandagedandwounded. Run together.

DAN (*thinking*): How is that *bandage* precedes *wound?*

SNOW WHITE: A metaphor for the self armoring itself against the gaze of The Other.

DAN: The theme is Loss, then.

SNOW WHITE: What . . . else?

HENRY: Are you specific as to what is lost?

SNOW WHITE: Brutally.

(*The* MEN *nervously talking among themselves.* CLEM *steps into the breach, talking to paper things over.*)

CLEM (*to audience*): Sometimes I see signs written on the walls which say "Kill the Rich." And sometimes "Kill the Rich" has been rubbed out and "Harm the Rich" written underneath. A clear gain for civilization, I'd say. And then the one that says "Jean-Paul Sartre Is a Fartre." Something going on there, you must admit. Dim flicker of something. (*Pause*) I see a great many couples, men and women, walking along. When I see a couple fighting, I give them a dollar, because fighting is interesting. Thank God for fighting. But if we can't fight, we can at least fornicate. (*Pause*) Hard to tell which is preferable.

(CLEM *joins* SNOW WHITE *in the shower space.*)

SNOW WHITE: This water is marvelous. When it falls on my tender back. The white meat there. Give me the needle spray. First the hot, then the cold. A thousand tiny points of perturbation. More perturbation! And who is it with me, here in the shower? It is Clem. The approach is Clem's, and the technique, or lack of it, is Clem, Clem, Clem. And Hubert waits outside, on the other side of the shower curtain, and Dan in the hall, before the closed door, and Edward is sitting downstairs, waiting. But what of Bill? Why is it that Bill, the leader, has not tapped on my shower stall door, in recent weeks? Clem, you are downright antierotic, in those blue jeans and chaps! Everything in life is interesting except Clem's idea of sexual congress—his Western confusion between the concept "pleasure" and the concept "increasing the size of the herd."

MEN (*in chorus*): Skidmore College is where she got her education. She studied "Modern Woman, Her Privileges and Responsibilities"! the nature and nurture of women and what they stand for, in evolution and in history, including householding, upbringing, peacekeeping, healing, and devotion.

SNOW WHITE (*complaining*): I am tired of being just a horsewife!

MEN (*in chorus*): Then she studied "Classical Guitar One," the methods and techniques of Sor, Tárrega, Segovia. Then she studied "English Romantic Poets Two": Shelley, Byron, Keats.

SNOW WHITE: I am tired of being a horsewife!

MEN (*in chorus*): Skidmore College is where she got her education. She studied "Theoretical Foundations of Psychology": mind, consciousness, unconscious mind, personality, the self, interpersonal relations, psychosexual norms, social games, groups, adjustment, conflict, authority, mental health.

SNOW WHITE: Oh I wish there were some words in the world that were not the words I always hear!

MEN (*in chorus*): Then she studied "Realism and Idealism in the Contemporary Italian Novel": Berto, Cassola, Ginzburg, Malaparte, Calvino, Gadda, Bassani, Landolfi. Then she studied . . .

(BILL *enters on the platform, right, and crosses to the edge of* SNOW WHITE*'s space, making it clear that he stands outside the shower area.*)

SNOW WHITE: But the water on my back is interesting. It is more than interesting. Marvelous is the word for it.

BILL (*to audience*): Well it is a pleasure to please her, when human ingenuity can manage it, but the whole thing is just trembling on the edge of monotony, after several years. And yet . . . I am fond of her. Yes, I am. For when sexual pleasure is had, it makes you fond, in a strange way, of the other one, the one with whom you are having it.

SNOW WHITE (*to audience*): But who am I to love? I love *them*, in a way, but it isn't enough.

BILL: And the psychiatrist?

SNOW WHITE: He was unforgivable.

BILL: Unforgivable?

SNOW WHITE: He said I was uninteresting.

BILL: Uninteresting?

SNOW WHITE: He said I was a screaming bore.

BILL: That's less than kind.

SNOW WHITE: He said, "Let's go to a movie," for God's sake.

BILL: And?

SNOW WHITE: We went to a movie.

BILL: Which?

SNOW WHITE: A Charlton Heston.

BILL: How was it?

SNOW WHITE: Excellent.

BILL: Was there popcorn?

SNOW WHITE: Mars Bars.

BILL: Did you hold hands?

SNOW WHITE: *Naturellement.*

BILL: And after?

SNOW WHITE: Drinks.

BILL: And after that?

SNOW WHITE: Don't pry.

BILL: But . . . *three days* at the psychiatrist's . . .

MEN (*in chorus*): What is Snow White thinking? No one knows.

(HENRY *moves downstage, right, adjusting his tie, looking in a mirror, etc.*)

HENRY: Now it is necessary to court her, and win her, and put on this clean dressing gown, and cut my various nails, and drink something that will kill the millions of germs in my mouth, and say something flattering, and be witty and bonny, and hale and kinky, all just to ease this wrinkle in the groin. It seems a high price.

DAN: You live in a world of your own, Henry.

HENRY: I can certainly improve on what was given.

(HENRY *turns and climbs up on the platform to* SNOW WHITE's *shower space. He stands behind her and puts his arms around her.*)

BILL (*to audience*): Snow White knows a singing bone. The singing bone has told her stories which have left her troubled and confused: of a bear transformed into a king's son, of an immense treasure at the bottom of a brook, of a crystal casket in which there is a cap that makes the wearer invisible. This must not continue. The behavior of the bone is unacceptable. The bone must be persuaded to confine itself to events and effects confirmable by the instrumentarium of the physical sciences. Someone must reason with the bone!

MEN (*in chorus*): What is Snow White thinking? No one knows.

SNOW WHITE: Those men . . . hulking . . . hulk in closets . . . and outside . . . gestures eventuating against a white screen . . . difficulties . . . intelligence. . . . I only wanted one plain hero of incredible size . . . soft, flexible manners . . . parts . . . thought . . . dissembling . . . add up the thumbprints on my shoulders . . . seven is . . . different levels of emotional . . . mirror . . . daytime . . . Bill . . . thank you.

(PAUL *enters carrying a very large painting, painfully abstract.*)

PAUL: Is there someplace I can put this? It's a new thing I just finished today, still a little wet I'm afraid.

(PAUL *leans canvas against chair.* SNOW WHITE *inspects it.*)

SNOW WHITE: It's poor. Poor, poor.

PAUL (*complacently*): Yes. One of my poorer things, I think.

SNOW WHITE: *Wonderfully* poor.

PAUL: Yes, it has some of the qualities of poorness. I just took up painting yesterday. This is only my fourth canvas.

SNOW WHITE: Especially poor in the lower-left-hand corner.

PAUL: I would go so far as to hurl it into the marketplace.

SNOW WHITE: What is your name, handsome stranger? You have a certain . . . princeliness.

PAUL: Paul. I am princely. There is that. At times, when I am down, I am able to pump myself up again by thinking about my blood. It is blue, the bluest this fading world has known, probably. At times I startle myself with a gesture so royal, so full of light, that I wonder where it comes from. (*Pause*) It comes from my father, Paul the Seventeenth, a most kingly man and personage. Even though his sole accomplishment during his long lack of reign was the de-deification of his own person. The one thing they could not take away from him, there in that hall bedroom in Montreux, was his blood. And the other thing they could not take away from him was his airs and graces, which I have inherited, to a sickening degree. Even at fifty-five he was still putting cologne in his shoes. The height of his ambition was to tumble the odd chambermaid now and then, whereas I have loftier ambitions, only I don't know what they are, exactly. Probably I should go out and effect a liaison with some beauty who needs me, and save her, and ride away with her flung over the pommel of my palfrey. But on the other hand . . . that's an awful lot of trouble. (*Pause*) He was peculiar, my father. He knew some things other men do not know. He heard the swans singing just before death, and the bees barking in the night. That is what he said, but I didn't believe him then. Now I don't know.

SNOW WHITE (*looking at the picture*): Sublimely poor!

PAUL: Wallpaper!

(SNOW WHITE *jumps down from the platform. She walks slowly up to* PAUL *and looks at him very carefully, then goes off opposite side.*)

(*Blackout*)

SCENE THREE

(*The platform has been hoisted about halfway up the back of the stage. A grid suggesting windows is seen behind it. On the platform are* EDWARD, KEVIN, DAN, *and* BILL, *with buckets, squeegees, etc.* HUBERT, HENRY, *and* CLEM *are onstage, backs to the audience, miming building-washing. At right are* JANE

and HER MOTHER, *with an ironing board [for instance].* JANE
addresses the audience)

JANE: I was fair once. I was the fairest of them all. Men came from
miles around simply to be in my power. But those days are gone.
Those better days. Now I cultivate my malice. It is a cultivated
malice, not the pale natural malice we knew, when the world
was young. I grow more and more witchlike as the hazy days
imperceptibly slip into one another, and the musky months
sink into memory as into a sough, sump, or slime. But I have
my malice. I have that. I have even invented new varieties of
malice, that men have not seen before now. Were it not for the
fact that I am the sleepie of Hogo de Bergerac, I would be *total
malice*. But I am redeemed by this hopeless love, which places
us along the human continuum, still. (*Pause*) Mother, can I go
over to Hogo's and play?

MOTHER: No, Jane, Hogo is not the right type of young man for
you to play with. He is forty now and that is too old for innocent
play. I am afraid he knows some kind of play that is not innocent, and will want you to play it with him, and you will agree
in your ignorance, and then the fat will be in the fire. That is
the way I have the situation figured out. That is my reading of
it. That is the way it looks from where I stand. (*Pause*) What is
that apelike hand I see reaching into my mailbox?

JANE: Mother, all this false humility does not become you. Neither does that mucky old poor-little-match-girl dress.

MOTHER: This dress I'll have you know cost two hundred and forty
dollars when it was new.

JANE: When it was new?

MOTHER (*elegiac*): It was new in 1918, the year your father and I
were in the trenches together, in the Great War. That was a war,
all right. Oh I know there have been other wars since, better-
publicized ones, more expensive ones, but our war is the one
I'll always remember. Our war is the one that means *war* to me.

JANE: Mother, I know Hogo is forty and thoroughly vile through
and through, but there is something drawing me to him. To his
house. To the uninnocence which awaits me there.

MOTHER: Simmer down, child. I know how you feel. I was a person myself, once. (*Pause*) What is that apelike hand I see reaching into my mailbox?

JANE: That's nothing. Think nothing of it. It's nothing. It's just one of my familiars, Mother. It's just an ape, that's all. Just an ordinary ape. Don't give it another thought.

MOTHER: I think you dismiss these things too easily, Jane. It's unusual. It *means* something.

JANE: No, Mother. It doesn't mean anything. It's just what I said it was.

MOTHER: I'm sure it means more than that, Jane.

JANE: No, Mother, it does not mean more than that. Don't go reading things into things, Mother.

MOTHER: I wish you wouldn't surround yourself with such strange creatures, Jane. The ape . . . Hogo . . .

JANE: Shhh, Mother. I have work to do. (MOTHER *exits.* JANE *picks up telephone book. Closes her eyes. Stabs telephone book with her forefinger. Opens her eyes. Memorizes number. Puts book down. Picks telephone up, dials.*) Mr. Quistgaard? (*Pause*) Hello, Mr. Quistgaard. (*Pause*) Although you do not know me, my name is Jane. (*Pause*) Jane. (*Pause*) I am a witch. (*Pause*) A witch. I am a *very good* witch. (*Pause*) I have seized your name, Mr. Quistgaard, from the telephone book. (*Pause*) From the telephone book. It was right there, in the telephone book. (*Pause*) You are correct, Mr. Quistgaard, in seeing this as a threatening situation. Who knows what I might say? Who knows what I might ask? Who knows what I might tell? Who knows what I might be told? (*Settling down; cozy*) Now, Mr. Quistgaard, let's *chat* for a bit.

(HOGO *enters.* JANE *continues to whisper threats during* HOGO's *speech but hangs up before he is finished.*)

HOGO: God, what filthy beasts we were, then! And what a thing it must have been to be a Hun! A filthy Boche! And then to turn around and be a Nazi! A gray vermin! And today? (*Pause*) Filthy deutschmarks! That so eclipse the very mark and texture of a man . . . That so eclipse the very mark and bosom of a man, that vileness . . . that vileness itself is vilely o'erthrown. That so enfold . . . that so enwash . . . Bloody deutschmarks! That so enwrap the very warp and fiber of a man, that what we cherished in him, vileness, is—*Dies*, his ginger o'erthrown. Bald pelf! That so encapsulates the very wrack and mixture of a man, that *in him* the sweet stings of vileness are . . . all ginger fled, he . . .

(HOGO *winds down*.)

JANE (*to audience*): He knows when I tremble. That is what he likes best. (*To* HOGO) What is to become of us, Hogo? Of you and me?

HOGO: Nothing is to become of us, Jane. Our becoming is done. We are what we are. Now it is just a question of rocking along with things as they are until we are dead.

JANE: You don't paint a very bright picture, Hogo.

HOGO: It's not my picture, Jane. I didn't think up this picture that we are confronted with. The original brushwork was not mine. I absolutely separate myself from this picture. I operate within the frame, it is true, but the picture—

JANE: You are forty, Hogo.

HOGO: A not unpleasant age to be.

JANE: You don't mind, then. That you are not young.

HOGO: It has its buggy aspects, as what does not?

JANE: You don't mind then that you are sagging in the direction of death?

HOGO: No, Jane.

(JANE *exits, crossing* BILL, *who is limping*. KEVIN *speaks from the platform*.)

KEVIN: Bill, our leader, has developed a shamble. The consequence, some say, of a lost mind. But this is not true. In the midst of so much that is true, it is refreshing to shamble across something that is not true. He does not want to be touched. But he is entitled to a quirk. He has earned it by his vigorous leadership in that great enterprise, his life. And in that other great enterprise, our love for Snow White.

BILL: This thing is damaging to all of us. We were all born in national parks. Clem has his memories of Yosemite, inspiring gorges. Kevin remembers the Great Smokies. Henry has his Acadian songs and dances, Dan his burns from Hot Springs. Hubert has climbed the giant Sequoias, and Edward has climbed stately Rainier. And I, I know the Everglades, which everybody knows. These common experiences have yoked us together forever under the red, white, and blue. (*Pause*) Love has died here, apparently. And it is our task to infuse it once more with the hot orange breath of life. With that in mind I have asked Hogo de Bergerac to come over and advise us on what should be done. He knows the deaths of the heart, Hogo does. And he knows the terror of aloneness, and the rot of propinquity, and the absence of grace. That equips him to talk to us about this problem. That and his vileness.

HOGO: Well, chaps, first I'd like to say a few vile things more or less at random, not only because it is expected of me but also because I enjoy it. One of them is that this cunt you've got here, although I've seen her with my own eyes, is probably not worth worrying about. Now excuse me if I'm treading on your toes in this matter. God knows I love a female gesture as much as any man. The only thing worth a rap in the whole world, in my opinion, is the beauty of women, and maybe certain foods, and possibly music of all kinds, especially parade music, which can reduce you to tears, in the right light, by speaking to you from the heart about your land, and what a fine land it is, and that it is *your* land really, and my land, this land of ours—that particular insight can chill you, rendered by a marching unit. But I wander. The main thing I want to say is that the world is full of cunts, that they grow like clams in all quarters of the earth, cunts as multitudinous as cherrystones and littlenecks burrowing into the mud in all the bays of the world. The point is that the loss of any particular one is not to be taken seriously. She stays with you as long as she can put up with your shit and you stay with her as long as you can put up with her shit. That's the way it is. (*Pause*) Of course they change. They age. Ruin of the physical envelope is our great theme here, and if we keep changing girls every four or five years, it is because of this ruin, which I will never agree to, to my dying day. And that is why I keep looking out of the window, and why we all keep looking out of the window, to see what is passing, what has been cast up on the beach of our existence. Because something is always being cast up on that beach, as new classes of girls mature. My main point is that you should bear in mind multiplicity, and forget about uniqueness. The earth is broad, and flat, and deep, and high. And remember what Freud said.

EDWARD: The value the mind sets on erotic needs instantly sinks as soon as satisfaction becomes readily available.

ALL (*in chorus*): THE VALUE THE MIND SETS ON EROTIC NEEDS IN-STANTLY SINKS AS SOON AS SATISFACTION BECOMES READILY AVAILABLE.

(HOGO *exits.*)
(SNOW WHITE *appears on the platform. She appears to be looking out of second-story window.*)

SNOW WHITE: My suffering is authentic enough but it has a kind of low-grade concrete-block quality. The seven of them only add up to the equivalent of about two *real men*, as we know them from the films of our childhood, when there were giants on the earth. It is possible of course that there are no more *real men* here, on this ball of half-truths, the earth. *I am tired of being just a horsewife!* Which prince? Which prince will come?

(*Light goes down on the platform*)

HENRY: I understand all this about Bill. Nevertheless, I think somebody ought to build a fire under him. He needs a good kick in the back according to my way of thinking.

HUBERT: We are little children compared to him, in terms of possibility, yet all he seems to want to do is sit around the game room, and shuffle the bezique cards, and throw darts and that sort of thing, when he could be out realizing his potential.

EDWARD: We are little balls of dust under his feet, potentially, and he merely sits there making ships inside bottles, and doing scrimshaw, and all that, when he could be out maximizing his possibilities.

CLEM: Boy I would like to build a fire under that boy. I'll be damned if I know what to do about this situation, which is vexing me in a hundred ways.

DAN: It's just such a damned shame and crime I can't stand it, the more I think about it. I just want to go out and rage against fate, that one so obviously chosen to be the darling of the life principle should be so indolent, impious, and wrong. I am just about at the end of my tether, boys, and I'll say that to his face, too!

(*Lights up on* SNOW WHITE, *on platform*)

SNOW WHITE: Paul? Is there a Paul, or have I only projected him in the shape of my longing, boredom, ennui, and pain? Have I been trained in the finest graces and arts all my life for nothing but this? Is my richly appointed body to go down the drain, at twenty-two, in this, in this . . . (*Pause*) Of course, there is a Paul! There is a Paul somewhere, but not here. Not under my window. Not yet. (*To Bill*) What is it?

BILL: I wish I knew. It's something.

SNOW WHITE: I don't doubt it. I mean, I think it's real, whatever it is.

BILL: It's real but I can't put my finger on it. (*Pause*) I think it's fear.

SNOW WHITE (*taken aback*): Oh! (*Pause*) What kind? (*Pause*) Specific or nonspecific?

BILL: Early morning. And then again at four.

SNOW WHITE: I've noticed that your coffee cup rattles a good bit, at breakfast.

BILL: And my teacup, at teatime.

SNOW WHITE: But what is it that is rattling you?

BILL: Things.

SNOW WHITE: It's not . . . me?

BILL: Not you.

SNOW WHITE: You're sure?

BILL: I'm sure.

SNOW WHITE: You've exhausted me . . . as a possibility?

BILL: No, Snow White. You are still . . . You are the game and the object of the game and the prize for winning the game and the referee. (*Pause*) And the other team. (*Pause*) Busy, busy, dummy.

SNOW WHITE: All I wanted was one immense hero with soft, flexible hands . . .

BILL: Entirely reasonable.

SNOW WHITE: All I wanted was to lose my head . . . (*thinking*) really, to be mad, to be driven mad. To have . . . me . . . unravel. To dissolve. Melt.

BILL: Yes, I can see that.

SNOW WHITE: And to be able to do that for you.

BILL: Yes, yes, I see how it works. (*Pause*) Or did, once. (*Pause*) Or did it ever?

SNOW WHITE (*thinking*): It sort of worked. It almost worked. It worked for a while. In a way.

BILL: Dismal words.

SNOW WHITE: Quite, quite dismal. I am tired of being just a horsewife!

KEVIN: THE HORSEWIFE IN HISTORY!

HENRY: FAMOUS HORSEWIVES!

HUBERT: THE HORSEWIFE: A SPIRITUAL PORTRAIT!

DAN: THE HORSEWIFE: A CRITICAL STUDY!

EDWARD: THE FIRST MOP, 4000 B.C.!

BILL: VIEW OF ST. AUGUSTINE!

KEVIN: EMERSON ON THE AMERICAN HORSEWIFE!

HENRY: OXFORD COMPANION TO THE AMERICAN HORSEWIFE!

HUBERT: INTRODUCTION OF BON AMI, 1892!

DAN: HORSEWIVES GET THE VOTE!

EDWARD: ACCEPT ROLE, PSYCHOLOGIST URGES!

BILL: THE PLASTIC BAG!

CLEM: THE GARLIC PRESS!

BILL: Most life is unextraordinary.

SNOW WHITE: Yes. Most life is unextraordinary looked at with a woman's desperate eye, too, it might interest you to know.

BILL: Snow White, why do you remain with us? Here? In this house?

SNOW WHITE: It must be attributed, I suppose, to a failure of the imagination. I have not been able to imagine anything better. (*Pause*) But my imagination is stirring. Be warned. (*Pause;* SNOW WHITE *fingers her long black hair.* BILL *exits.*) I could fly a kite with this hair, it is so long. The wind would carry the kite up into the blue, and there would be the red of the kite against the blue of the blue, together with my hair black as ebony, floating there. That seems desirable. This motif—the long hair streaming from the high window—is a very ancient one, I believe, found in many cultures, in various forms. (*Pause*) Now I recapitulate it—for the astonishment of the vulgar and the refreshment of my venereal life!

(SNOW WHITE *begins to unwind her hair.*)

(*Blackout*)

ACT TWO
SCENE ONE

(*Seven brilliant red-and-yellow shower curtains spread across the stage.*)

HENRY (*to the other* MEN, *who are standing in front of the shower curtains, inspecting them, feeling them, etc.*): She still sits there in the window, dangling down her long black hair black as ebony. The crowds have thinned somewhat. The new shower curtain has not swayed her noticeably. We've asked an expert in to make sure it's the *right sort* of shower curtain. We have returned the red towels to Bloomingdale's. (*All look at* DAN, *who vomits*) The grade of pork ears we are using in the Baby Ding Sam Dew cannot meet the U.S. government standards, or indeed, any standards. Our man in Hong Kong says that the next shipment will be superior. Sales nationwide are brisk, brisk, brisk. The weather tomorrow, fair and warmer.

DAN (*elegiac*): Standing in the splendid bathroom, we regard the new shower curtain.

KEVIN: It has two colors, a red and a yellow. The red the red of red cabbage, the yellow the yellow of yellow beans.

HUBERT: It has two figures—a kind of schematic peahen, a kind of schematic vase.

EDWARD: We know that it is adequate. We know that it is "nice." We even know that it is "splendid," more or less. That is the idea, that it be "splendid."

PAUL (*entering*): This is the best-looking shower curtain in town!

HENRY: Paul says that it is the best-looking shower curtain in town. That is a chiller. That gives us a problem. How can we determine if it is true, what he says? That ours is the best-looking shower curtain in town?

DAN: Our city, the arena of the proposition, is not large but on the other hand not small; in excess of a hundred thousand souls swelter here awaiting the Last Day and God's mercy. A census of shower curtains is possible—

320

CLEM (*to audience*): But to conduct it, we would have to neglect the vats, and that is something we have sworn never to do, neglect the vats. And to conduct it, we would be forced to leave the buildings unwashed, and that is something else we have sworn never to do, leave the buildings unwashed.

DAN: And granting we manage to gain access to the rotten bathrooms of all hundred thousand souls who swelter here, by what standards are the hundred thousand shower curtains hanging there, on little silver rings, to be assessed?

EDWARD: That's not the point. The point is, does *she* like it?

DAN: If it's the best-looking shower curtain in town, she must.

ALL (*a babble*): She must, she must.

HUBERT: If it gets out—that we have the best-looking shower curtain in town—won't other people come and take it away from us?

DAN: Before it has had time to work its magic on Snow White?

EDWARD: There is a solution: destruction of Paul, who made the original remark.

(ALL *gather menacingly around* PAUL.)

PAUL: I have decided to become a monk.

(PAUL *exits left.*)
(*Blackout*)
(*Lights up on* SNOW WHITE, *who is sitting on a stepladder or whatever behind the shower curtains, with her hair falling in front of one of them.*)

SNOW WHITE (*angry*): Oh, if I could just get my hands on the man who dubbed those electrical connections male and female! He thought he was so worldly! And if I could just get my hands on the man who called that piece of pipe a nipple! He thought he was so urbane. (*Pause*) No one has come to climb up. That says it all. This time is the wrong time for me. There is something wrong with all those people standing there, gaping and gawking.

And with all those who did not come and at least *try* to climb up. To fill the role. And with the very world itself, for not being able to supply a prince. For not being civilized enough to supply the correct ending to the story.

(Blackout)
(When the lights come up, the shower curtains are gone, and DAN *stands in front of* SNOW WHITE'S *stepladder, ignoring her.)*

DAN: Bill has dropped the money. A bundle totaling *a great deal of money.* I can tell you that. He was on his way to the vault with the money bundled into his armpit, wrapped in a red towel. Henry had wrapped it in a red towel. Hubert had bundled it into Bill's armpit. I had opened the door. Kevin had pointed Bill toward the vault. Clem had given Bill a kick in the back, to get him started.

HUBERT: But somewhere between the house and the vault the money rushed out of Bill's armpit in a direction known only to it. We all rushed out into the air, to recover the money. But it was nowhere. The loss of money is not serious. We have more money. But the loss of equanimity is serious. We prize equanimity, and a good deal of equanimity leaked away, today.

SNOW WHITE *(drinking a glass of orange juice)*: From now on I deny myself to them. These delights. No more do I trip girlishly to their beds in the night, or after lunch, or in the misty mid-morning. And no more will I chop their onions, boil their fettucini, or marinate their flank steak. No more will I trudge about the house pursuing stain. No more will I fold their lingerie in neat bundles and stuff it away in the highboy. I don't know what such a policy will win me. I am not even sure I wish to implement it. It seems small and meanspirited. I have conflicting ideas. But the main theme that runs through my brain is that what is, is insufficient.

DAN *(holding a bottle of wine)*: I have killed this whole bottle of Chablis by myself. And that other bottle of Chablis too—that one under the bed. And that other bottle of Chablis too—the one with the brown candle stuck in the mouth of it. I feel abandoned. After a hard day tending the vats, one wants to come home and find a leg of mutton on the table, in a rich gravy, with little pearly onions studded in it, and perhaps a small pot of Irish potatoes somewhere about. Instead I come home to all this nothingness.

HENRY (*holding a glass of whiskey*): Now she sits in her room reading *Liberation* and admiring her figure in the mirror. She still loves us, in a way, but it isn't enough. It is a failure of leadership, I feel. We have been left sucking the mop again. True leadership would make her love us fiercely, excitingly. As in the old days. True leadership would find a way out of this hairy imbroglio. I am tired of Bill's halting explanations, promises. If he doesn't want to lead, then let us vote.

CLEM (*holding four bottles of beer, two in each hand*): They can treat me like a rube if they wish. I suppose I am a rubish hayseed in some sense, full of down-home notions that contradict the more sophisticated notions of my colleagues. But I notice that it is me they come to when it is a question of grits or chitlins or fried catfish. Of course these questions do not arise very often. I have not had a whiff of fried catfish these twelve years! How many nights have I trudged home with my face fixed for fried catfish, only to find that we were having fried calimaretti or some other Eastern dish. (*Pause*) But why am I talking about dishes? Dishes are not what is troubling me. I am worried by the fact that no one has responded to Snow White's hair. Even though I am at the same time relieved. But it suggests that Americans cannot or will not see themselves as princely. Even Paul, that most princely of our contemporaries, did not respond appropriately. I hope he's doing well in the monastery. Be-damned if I don't feel like maybe goin' and joinin' him.

KEVIN (*semihysterical*): THE VALUE THAT THE MIND SETS ON EROTIC NEEDS instantly sinks as soon as satisfaction is readily available! An obstacle is needed to swell the tide of the libido to its height! (KEVIN *holds up a red towel, then begins waving it like a flag.*) And at all periods of history, whenever natural barriers have not sufficed, men have erected conventional ones!

(Blackout)
(Lights up on the seven MEN *and* SNOW WHITE, *all wearing pajamas)*

SNOW WHITE: If Bill takes off his pajamas, I will remove my own pajamas, and allow you to remove all of your pajamas, and who knows what will happen then? *(She flirts with her pajama top, buttoning and unbuttoning.)* Take off your pajamas, Bill.

BILL *(austere)*: I will not. I will not take off my pajamas. *(The others crowd around him, angry, urging him to take off his pajamas.)* I won't. I will not.

SNOW WHITE: Take off your pajamas, Bill. *(More pajama business by* SNOW WHITE*)*

BILL *(to audience)*: I must hold the whole thing together. Everything depends on me. I cannot fall apart, yet. I must conceal my wounds, contrive to appear unwounded. The bloody handkerchief stuffed under the shirt. Under the pajamas. They must not know. *(Music, the opening bars of "The Ride of the Valkyries," is heard for a moment, then fades)* The great black horse! For which I have waited all my days, since I was twelve years old! I know that the great black horse may appear at any moment. They don't know that. That is the difference between me and them—I know that and they don't know that.

ALL: Take off your pajamas Bill!

BILL *(to audience)*: Don't think about it. Think about leadership. No, don't think about leadership. Don't think. We are what we have been told about ourselves. We are the sum of the messages we have received. The true messages. The false messages.

*(*SNOW WHITE *turns her back to the audience, removes her pajama top, stretches luxuriously.)*

DAN: Bill are you going to take off those . . . goddamn . . . *pajamas?*

BILL *(to audience)*: Leadership means . . .

(*He begins unbuttoning his pajama top. Again, "The Ride of the Valkyries." He approaches* SNOW WHITE. *He places a hand on her shoulder. She turns and embraces him.*)

SNOW WHITE: No.

BILL: No?

SNOW WHITE: No.

BILL (*aside*): Unbearable beauty.

SNOW WHITE (*drawling*): Nooooo.

BILL: They'll blame . . . me.

SNOW WHITE: As do I.

BILL: What did I do wrong?

SNOW WHITE: I don't know. I only know that it's . . . not enough.

BILL: More.

SNOW WHITE (*agreeing*): More.

BILL: You want more.

SNOW WHITE: Much more.

BILL: Your demands are great.

SNOW WHITE: Average.

DAN (*thrusting himself between them*): Bill, if you don't—

SNOW WHITE (*sarcastic*): Dan, I believe I hear the market falling. Two points. One, two. (*Mimes listening*) Three. Hadn't you better call your broker? (DAN *rushes from the room*) Four. (*All the others except* BILL *rush out.* SNOW WHITE *speaks to* BILL) You see?

BILL: Freud said . . .

SNOW WHITE: I don't want to know what Freud said.

BILL: Freud said that the two values left to this civilization were money and the beauty of women.

SNOW WHITE: Clever devil.

(Blackout)
(Lights up on HOGO *holding a telephone)*

HOGO: Hello, is this the IRS? Hogo de Bergerac here. I have your reply to my letter of the sixteenth, in which I offer to inform on Bill, Kevin, Edward, Hubert, Henry, Clem, and Dan for 17 percent of the monies collected. *(Pause)* The what? *(Pause.* HOGO *looks at letter)* Your reference number is 175 dash 05 dash 1272. *(Pause.* HOGO *scowls.)* 175 dash 05 dash 1272. *(Pause.* HOGO *is growing angrier.)* Yes, well, I have your letter stating that you may only pay 8 percent to informers, but my fee is 17 percent and that's that. *(Pause)* I am *aware* that if you paid me 17 percent all the other informers would want the same, but that's not my problem, is it? Good God, 8 percent. That's damn little for doing such a vile and dishonorable thing, damned little. *(Pause)* There's what involved? *(Pause)* There's patriotism involved? *(Pause)* It's my duty as an American citizen to come forward with this information if I have it? Well, listen here, IRS. I am not an American citizen. I am under Panamanian registry. So just forget my duty as an American citizen. Eight percent. No, I don't think I'm talking to you anymore, IRS. There would be some pleasure in doing the thing just for the pure vileness of it, but there is more pleasure in spitting on your 8 percent. Eight percent. Goodbye, IRS. Eight percent. Goodbye, IRS and bad cess to you.

(Blackout)

SCENE TWO

*(*SNOW WHITE*'s bedroom. A large mirror, a bed, a window.* SNOW WHITE *removes her blouse, then her slip, then her bra. Standing by the mirror, she regards her bare breasts, by pointing her head down.)*

SNOW WHITE: Well, what is there to think about them? These breasts? *(Pause)* Usually I don't think about them at all. But recent events, or lack of events, have provoked in me a crisis of confidence. But let us take stock. These breasts, my own, still stand delicately away from the trunk, as they are supposed to do. And the trunk itself is not unappealing. In fact, *trunk* is a rather mean word for the main part of this assemblage of felicities. The terrific belly smooth as sour cream! The stunning ass, in the rococo mirror! And then the especially good legs, including the important knees! I have nothing but praise from this delicious assortment! But my curly mind has problems distinct from, although related to, those of my scrumptious body. The curious physicality of my existence here on earth is related to both parts of the mind-body problem, the mind part and the body part. (*Pause*) Although I secretly know my body *is* my mind. The way it acts sometimes, spontaneously and scandalously hurling itself into the arms of bad situations, with never a care for who is watching or real values. This damned body! (*Pause*) Not the best I've ever seen. But not the worst.

(PAUL *enters and moves to the edge of* SNOW WHITE'S *space. He is wearing monk's robes.*)

PAUL: God Almighty! It's a good thing it occurred to me to stand under this tree and look through this window. It's a good thing I am on leave from the monastery. It's a good thing I had my reading glasses in my upper robe pocket. (PAUL *puts on glasses*) Now I can read the message written on Snow White's unwrapped breasts. What beauty! What torment! She is just like one of those dancers one sees from time to time on Bourbon Street in New Orleans, and in selected areas of other cities. Looking through this window is sweet. The sweetest thing that has happened to me in all my days. I savor the sweetness of human communication, through the window.

(HOGO *enters* PAUL'S *space and pushes him roughly aside, taking his position.*)

HOGO: You are slime, sir, looking through that open window at that apparently naked girl there, the most beautiful and attractive I have ever seen, in all my life. You are a dishonor to the robes you wear. That you stand here without shame, gazing at that incredible beauty, at her snowy buttocks and so forth, at that natural majesty I perceive so well, through the window, is endlessly reprehensible, in our society. I have seen some vileness in my time, but your action in spying upon this beautiful unknown beauty, whom I already love with all my heart until the end of time, is the vilest thing that the mind of man ever broached. I am going to set a rat chewing on your anus, false monk, for if there is anything this world affords, it is punishment.

PAUL: You have a good line, citizen. Perhaps next you would care to make a few remarks about unearned pessimism.

HOGO: It is true that I am in favor of earned pessimism, Paul. And I have earned mine. Yet at the same time I seem to feel a new vigor, optimism, and hope, simply through the medium of pouring my eyes through this window.

PAUL: It is strong medicine, this.

(*They stand gazing for a moment. Then* HOGO *wanders off, moonstruck.* PAUL *remains.*)

PAUL: Yes, this is a situation that requires careful study. And after that, more careful study. Let's see. I'll need four hundred feet of number ten cable . . .

(*Blackout*)
(HOGO, *at stool, and* JANE. HOGO *is sharpening a variety of knives.*)

JANE: What's this?

HOGO: Just some work I brought home from the office.

JANE: What are you thinking about?

HOGO: Edges.

JANE: It doesn't look like office work to me.

HOGO (*aside*): This cello-shaped girl still has some life left in her. Why don't I spend more time looking at her and drinking in her seasoned beauty? Why is it we always require "more"? Why is it that we can never be satisfied? It is almost as if we were designed that way. As if that were part of the cosmic design.

JANE: What are you thinking about?

HOGO: I love her, Jane. Whoever she is, she is mine, virtually if not actually, forever. I feel I have to tell you this, because after all I do owe you something for having been the butt of my unpleasantness for so long. For these years.

(*With an operatic cry,* JANE *runs off, passing* HENRY, *who is entering.*)

HENRY: Bill must be brought to justice for his bungling. This latest bit is the last straw absolutely. I see the trial as a kind of analysis really, more a therapeutic than a judicial procedure. When he threw those two six-packs of Miller High Life through the windscreen of that blue Volkswagen—

(SNOW WHITE'S *space. Kitchen setup.* SNOW WHITE *scoring meat with knife.*)

SNOW WHITE: Oh, why does fate give us alternatives to annoy and frustrate ourselves with? Paul has dug a pit outside the house, from which he is keeping watch, watching me, through a system of mirrors and trained dogs. Why, for instance, do I have the option of going out of the house, through the window, and sleeping with Paul in his pit? Luckily that alternative is not a very attractive one. Paul's princeliness has somehow fallen away, and the naked Paul, without his aura, is just another complacent bourgeois. But I thought I saw, over his shoulder, a dark and vilely compelling figure not known to me. Who is that?

(*Lights up on* JANE, *who is standing before what appears to be a six-foot-square spice rack, filled with little bottles. An ape stands by her side. This could be a stuffed ape if desired.*)

JANE: Now I have been left sucking the mop again. Hogo de Bergerac no longer holds me in the highest esteem. His highest esteem has shifted to another, and now he holds her in it, and I am alone with my malice at last. Face-to-face with it. For the first time in my history, I have no lover to temper my malice with healing, wholesome, older love. (JANE *picks a bottle and reads the label*) Dryshade. (*Replaces bottles and picks another*) Scumlock. (*Replaces bottles and picks another*) Hyoscine. (*Replaces bottle and picks another*) Azote. (*Replaces bottles and picks another*) Hurtwort. (*Replaces bottle and picks another*) Milkleg. (*Replaces bottle, fondles ape's head*) Now I must witch someone, for that is my role, and to flee one's role is bootless. But the question is, What form shall my malice take, on this occasion? This braw February day? Whose sweet life shall I poison, with the tasteful savagery of my abundant imagination and talent for concoction? I think I will go around to Snow White's house, where she cohabits with the seven men in a mocksome travesty of approved behavior, and see what is stirring there. If something is stirring, perhaps I can arrange a sleep for it—in the corner of a churchyard, for example.

(*Blackout*)

SCENE THREE

(*A courtroom setup.* BILL *in the dock.* DAN *as judge. The other five men as jury-spectators.*)

DAN: Bill, will you begin? Can you explain this most recent embarrassment, the hurlment of two six-packs of Miller High Life in a brown paper bag through the windscreen of a blue Volkswagen operated by I. Fondue and H. Maeght? Two absolute and utter strangers, so far as we know?

BILL: Strangers to you, perhaps. But not to me.

DAN: You were acquainted with them previously.

BILL: Yes. Sixteen years ago.

DAN: First, give me the circumstances of the hurlment.

BILL: It was about four o'clock in the afternoon.

DAN: What is your authority?

BILL: The cathouse clock.

DAN: Proceed.

BILL: I was on my way to the coin-operated laundry.

DAN: With what in view?

BILL: Laundering. Snow White being, as you know, reluctant in these days to—

DAN (*hastily*): As we know. And the Miller High Life?

BILL: I had in mind drinking it while watching the machines. (*Pause*) There was a lot of laundry.

DAN: Proceed.

BILL: I then apprehended, at the corner of Eleventh and Neat Street, the blue Volkswagen containing Fondue and Maeght.

DAN: You descried them through the windscreen.

BILL: That is correct.

HENRY (*interrupting*): The windscreen was in motion?

BILL: The entire vehicle.

EDWARD: Making what speed?

BILL: It was effecting a stop.

DAN: You were crossing in front of it.

BILL: That is correct.

DAN: What then?

BILL: I recognized, at the controls, Fondue and Maeght.

HENRY: This after the slipping away of sixteen years?

BILL: The impression was indelible.

EDWARD: What then?

BILL: I lifted my eyes.

EDWARD: To heaven?

BILL: To the cathouse clock. It said, four.

DAN: What then?

BILL: The hurlment.

DAN: You hurled said bag through said windscreen.

BILL: Yes.

DAN: And then?

BILL: The windscreen shattered. Ha ha.

DAN: Did the court hear you aright? Did you say ha ha?

BILL: Ha ha.

DAN: Outbursts will be dealt with. You have been warned. Let us continue. The windscreen was, then, imploded upon the passengers.

BILL: Ha ha.

DAN: Facial injurement resulted in facial areas a b c and d.

BILL: That is correct. Ha ha.

DAN: You then danced a jig—

KEVIN (*standing*): Objection!

DAN: What is the objection?

KEVIN: My client, your honesty, did not *dance a jig*. A certain shufflement of the feet might have been observed, product of a perfectly plausible nervous tension, such as all are subject to on great occasions, weddings, births, deaths, and so on. But nothing that, in all charity, might be described as *a gigue*, with its connotations of gaiety, carefreeness . . .

DAN (*irritated*): All right, all right. Now, Bill, to return to your entanglement of former times with the victims, Fondue and Maeght. In what relation to you did they stand, sixteen years ago?

BILL: They stood to me in the relation, scoutmasters.

DAN: They were your scoutmasters. Entrusted with your schoolment in certain lores.

BILL: Yes. The duty of the scoutmasters was to reveal the scout mysteries.

CLEM: You were a scout, then.

BILL: Yes. I was a patrol leader.

HUBERT: Which patrol?

BILL: The, uh, Beaver Patrol.

DAN: Proceed.

BILL: We were competing with the Wolf Patrol in a map-reading exercise. (*Pause*) Fondue and Maeght came to me before the exercise. (*Pause*) The Beaver Patrol had to win, they told me. (*Pause*) They had staked their reputations on it. (*Pause*) There was a great black horse, they told me. If the Beaver Patrol did not win, the great black horse would come to me by night. And devour me, they said.

CLEM (*taken aback*): They did!

BILL: I led the Beaver Patrol into a cornfield. It was the wrong cornfield. The Wolf Patrol won.

CLEM: And did the horse come?

BILL: No. But I awaited it. Lying on my cot listening.

DAN: You waited for it.

BILL: Yes. (*Pause*) I await it still.

HENRY: One more question: is it true that you allowed the fires under the vats to go out, on the night of February sixteenth, while pursuing this private vendetta?

BILL: It is true.

DAN: Vatricide! That crime of crimes. Well, it doesn't look good for you, Bill. It doesn't look *at all* good for you.

(*Blackout*)

SCENE FOUR

(SNOW WHITE *on stage*)

SNOW WHITE: Paul is frog. He is frog through and through. I thought he would, at some point, cast off his mottled wettish green-and-brown suit to reappear washed in the hundred glistering hues of princeliness. But he is *pure frog.* So. I am disappointed. Either I have overestimated Paul, or I have overestimated history. In either case I have made a serious error. So. There it is. I have been disappointed, and am, doubtless, to be disappointed further. Total disappointment. That's it. The red meat on the rug. The frog's legs on the floor.

(HOGO *enters.*)

HOGO: I love you, Snow White.

SNOW WHITE: I know, Hogo. I know because you have told me a thousand times. I do not doubt you. I am convinced of your sincerity and warmth. And I must admit that your suave brutality has made its impression on me, too. But this "love" must not be, Hogo, because of your blood. You don't have the blood for this love, Hogo. Your blood is not fine enough. Oh I know that in this democratic era questions of blood are little *de trop,* a little frowned upon. People don't like to hear people talking about their blood, or about other people's blood. But I am not "people," Hogo. I am me. I must hold myself in reserve for a prince or prince figure, someone like Paul. Paul has the blood of kings and queens and cardinals in his veins, Hogo. He has the purple blood of exalted station. Whereas you have only plain blood in your veins, Hogo, blood that anybody might have—the delivery boy from the towel service, for example.

HOGO: But what about love? What about love which, as Stendhal tells us, seizes the senses and overthrows all other considerations in a giddy of irresponsibility?

SNOW WHITE: You may well say "a giddy of irresponsibility," Hogo. That is precisely the state I am not in. I am calm. As calm as a lamp, as calm as a hat. As calm as you are giddy.

HOGO: Well Snow White your blood arguments are pretty potent, and I recognize there is a gap there, between my blood and the blood royal. Yet in my blood there is a fever. I offer you this fever. It is as if my blood were full of amperes, so hot and electrical does it feel, inside me. If this fever, this rude but grand passion, in any measure ennobles me in your eyes, or in any other part of you, then perhaps all is not yet lost. For even a bad man can set his eyes on the stars, sometimes. Even a bad man can breathe and hope. And it is my hope that, as soon as you fully comprehend the strength of this fever in me, you will find it ennobling and me ennobled, and a fit consort suddenly, though I was not before. I know that this is a slim hope.

(HOGO *kneels on ground at her feet.*)

SNOW WHITE: No, Hogo. It does not ennoble you, the fever. I wish it did, but it does not. It is simply a fever, in my view. Two aspirin and a glass of water. I know that this is commonplace, even cruel advice, but I have no other advice. Goodnight, Hogo. Take your dark appeal away. Your cunningly wrought dark appeal.

(HOGO *rises, bows, and leaves.*)
(JANE *and* SNOW WHITE, *stage center*)

JANE: Drink this. It will make you feel better.

(JANE *offers* SNOW WHITE *a glass.*)

SNOW WHITE: What is it?

JANE: Vodka Gibson on the rocks.

SNOW WHITE: I don't feel bad physically. Emotionally is another story of course.

JANE: Go on. Go on, drink it.

SNOW WHITE: No, I won't drink it now. Perhaps later. Although something warns me not to drink it at all. Something suggests to me that it is a bad scene, this Vodka Gibson on the rocks you proffer. Something whispers to me that there is something wrong with it.

JANE: Well that's possible. I didn't make the vodka myself, you know. I didn't grow the grain myself, and reap it myself, and make the mash myself. I am not a member of the Cinzano Vermouth Company. They don't tell me everything. I didn't harvest the onions. I'm not responsible for everything. All I can say is that to the best of my knowledge, this is an ordinary Vodka Gibson on the rocks. Just like any other. Further than that I will not go.

SNOW WHITE: Oh well then. It must be all right in that case. It must be all right if it is ordinary. If it is as ordinary as you say. In that case, I shall drink it.

(SNOW WHITE *takes the glass from* JANE. *As she is about to drink,* PAUL *enters and takes it away from her, drinking deeply.*)

PAUL: This drink is vaguely exciting, like a film by Lina Wertmuller. It is a good thing I have taken it away from you, Snow White. It is too exciting for you. If you had drunk it, something bad would probably have happened to your stomach. But because I am a man, and because men have strong stomachs for the business of life, and the pleasure of life too, nothing will happen to me. Lucky that I sensed you about to drink it, and sensed that it was too exciting for you, from my pit where—

(PAUL *falls to the ground.*)

SNOW WHITE: Look how he has fallen to the ground, Jane! And look at all that green foam coming out of his face! And look at those convulsions he is having! Why it resembles nothing else but a death agony, the whole picture! I wonder if there was something wrong with that drink after all? Jane? Jane?

(JANE *has slipped away.*)
(*Blackout*)
(*Lights up on* CLEM *and* EDWARD)

CLEM: Well I don't know . . . seems a little harsh.

EDWARD: I'm against it.

CLEM: We voted. The decision's made.

EDWARD: But is it the *right* decision?

CLEM: It's got to be the right decision because it was the decision that was, uh, decided.

EDWARD: Your logic is . . . interesting.

CLEM: Well I don't like to just go hang Bill lightly. Even though he's guilty, and when you're guilty, then you got to be hanged —no two ways about it. Still, I think the whole thing is going to be just *very* unpleasant.

EDWARD: It's a moral question, that's clear. Whether our leader, Bill—

CLEM: Our former leader, Bill—

EDWARD: Our former leader, Bill, guilty of fear and failure, should be . . . Whether fear and failure *in themselves,* qua fear and qua failure, are, in the light of present-day attitudes, and the prevalence of fear-inducing as well as failure-generating occasions—

CLEM: I wonder how many of us will hafta pull on the rope. I mean one can't do it, and two can't do it, and probably *three* can't do it . . . Probably about four will have to do it . . .

EDWARD: But! Looking at the matter in an entirely different way, from the point of view of the one who has not looked at it from this point of view previously—

CLEM: And let's see, it's probably gonna take two to hold him, that's one on each side, and them two will probably have to give him a little boost to get him started . . .

EDWARD: So the case is not clear. Not at all. Ambiguities, difficulties—

CLEM (*counting on his fingers*): Four and two are six, and probably we'll need somebody to stand close to Snow White, so if she swoons during the . . . the . . . so if she swoons, then he can ketch her . . . (*To* EDWARD) Hey, we're one short.

EDWARD (*wearily; giving up*): Hogo. You forgot Hogo.

(*Blackout*)
(*Lights up on a princely funeral scene,* PAUL'*s. A large purple coffin.* HOGO *is delivering the oration.*)

HOGO: One thing you can say about him is that Paul was straight. A straight arrow. And just by looking at him, on those occasions when our paths crossed, at the bus stop, for example, or at the discount store, I could tell that Paul had a lot of ginger. He must have had a lot of ginger, to have dug that great hole, outside the house, and to have put all those wires in it, and connected all those dogs to the wires, and all that. That took a lot of mechanical ingenuity, and a lot of technical knowledge too, that shouldn't be understated, when we are making our final assessment of Paul. And now his friends have gathered together here, waiting to see him tucked away under the earth, friends who have been deprived at a stroke of the Lord's pen, as it were, of a source of amusement and warmth and human intercourse, which we all regard so highly, and need so much. I leave that thought to stick in your minds. As for myself, I am only Hogo, a citizen spitted on a passion for Snow White, that girl in the first row there, seated next to Jane. But that is my business, and not the business we are gathered together here in the sight of God to execute, which is the burning of Paul, and the putting of him into a vase, and the sinking of the vase into the ground, in the niche that has been prepared for it. Some people like to be scattered on top, but Paul wanted to be put under the ground. That is like him. (*Pause*) Good night, sweet prince.

KEVIN: And now Bill moves toward his lack of reward.

(PAUL'*s coffin is carried off in a sort of parody of the final scene of the Olivier* Hamlet; *the pallbearers immediately reenter rolling on bicycle wheels a large gibbet.* BILL *is brought out from the other side of the stage with his arms tied behind his back.*)

EDWARD (*a clumsy attempt at casualness*): Hi, Bill.

BILL: Hi.

EDWARD: How are . . . things?

BILL: So-so.

HENRY: Now we must hang Bill. Bill is guilty of vatricide and failure, and when you are guilty, then you must be hanged. Bill's friend Dan is the new leader. We have decided to let Hogo live in the house. He is a brute perhaps but an efficient brute. He is good at tending the vats. Dan has taken charge with a fine aggressiveness. He has added three new varieties to the line: Baby Water Chestnuts, Baby Kimchi, and Baby Bean Thread. They are selling well, these new items.

(BILL *is placed on the gibbet, the rope adjusted around his neck, etc.* SNOW WHITE *and* JANE *enter, holding hands.*)

DAN (*to* BILL): Uh . . . I hope you don't have any last words?

BILL: Yes I do have a few words as a matter of fact. (*He pulls a large sheaf of papers from his shirt*) My topic for today (*Pause*) is Failure. (*Pause*) Failure. Many people fear failure, but it is a natural part of life. It is as natural as death. We prefer, of course, the boiling purity of success. We prefer, of course, the blessed grace of breathing. But failure, like death, is an ever-present possibility, and as we shamble through life, it is very likely that we shamble into it. We shamble into it by looking for "something better." How does this monstrous idea, "something better," arise, in our tidy lives? I could mention a certain individual whose raving beauty brought it to our door. But I will not. She was our idea, but we were not her idea. So be it. There's no use crying over spilt marble—the marble of her marble brow, for example. You must all strive for a positive adjustment. Failure will be among your possibilities, but can be minimized by lowered expectations. Failure. (*Pause*) How does it feel? It feels terrible. Thank you.

DAN: Goodbye, Bill.

ALL: Goodbye, Bill.

BILL: Fare thee well. And if forever, then forever, fare thee well.

(BILL *is hanged, to the first few bars of "The Ride of the Valkyries." His body is lifted out of sight. All onstage stare upward after him.*)

SNOW WHITE: I feel . . . I feel as if I never really knew him.

DAN: We shall not look upon his like again. Thank God.

(*They continue staring upward.*)

SNOW WHITE: I must leave you now. I will return to the forest, and wander there, until my prince finds me.

DAN: We know.

JANE: I'll accompany you. Who knows who might be holding the bridle of your prince's horse?

(*They embrace in sisterly fashion.*)

DAN: We'll remember you, Snow White. We'll continue to be part of your story, forever.

KEVIN: And in spite of what Bill said, we will continue to search for a new principle.

(*All look upward again. The sky releases a shower of red towels.*)

ALL (*a shout*): Heigh-ho!

(*Blackout*)

Notes

SATIRES, PARODIES, FABLES, AND ILLUSTRATED STORIES

THE TEACHINGS OF DON B.: A YANKEE WAY OF KNOWLEDGE

First appeared in *The New York Times Magazine*, February 11, 1973. Reprinted in *Guilty Pleasures* (Farrar, Straus and Giroux, 1974).

I WROTE A LETTER . . .

First appeared in "Notes and Comment," unsigned, *The New Yorker*, October 27, 1980. Previously uncollected.

CHALLENGE

First published in *The New Yorker*, October 5, 1981, signed "William White," one of Barthelme's pseudonyms. Previously uncollected.

THREE GREAT MEALS

First published in *The New Yorker*, June 1, 1987, signed "William White." Previously uncollected.

LANGUISHING, HALF-DEEP IN SUMMER . . .

First published in "Notes and Comment," unsigned, *The New Yorker*, July 30, 1979. Previously uncollected.

Notes

THE PALACE

First appeared as an untitled, unsigned "Notes and Comment" piece in *The New Yorker*, December 24, 1973. It was reprinted in *Guilty Pleasures* as "The Palace," with minor changes.

MR. FOOLFARM'S JOURNAL

First published in *The Village Voice*, May 16, 1974. Reprinted in *Guilty Pleasures* with minor changes and one elision.

NATURAL HISTORY

First published in *Harper's*, August 1971. Previously uncollected.

THE JOKER'S GREATEST TRIUMPH

First published in *Come Back, Dr. Caligari* (Little, Brown, 1964).

THE AUTHOR

First published in *The New Yorker*, June 15, 1987. Previously uncollected.

I WAS GRATIFIED THIS WEEK . . .

First published in "Notes and Comment," unsigned, *The New Yorker*, November 18, 1974. Previously uncollected.

WHEN I DIDN'T WIN . . .

First published in "Notes and Comment," unsigned, *The New Yorker*, September 2, 1985. Previously uncollected.

RETURN

First published in the Houston *Post*, March 23, 1984. The Houston Festival Committee commissioned Barthelme for a "prose piece about some aspect" of Houston, and "Return" was his response. Barthelme read the piece on March 26 at the Museum of Fine Arts in conjunction with the Houston Festival. It is previously uncollected.

AT LAST, IT IS TIME . . .

First published in "Notes and Comment," unsigned, *The New Yorker*, November 27, 1978. Previously uncollected.

Notes

THE INAUGURATION

First published in *Harper's*, January 1973. Previously uncollected.

THE ART OF BASEBALL

First published in *The Spirit of Sport*, edited by Constance Sullivan (New York Graphic Society/Little, Brown, 1984). It originally appeared with photographs by Nicholas Nixon. Previously uncollected.

GAMES ARE THE ENEMIES OF BEAUTY, TRUTH, AND SLEEP, AMANDA SAID

First published in *Mademoiselle*, November 1966. Reprinted with some minor changes and one elision in *Guilty Pleasures*.

AN HESITATION ON THE BANK OF THE DELAWARE

First appeared as "A Dream" in *The New Yorker*, September 3, 1973, signed by "Lily McNeil," another of Barthelme's pseudonyms. It was reprinted in *Guilty Pleasures* under the current title.

I HAVE FOR SOME TIME . . .

First published in "Notes and Comment," unsigned, *The New Yorker*, October 10, 1977. Previously uncollected.

THE GREAT DEBATE

First appeared in *The New Yorker*, May 3, 1976. It is previously uncollected.

SNAP SNAP

First appeared in *The New Yorker*, August 28, 1965. Reprinted in *Guilty Pleasures*.

MING

Previously unpublished. "Ming" was found on a computer disk early in 1990. Barthelme had worked on it in 1989, perhaps with *The New Yorker*'s "Notes and Comment" in mind. The draft stage of the piece is unknown.

DONALD BARTHELME'S FINE HOMEMADE SOUPS

First published in *The Great American Writer's Cookbook*, edited by Dean Faulkner Wells (Oxford, Miss.: Yoknapatawpha Press, 1981). Wells solicited Barthelme for a recipe to include in the book, which includes contributions from, among others, Norman Mailer ("Stuffed Mushrooms"), Eudora Welty ("Charles Dickens's Eggnog"), Walker Percy ("Salt Steak"), John Hawkes ("Sanglier"), John Barth ("Five Chesapeake Bay Recipes"), and E. L. Doctorow ("The Miracle of *His* Instant Potatoes"). Despite an introduction by Craig Claiborne and two staunch assistants who tested recipes, readers should be aware that writers often eat hurriedly. Previously uncollected.

ADVENTURE

First published in *Harper's Bazaar*, December 1970. Previously uncollected.

HELIOTROPE

First appeared as an untitled, unsigned "Notes and Comment" piece in *The New Yorker*, April 1, 1974. It was later published as "Heliotrope" in *Guilty Pleasures*, with minor changes.

THE ANGRY YOUNG MAN

First appeared in *Fiction* 2, no. 2, 1973. It was reprinted in *Guilty Pleasures* with a significant rearrangement of the paragraphs and other minor changes.

CORNELL

First appeared as text in the *Joseph Cornell Exhibition Catalogue*, Leo Castelli Gallery, New York City (February–March 1976). It was reprinted in *Ontario Review* 5 (Fall/Winter 1976) and again in 1983 as an interchapter in *Overnight to Many Distant Cities* (Putnam's, 1983).

I AM, AT THE MOMENT . . .

First appeared as an interchapter in *Overnight to Many Distant Cities*.

NOW THAT I AM OLDER . . .

First appeared as an interchapter in *Overnight to Many Distant Cities*.

SPEAKING OF THE HUMAN BODY...

First appeared as an interchapter in *Overnight to Many Distant Cities*.

A WOMAN SEATED ON A PLAIN WOODEN CHAIR...

First published in this form as an interchapter in *Overnight to Many Distant Cities*. Certain sections appeared earlier in "Presents" (*Penthouse*, December 1977).

THAT GUY IN THE BACK ROOM...

First appeared as an interchapter in *Overnight to Many Distant Cities*.

THEY CALLED FOR MORE STRUCTURE...

First appeared as an interchapter in *Overnight to Many Distant Cities*.

A NATION OF WHEELS

First appeared in *The New Yorker*, June 13, 1970. Reprinted in *Guilty Pleasures* with paragraphs 4 and 5 reversed. *The New Yorker* version is reprinted here.

KISSING THE PRESIDENT

First appeared in *The New Yorker*, August 1, 1983. Previously uncollected.

AND NOW LET'S HEAR IT FOR THE ED SULLIVAN SHOW!

First published in *Esquire*, April 1969. Reprinted in *Guilty Pleasures*.

BLISS...

Previously unpublished. The date of composition is uncertain. It was, however, found in 1990 among unused drafts of work associated with *The Dead Father*, making the likely date of writing about 1973–75.

BRAIN DAMAGE

First appeared in *The New Yorker*, February 21, 1970. Reprinted in *City Life* (Farrar, Straus and Giroux, 1970) with substantial changes. "Brain Damage" incorporates the uncollected fable "Blue Flower Problem," *Harvest* 31: 2, May 1967.

MANY HAVE REMARKED . . .

First published in "Notes and Comment," *The New Yorker*, unsigned, June 13, 1970. Parts of the piece were later incorporated into "Flying to America" (*The New Yorker*, December 4, 1971) which itself later became part of "A Film" (*Sadness*, 1972). The title "A Film" was changed to "The Film" in *Forty Stories*, 1987, but is otherwise identical. The textual history of the *Sadness* version of "A Film"—there was also a *New Yorker* story with the same title (September 26, 1970)—has been called by Barthelme's bibliographer "the most complex of any Barthelme story." In short, this "Comment" piece was intercut and combined with "Flying to America" and *The New Yorker* "A Film" to create the *Sadness* "A Film." In addition, a part of "Flying to America" not used in the *Sadness* "A Film" was later resurrected as "Two Hours to Curtain" (published in *Guilty Pleasures* and reprinted here), and other parts of "Flying to America" were used in *The Dead Father*. "Many have remarked . . ." is previously uncollected in its original form.

SWALLOWING

First appeared on *The New York Times* op-ed page, November 4, 1972. It was reprinted in *Guilty Pleasures* with minor changes.

THE YOUNG VISITIRS

First appeared as an unsigned "Notes and Comment" piece titled "A Made Up Story" in *The New Yorker*, February 10, 1973. It was reprinted as "The Young Visitirs" in *Guilty Pleasures*. The spelling of "Visitirs" is an allusion to nine-year-old Daisy Ashford's extraordinary "novel" *The Young Visiters*, published in 1919.

MY LOVER SAID TO ME . . .

First published in "Notes and Comment," unsigned, *The New Yorker*, August 11, 1986. Previously uncollected.

THAT COSMOPOLITAN GIRL

First appeared in *The New Yorker*, July 16, 1973, signed "Lily McNeil." Reprinted in *Guilty Pleasures*.

L'LAPSE

First appeared in *The New Yorker*, March 2, 1963. "L'Lapse" was Barthelme's first publication in *The New Yorker*. Reprinted in *Guilty Pleasures* with minor changes.

MORE ZERO

First appeared in *The New Yorker*, July 7, 1986, signed "William White." Previously uncollected.

THE STORY THUS FAR:

First published in *The New Yorker*, May 1, 1971. Previously uncollected.

BUNNY IMAGE, LOSS OF: THE CASE OF BITSY S.

First appeared in *Guilty Pleasures*.

TWO HOURS TO CURTAIN

"Two Hours to Curtain" originally appeared as part of "Flying to America" (*The New Yorker*, December 4, 1971), then appeared under its current title in *Guilty Pleasures*.

THE ROYAL TREATMENT

First appeared in *The New York Times*, November 3, 1973, signed "Lily McNeil." It was reprinted in *Guilty Pleasures*, with minor changes.

MAN'S FACE

First published in *The New Yorker*, May 30, 1964. It is previously uncollected.

WASTELAND!

"Wasteland!" is an unpublished piece found among Barthelme's papers in 1990. There are two versions. The version not published here is longer by some two typescript pages, and—not unlike T. S. Eliot's "Notes on *The Waste Land*"—is organized by references to the "pages" of Lionel Bart's imaginary script. Barthelme apparently scrapped this idea for organizing the piece and condensed the material for the version published here.

Although dating the piece with absolute accuracy has proven to be impossible, it can be said that it was written between 1964 and 1967, with the strong likelihood that it was written in 1965.

The British lyricist/composer Lionel Bart could read no music, but he nevertheless wrote a number of hit, near-hit, and nonhit musicals during the late 1950s and throughout the 1960s. Most of them were adapted from well-known sources with new titles featuring a breathless exclamation point for emphasis. *Lock Up Your Daughters!* (based on Henry Fielding's *Rape upon Rape*) was produced in 1959, followed by the major hit *Oliver!*—based on Dickens's *Oliver Twist*—in 1960 (New York, 1963, with an Academy Award for Best Picture in 1968); *Blitz!* appeared in 1962; *Maggie May* in 1964; the disastrous failure *Twang!* (a Robin Hood musical) in 1965; and *La Strada*, based on the Fellini film, in 1969. In 1977 Bart offered *Lionel*, which was based on his own career and works!

Barthelme refers to his unpublished "Wasteland!" in "Games Are the Enemies of Beauty, Truth, and Sleep, Amanda Said" when Hector suggests to Amanda that one of the games they could play is "Broadway Flop" or "The Game of Ill-Conceived Musical Comedy."

THE EDUCATIONAL EXPERIENCE

First appeared in *Harper's*, June 1973. Reprinted in *Amateurs* (Farrar, Straus and Giroux, 1976) without collages, and again—without collages—in *Forty Stories*. The collages have been restored for this printing.

THE DRAGON

First appeared in "Notes and Comment," unsigned, *The New Yorker*, February 26, 1972. Reprinted with minor changes in *Guilty Pleasures*.

NEWSLETTER

First published in *The New Yorker*, July 11, 1970. Previously uncollected.

THE PHOTOGRAPHS

First published in *The New Yorker*, January 28, 1974. Reprinted in *Guilty Pleasures*.

WE DROPPED IN AT THE STANHOPE . . .

First published in "Notes and Comment," unsigned, *The New Yorker*, December 25, 1978. Previously uncollected.

WELL WE ALL HAD OUR WILLIE & WADE RECORDS . . .

First appeared in *Harper's*, June 1979, with illustrations by James Stevenson. It was reprinted, without illustrations, as an interchapter in *Overnight to Many Distant Cities*.

DOWN THE LINE WITH THE ANNUAL

First published in *The New Yorker*, March 21, 1964. Reprinted with minor changes in *Guilty Pleasures*.

MONUMENTAL FOLLY

First appeared in *The Atlantic*, February 1976, with illustrations by Edward Sorel. The text only is reprinted here. Previously uncollected.

THE DASSAUD PRIZE

First appeared in *The New Yorker*, January 12, 1976. Previously uncollected.

PLAYS

The plays, perhaps, require special attention here, since they are practically unknown. Barthelme published no plays during his lifetime, even though he wrote quite a large number of pieces in dramatic form. Many, of course, appear as dialogue stories in *Great Days*, *Forty Stories*, and elsewhere. The three plays that appear here—only one of which, *Snow White*, appears to have been intended for actual stage production—are reworkings and recombinations of stories that Barthelme had published previously. They have been included in this volume because of their intrinsic interest, but also because they differ in significant ways from the prose pieces from which they were adapted.

In addition to these three, however, Barthelme wrote something in the way of seventeen dramatic adaptations of various kinds, most of which duplicate the prose versions almost verbatim. He worked with Wynn Handman at New York's American Place Theatre on at least four different occasions: *Snow White* was given a full-scale rehearsed reading there in 1976; in 1975 American Place produced *Straws in the Wind: A Revue by Various Authors and Composers*, which included adaptations of "The Photographs" and "The School"; 1976 saw *Conversations with Don B.: An Entertainment with Music Drawn from the Writing of Donald Barthelme*, which included—among other things—adaptations of "That Cosmopolitan Girl" and "The Balloon." The same theater presented a full main-stage production of *Great Days* in the spring of 1983. *Great Days*, the stage production, included "Momma," "On the Steps of the Conservatory," "Grandmother's House," "The Apology," "Morning," Great Days," and "The Leap." All these pieces, with the exception of "Grandmother's House," had earlier appeared in prose form in *Great Days*, the book. "Momma" was adapted from the story published first in 1978 in *The New Yorker*, and later became part of "The New Music" (the first half of which, it should be noted, was originally written as an unpublished story entitled "Pool"). "Grandmother's House" had appeared previously in *Sixty Stories*.

"The Emerald," an adaptation of the story first published in *Esquire* and reprinted in *Sixty Stories*, was proposed for the Corporation for Public Broadcasting's *National Television Theatre* in 1981. In the synopsis of "The Emerald," by Barthelme and Harrison Starr, they suggest that the "adaptation of the basic story would be enriched and elaborated to take advantage of the special opportunities for visual effects offered by the medium, but also, and most importantly, to provide a sense of the importance of the presence or absence of myth and the magical in contemporary life." The adaptation targeted for *National Television Theatre* did not, apparently, get much beyond the draft stage (an unfinished twenty-four-page typescript exists, along with many pages of notes), but a full-length version of "The Emerald"—verbatim with the published story—does exist, and in March 1992 was performed at the Cardiff Giant Theater in Chicago. The two "Emerald" 's may have been two different, though perhaps related, projects.

Some of Barthelme's other dramatic work—like *The Friends of the Family* and *The Conservatory*—were written for National Public Radio's *Earplay* and are discussed below.

Notes

THE FRIENDS OF THE FAMILY

The Friends of the Family was written as a radio play in the early 1970s. It intercuts sections from "For I'm the Boy Whose Only Joy Is Loving You" (*Come Back, Dr. Caligari*, 1964) and "The Big Broadcast of 1938" (*Come Back, Dr. Caligari*) along with some apparently new material (the dialogue between Bloomsbury and the Woman beginning with the line "Differentiation" and ending with "Perhaps a bucket of fun?"). Previously unpublished.

THE CONSERVATORY

The Conservatory was written as a radio play in the 1970s. It uses intercut sections from "On the Steps of the Conservatory" and "Great Days," both published in *Great Days* (Farrar, Straus and Giroux, 1979). It is previously unpublished.

SNOW WHITE

Previously unpublished. Barthelme's adaptation of *Snow White* was begun in 1974, using selected lines from the published novel almost verbatim. He rewrote the play at least once between 1974 and 1976, making major cuts and adding entirely new material. In 1976 Barthelme reworked it again—with the help of American Place Theatre director Wynn Handman—for a rehearsed reading which was performed before an audience at the American Place Theatre in New York City on June 10. The purpose of the reading, according to the program note, was to give Barthelme "an opportunity to participate in rehearsals, see his play with an audience and hopefully use this experience to further the development of the play and of himself as a playwright." Barthelme was apparently not happy with the result. He wrote to thank Handman for his help on June 21: "The experience was invaluable to me. Not only did I learn what a poor play I had written, but also I got what I consider invaluable assistance in figuring out how it might be improved." Despite Handman's urging that he continue to work on the play, Barthelme apparently decided that he'd had enough. It is, of course, difficult to say exactly why Barthelme decided his play was so "poor," though it should be noted that authors are often discouraged by difficulties in staging and dramatic effect quite separate from the script. Readers, we think, will find the reading script interesting indeed, and an important complement to the novel from which it was adapted.

The text for this printing is that which was used for the rehearsed reading and was kindly made available by Mr. Handman. The typescript bears the evidence of a number of last-minute changes. Most of Handman's stage directions, since they were specifically for the New York production, have been eliminated; all of Barthelme's stage directions have been retained.

VINTAGE INTERNATIONAL

THE INFORMATION
by Martin Amis

Fame, envy, lust, violence, intrigues literary and criminal—
they're all here in this deliriously entertaining, blackly hilarious
novel, in which a failed writer, Richard Tull, is out to mess up
his overly successful friend, Gwyn Barry.

"Satirical and tender, funny and disturbing . . . wonderful."
—Michiko Kakutani, *The New York Times*

Fiction/Literature/0-679-73573-9

POSSESSION
by A. S. Byatt

An exhilarating novel of wit and romance, at once an intellectual mystery and a triumphant love story, *Possession* is the tale
of a pair of young scholars, who, through a treasure trove of
letters, journals, and poems, trace the mysterious lives of two
Victorian poets.

"Gorgeously written . . . dazzling . . . a tour de force."
—*The New York Times Book Review*

Winner of the Booker Prize
Fiction/Literature/0-679-73590-9

THE FIRST MAN
by Albert Camus

A moving journey through the lost landscape of youth that also
discloses the wellsprings of Camus's aesthetic powers and moral
vision, *The First Man* is the brilliant consummation of the life
and work of one of the twentieth century's greatest novelists,
published more than thirty years after his death.

"A masterpiece. . . . One of the most extraordinary evocations
of childhood that exists in any language."   —*Boston Globe*

Winner of the Nobel Prize
Fiction/Literature/0-679-76816-5

THE UNCONSOLED ·
by Kazuo Ishiguro

The Unconsoled is at once a gripping psychological mystery, a wicked satire of the cult of art, and a poignant character study of a man whose public life has accelerated beyond control, by the author of *The Remains of the Day*.

"Ishiguro is an original and remarkable genius. . . . *The Unconsoled* is a work of art."

—*The New York Times Book Review*

Fiction/Literature/0-679-73587-9

THE CROSSING
by Cormac McCarthy

A novel with the unstoppable momentum of a classic Western and the elegiac power of a lost American myth, *The Crossing* is luminous and appalling, a book that touches, stops, and starts the heart and mind at once.

"A miracle in prose, an American original."

—*The New York Times Book Review*

Fiction/Literature/0-679-76084-9

THE ENGLISH PATIENT
by Michael Ondaatje

During the final moments of World War II, four damaged people come together in a deserted Italian villa. As their stories unfold, a complex tapestry of image and emotion is woven, leaving them inextricably connected by the brutal circumstances of war.

"A rare and spellbinding web of dreams."   —*Time*

Winner of the Booker Prize

Fiction/Literature/0-679-74520-3

VINTAGE INTERNATIONAL
Available at your local bookstore, or call toll-free to order:
1-800-793-2665 (credit cards only).